Therapy at Lightning Speed

Case Studies of EMDR

Rachel B. Aarons MSW, PhD

Therapy at Lightning Speed:
Case Studies of EMDR
Rachel B. Aarons MSW, PhD

Printed in the United States of America

Published by Journey Press
Santa Barbara, California 93101

Library of Congress Control Number: 2011910201

ISBN 978-0-9842327-2-7

Book Design by www.KarrieRoss.com
Cover Photos from istockphoto.com

First Edition
10 9 8 7 6 5 4 3 2 1

Dedication

This book is dedicated to my clients
who put their trust in me
and honored you, the reader, by opening their struggles
so that you might learn and grow from them.

In deepest gratitude and love,
Rachel

Contents

Introduction:

Protocol, Resources and Set up

Introduction

I am passionate about EMDR – passionate enough to write a book about it. This book provides case studies of actual EMDR therapy sessions conducted with clients in my practice. I believe that a book like this will offer you the inside story about why I am so excited about this work and the powerful positive impact it is having. It allows you to go "behind the scenes" to see what really happens in an EMDR session as if you are right there in the room watching as the process unfolds. You will be able to witness the therapeutic process firsthand from beginning to end. You will see people changing right before your eyes, as I did, in a radically short time frame. EMDR has the capacity to resolve in one processing session issues that could take years using traditional approaches. After more than thirty-five years of experience as a therapist and extensive training in a diversity of methods such as Gestalt therapy, psychodynamic therapy, conjoint family therapy, and hypnotherapy, I can state unequivocally that EMDR is the fastest and most transformative therapy I have ever seen.

This is not a textbook of EMDR theory and methodology. To get the full story about Eye Movement Desensitization and Reprocessing, I strongly recommend you go to the source and read what Dr. Francine Shapiro, the originator and developer of EMDR, has to say about it.[1]

You may also want to look at the work of my teacher, Dr. Laurel Parnell,[2] and at the EMDRIA website[3] for a large collection of articles on EMDR theory and research. Given that

---

[1] See: Francine Shapiro, *Eye Movement Desensitization and Reprocessing: Basic Principles, Protocols, and Procedures* (New York: The Guilford Press, 1995) and numerous articles.

[2] See: Laurel Parnell, *Transforming Trauma: EMDR*, (New York: W.W. Norton, 1997) and *EMDR in the Treatment of Adults Abused as Children*, (New York: W.W. Norton, 1999) and numerous articles.

[3] International Association for EMDR at www.emdria.org.

EMDR is the most researched methodology on trauma, you can expect to see an impressive amount of scholarly material. It is not my intention to do a review of the literature here.

However, I do see the need for a brief general introduction to the topic of the book so that you are able to orient to what I am talking about when I refer to EMDR terminology, and you have some basic knowledge of the concepts that are essential to the work.

Eye Movement Desensitization and Reprocessing was discovered in 1987 by a research psychologist named Francine Shapiro who was taking a walk in a park. As she walked, she was thinking about a personal matter that was bothering her. She happened to notice that her eyes were going back and forth and that, as they did, her level of disturbance went down. Intrigued by this discovery, she began the extensive research and formulation that culminated in EMDR theory and methodology.

In the beginning, it was assumed that eye movements were essential to the process. Then tapping on two sides of the body was found to be effective and, finally, alternating audio stimulation through headphones and a scanner. What is common to all these different modalities is that they all constitute *bilateral stimulation* – that is, stimulation on two sides of the body.

Why is bilateral stimulation effective? The bottom line is: there is no definitive, finally agreed upon explanation at this time. However, what makes sense to me is that bilateral stimulation seems to allow trauma to process through in such a way that it no longer produces a high level of disturbance for the client. What we mean by "trauma" is an experience or pattern of experiences that are overwhelming to the coping structures that are available to the client at that moment in time. As a result, trauma of this sort gets locked away in the nervous system and cordoned off in certain areas of the brain that are only minimally connected to the rest of the brain and its circuitry.

The use of bilateral stimulation allows this traumatic experience to become connected with the bulk of experience and learnings that have been developed in the course of the client's life history and stored in the other parts of their brain. Consequently, clients will no longer continue to experience the recurrence of such traumatic experience in their nervous system and limbic system exactly as if it were happening again. With lowered disturbance and new under-standing, the bilateral processing enables them to convert compulsive behavior patterns into decisions based on choice. We will see how this change emerges in every case study that follows. Each individual client's processing will be different from every other in as much as each client's learnings and life history are different. Therefore, although the fundamental principles are the same, each case study will be unique.

I know that every therapist works differently and I am not implying that every therapist should work the way I do. I have been trained and certified as an EMDR therapist and I believe that my work is compatible with acceptable EMDRIA protocol. But not every EMDR therapist works the way I do. I realize that there is no one "right" way to proceed. I am happy if what I do works for the client.

What motivated me to write this book is that the results I am getting seem almost like a miracle, even to me. People have been asking how it is possible to resolve an issue using only *one processing session* – not just once (as if it were a fluke) but repeatedly.

To use an analogy, it is as if I threw down seeds in my garden and then sat back and watched them sprout and bloom right in front of my eyes, not over a period of months or weeks or even days, but in just two hours. It's impossible, isn't it?

I would have said the same as a therapist about resolving clinical issues. But it is happening consistently in my practice.

Let me be very clear. I am *not* saying that two hours is the total time I spend with each client – as if they were to walk into my office for the first time and then walk out two hours later healed. That *would* be impossible. The Eight Phase model for EMDR[4] requires a psychosocial assessment, development of rapport and a therapeutic alliance, as well as an explanation of EMDR theory and practice. The EMDR model I use begins with a one-and-a-half-hour preparation session and ends with a one-and-a-half-hour follow-up session. However, the actual healing process – i.e. the processing time for each trauma – is *two hours*, not a series of twelve to twenty sessions as has been reported in the literature. That in itself is remarkable enough.

I was trained in EMDR in 1997 and have been using it regularly in my practice since 2003. I developed the format I will outline here in the last four years. In my results to date using this format, (with one possible exception,[5]) all of my EMDR clients have successfully resolved the issue they were working on within this time frame. Client follow-up forms indicate that the results are holding. None of my EMDR clients have returned to work on the same issue again.

Unlike many other EMDR trained therapists I have talked to, I do not do twenty or thirty minutes of EMDR during a one-hour counseling session. I follow a very definite structure as to how I utilize the time. My time structure is:

1. a one-and-a-half-hour preparation session,

2. a two-hour processing session,

3. a one-and-a-half-hour follow-up session.

---

[4] Francine Shapiro, *Eye Movement Desensitization and Reprocessing,* 67- 74.

[5] See Chapter Six.

I do not believe I could get the same results in a shorter period of time.

Understanding the process I will present in this book does *not* mean that you will thereby be ready and able to use it with clients yourself or on yourself as a client. If you are a licensed therapist, you will need to be trained in an EMDRIA approved Basic Training course. You can find information about this training on the EMDRIA website. If you are not a licensed therapist, you should not use the methods on yourself or on anyone else. You should seek out a properly trained EMDR therapist to work with. Listings of EMDRIA approved therapists are available on the website[6] or in the *EMDRIA Membership Directory* which is updated annually.

I have modified the protocol somewhat over the years that I have worked with it. I use the same basic ingredients, but have changed the order and added some precision that I felt was helpful. I will indicate these modifications as I go along.

I have to acknowledge that my work does not always adhere to the precise specifications taught in the basic EMDR training. As a seasoned therapist, I tend to follow my therapeutic instincts as to what will move the process forward for each client. Reviewing transcripts of what actually occurs in my EMDR sessions brought some of these details to light. For example, I do not return regularly to the target to assess the current level of associated disturbance unless I feel a need to check in with where the client is at. Similarly, I do not remind the client to breathe after each experience of bilateral stimulation. It is not that I have any objection to this procedure. It is simply not something I have incorporated (or remembered to incorporate) in my practice. Overall, I would say of my relationship to my EMDR training what Salvador Minuchin says of his relationship to the work of Carl Whitaker:

---

[6] www.emdria.org

> (W)hen I copied from Carl Whitaker ... - I was not impersonating Carl; I was incorporating him, with a Spanish accent and subtleties that were mine, not his.[7]

I like to think that I have "incorporated" EMDR in much the same way. I utilize the invaluable insights of EMDR theory in combination with my own style of doing therapy.

It is generally agreed that all therapy begins with a psychosocial assessment. I would never bring a client in off the street and start doing EMDR with them. I would have to know about their current functioning as well as their past history and, in particular, what past traumas might be triggered by our work. I also have to develop a therapeutic alliance with the client. We have to have mutual agreement on our goals.

For each case study, I will first give background information that places the EMDR work in a context and orients you to the issue that is being addressed. It is not depression or anxiety in general that is the subject of the work, but this particular client's depression or anxiety that I am working with. Just as each client is unique, each client's EMDR work will be unique. We may see themes, but we must never lose sight of the individual.

Protocol

In the preparation session, we set up the protocol for the EMDR work. I find it very important to pay close attention to each step. If poorly defined or badly articulated, it could have a negative impact on the processing and, therefore, on the outcome of the work.

---

[7] Salvador Minuchin, Michael P. Nichols and Wai-Yung Lee, *Assessing Families and Couples* (Boston: Pearson Education, 2007), 5.

The first step is for the client to state **the issue** he/she wants to work on in their own words. I will sometimes try on several different formulations with a client in order to ensure that the issue as stated is clear, specific, and realizable.

The next step is to determine a **target.** This will be the earliest or most disturbing example of the issue. For clients who have the ego strength to tolerate their negative feelings, it is generally true that the higher the level of disturbance, the more likely it will process through. It is as if emotional disturbance is the lubricant for the healing.

The subsequent step is to identify the **feelings** that come up for the client as this disturbing experience is remembered. I place this before the negative cognition (rather than after), as I find it helps clients get in touch with the experience that traumatized them. I also determine the somatic base of each of these emotions, since each individual feeling is found to be experienced in a specific place in the body. Some clients have difficulty in locating their feelings, but it is important to persevere, as I believe the somatic component is essential to the work.

As a next step, we then want to identify the negative belief about him or herself that is associated with the traumatic experience for the client. This is called the **negative cognition** and it is intrinsically related to the issue the client is there to heal. Again, we may need to entertain several possibilities until we find the one that is the best fit.

Holding all three of the above in their mind (i.e. the target, the associated feelings, and the negative cognition,) the client then rates their level of disturbance on a scale from zero to ten where ten represents the most disturbing experience they can imagine and zero represents no charge, neutral or flat. We call this the **SUDS (Subjective Units of Disturbance Scale).** I usually bring it in at this point in the protocol.

We then ask the client what they would like to believe about themselves if the work is successful. This belief, called the **positive cognition,** encapsulates the goal of the work. It should be something that is possible and realistic, something that the client can imagine being true, even if it doesn't feel true in the moment. Based on the processing work, the positive cognition can be modified, if necessary, at a later point in the work.

We then rate the degree to which this positive cognition seems true to the client at the present moment on a scale from one to seven where one is completely false and seven is completely true. This is called the **Validity of Cognition** or **VOC.**

This completes the protocol for the EMDR work.

Resources

Next, I routinely set up a list of resources that can be brought in and utilized, if necessary, in the course of processing. Here I largely follow the work of my individual EMDR consultant, Roy Kiessling.[8] Some EMDR therapists do not use resources of this sort, but I find that, in certain cases, they can be invaluable. You will notice that resources are brought in during some, but not all, of the case studies that follow.

The client can choose one or two resources in each of the following categories:

1. nurturing and support,

2. strength (physical and/or moral),

3. wisdom.

---

[8] Roy Kiessling, Consultation for EMDR certification, by telephone, 2003.

Let me explain each category in turn.

Nurturing figures welcome you. They care about you and support you. They feel safe and, as closely as possible, treat you with unconditional positive regard.

Figures of strength are protectors. They may be physically strong and able to defend you from attack. Or they may be models of emotional strength – for example, people who have suffered and maintained their principles, have high levels of integrity, or long experience in the school of hard knocks.

Figures of wisdom are sources of guidance and advice. They may have a deep understanding of people and how they function. They may be perceived as having a greater comprehension of life in the eyes of the client. They may be human or superhuman or divine.

Resources in each of these categories may be people selected from the client's past or present life, well-known figures from history, movies or literature. They may be animals, objects of nature, angels, spirits or some type of higher power. What is important is that each figure selected strongly represents the category in question and is neither ambiguous nor ambivalent in the client's mind.

When a resource is chosen, I ask of each one: "What do you admire about this figure in this regard?"

I then add a fourth category in response to the question: "If you were able to resolve this issue on your own, what quality would you need to possess that would be the most helpful and significant?"

Once the client has identified the requisite quality, I ask: "Can you think of a time when you exemplified this quality to a striking degree in the way you behaved in the past?" Then I get the significant details of this past situation. If the client is unable to think of a time when they demonstrated this quality, they can choose another figure who exemplifies it for them.

Again, this can be someone known to them personally or by reputation.

The fifth resource is a safe place. Laura Parnell points out[9] that, for very highly traumatized clients, the word "safe" can potentially be triggering and can bring up pain instead of comfort if nowhere ever seemed safe. Therefore, in such a case, we can use the term "calm and peaceful place."

This can be a place the client has visited in the past or goes to in the present when they want to be alone and nurture themselves. It can be a place they have never visited in person, but have seen in a movie or in a magazine or read about in a book. Or it can be a place they create in their imaginations, a perfect getaway place where they might go if they could. I direct them to notice all the visual details, the sounds, the smells, the sensations in their body and the feelings they have inside. Depending on the particular client, I might have them simply close their eyes and visualize such a place or I may use hypnosis to install it. I make it clear that, at any time in the processing if the client feels overwhelmed or frightened, we can take them to this safe place to ground and center and get a break.

Set Up

In the processing session, I give the client options about the procedures we will use. I want them to take an active role from the start.

For bilateral stimulation, I use auditory stimulation through headphones and a Neurotek scanner.[10] Our first task is to

---

[9] Laurel Parnell, Workshop entitled "Integrating an Attachment Repair Orientation into EMDR Treatment for Clients with Relational Trauma," (San Francisco: June 17, 2010).

[10] One important advantage of the audio stimulation is that clients can close their eyes and focus on their inner experience during the processing.

determine the settings on the scanner – the speed, the volume, and the intensity of the sensors.[11] I point out to the client that these decisions are based simply on personal preference. There is nothing good or bad, right or wrong, better or worse about the choices they make. Nor should they be influenced by the settings of the previous person. To use an analogy, if they walked into an ice cream store and the person ahead of them ordered butterscotch, this would not imply that they should order butterscotch too. It is purely a matter of personal taste. So, too, with the settings. The message I want to convey from the outset is that responses based on their own feelings in the moment will be honored in this process. I reassure them that I will be as patient as they need me to be while they decide what settings feel best to them.

Then, I ask them to make a personal choice about the way we use the scanner in the processing. Knowing that they will likely have no previous experience to go by, I make the point that, in the absence of evidence or experience, they can choose by instinct or gut feel. This helps them prepare for and acclimate to attending to what they feel in the moment without having to utilize intellectual analysis or prior belief systems to govern their response.

The client can either:

    1. opt to control the scanner themselves,

    2. nod to me when they want the scanner turned off,

    3. leave it on the whole time, or

    4. let me determine the length of each set.

The majority of my clients opt for the latter option. I encourage them to give me feedback about whether I am going too fast or too slow for them. At the same time, I indicate that there may be times when it feels right to

---

[11] Sensors add kinesthetic reinforcement to the auditory stimulation of the headphones.

them – or to me – to leave the scanner on continuously. This is something that becomes evident intuitively during the actual processing experience.

With the client's permission, I close the blinds and darken the lights for the processing experience. I explain that what is going on in the outside world does not matter for this period of time. Their focus will be inward, on their own experience. I have the sense that the place where we meet and dialogue is in their inner process more than it is in the room.

I also remind my clients that their one and only job – but it is *crucial* – is to be an observer of whatever comes up in their experience when the scanner is on. This means that they are not to censor or delete anything that arises because they find it shameful or think it is irrelevant. Whatever comes up is there for a reason. And their experience is considered to include all their thoughts, feelings, bodily sensations, memories, images, fantasies – literally anything that is going on in their experience during the bilateral stimulation. Holding the observer or witness position is a key element of the EMDR experience for the client.

When we are ready to begin, I review the elements that we have set up in the preparation session. Then I ask the client to hold the target, associated feelings, and negative cognition in their minds and ramp up the level of disturbance to the highest level that is tolerable for them at that moment in time. When they report their SUDS, it is the signal for me to start the scanner.

During the processing, I always take handwritten notes and, more recently, I have used audio recording as well. Half of the case studies are based on my notes and half have been taken from transcripts of the audio recordings. Had I chosen to use transcripts for all the cases, this would have been a much, much longer book.

In all the case studies, I have retained the bulk of what was said. My directions to the client have been deleted or substantially abbreviated to include only the most significant. My "go with that" or "focus on that" directions are assumed.

I invite you to engage with the experience of each client. Try to see what he/she is seeing, hear what he/she is hearing, and feel what he/she is feeling. Get ready to take a unique journey with each person by watching as his or her therapeutic process unfolds.

Summary

Modified EMDR PROTOCOL

1. THE ISSUE

2. THE TARGET

3. FEELINGS AND THEIR LOCATION IN THE BODY

4. NEGATIVE COGNITION

5. SUBJECTIVE UNITS OF DISTURBANCE SCALE (SUDS)

6. POSITIVE COGNITION

7. VALIDITY OF COGNITION (VOC)

RESOURCES

1. NURTURING AND SUPPORT

2. STRENGTH - PHYSICAL AND/OR MORAL

3. WISDOM

4. QUALITY & EXAMPLE

5. SAFE PLACE

CHAPTER ONE

Acute Recent Trauma:

The Suicide of a Loved One

Case of Thea

When one thinks of EMDR therapy, one often thinks of acute traumatic experiences such as rape, molestation, physical assault, armed robbery, murder, multiple horrors of war, tornadoes, fires, earthquakes and floods. One thinks of trauma with a capital "T." These are not the minor defeats and challenges of ordinary life, but events that make headline news.

Historically, EMDR was first identified in the literature as a treatment modality for Post-Traumatic Stress Disorder. Certainly, much of the energy and attention of EMDR therapy and research has been directed toward these catastrophic events and, of necessity, continues to be. There are trained therapists with the International Association for EMDR who go to troubled areas and help train local therapists to provide services for the masses of people affected by natural and human disasters around the globe.

Given this association, it seems fitting to begin with a case of acute recent trauma in one person's life. I think you will agree that this woman had a devastating experience that no one would handle easily.

Background Information

Thea was a thirty-two-year-old hairstylist who came to see me within a couple of weeks of her traumatic experience. She had lost her significant other to suicide.

Thea reported that, since the death of her partner, she was having difficulty falling asleep at night and she would wake up very early in the morning. She felt compelled to go through the trauma she had experienced in her head, in detail, every morning before she opened her eyes. Then, she would cry for an hour or more before she got out of bed.

She told me that she had been eating less since the traumatic event and had lost some weight. She took no pleasure in activities that she had previously enjoyed such as bike riding. She felt exhausted all the time and was unable to make a decision. She did not know what she wanted to do in the future. She complained that she was just "going through the motions" in her life.

Immediately following the traumatic incident, Thea had quit her job and left the town in Colorado where she lived when the suicide occurred. She never returned to the house she and her partner had lived in together. With the help and support of her parents who were visiting her at the time, she moved to Santa Barbara and was staying with her mother and stepfather (whom she called "Dad").

Thea's biological father was an alcoholic. Her mother had left him when Thea was three years old. She had regular contact with him during her childhood, with the exception of the two years when he was in prison for armed robbery. Apparently, when he was drinking and using cocaine, he had held up bars where he was known to the bartenders. It was no surprise that he was caught. She described him as a "nice guy," but she did not feel close to him. He married a woman who, she said, talked and swore incessantly. Her father had continued to drink and smoke pot, although "less than he used to."

Thea had been married when she first met her partner, Tom. They had socialized as couples and then, when her marriage broke up, she started dating Tom. Then they moved in together. Thea acknowledged that she and Tom had been drinking heavily during the time of her divorce. However, she quit drinking and Tom kept on.

"I never realized how big a problem with alcohol Tom had," Thea lamented. He had seizures when he tried to stop drinking and was in and out of hospital. She got him into a residential program and he did well for six months. Then he started drinking again. She called his father and got him into an outpatient program for two months. According to Thea: "It was on and off after that." The last time, nine months prior, she had taken him into Detox in hospital. He remained sober until he died.

"I was in charge of his life and I didn't realize how *huge* his problems were," Thea said. She felt guilty and responsible. "We were codependent and that was my pattern in every relationship. I 'took it on' and didn't see what was coming."

As well as his problem with alcohol, Tom was unemployed and unable to find a job. Thea said he felt rejected because, no matter how hard he tried, no one would hire him. It was very upsetting to him that he could not fill the provider role. Thea owned the house they lived in and the car they drove. Tom had made a lot of money in the past and felt like he needed a job to be a man. She knew this was very depressing to him. Consequently, she "had him in therapy" and on medication. She thought it was helping his depression. "I never thought he would do this!" she lamented repeatedly.

The Trauma

Tom was in a good mood that day. They went for a walk and "it was good," Thea reported. She went to work at 1:00 p.m. and talked to him on the phone from work. Tom came over at 4:30 p.m. to bring her cigarettes and told her he loved her very much. At 6:30 p.m. they talked on the phone about dinner and decided to order pizza that night. At 8:00 p.m. she called and he didn't answer so she texted him. He did not text back. At 8:30 p.m., she got "a sinking feeling" and ran home.

She walked up the stairs and found him hanging. "I tried to lift him, but I couldn't. Then, I got scissors to cut the rope. He dropped. I called 9-1-1 and started CPR, but he was gone. The police came, but it was too late."

Tom left a note that Thea showed me. It was addressed to his mother, his sister and "especially" her.

> "Love you all. Sorry for the shame. I dropped the ball and only I can be blamed."

Then, he added a note to Thea's parents:

> "Here's your girl back. I know she'll be a mess but get her on the right path."

Thea was hoping our EMDR therapy would help her get on that right path.

Preparation Session (1 1/2 hours)

I had some concern about how ready Thea would be to process this trauma given its severity and the short time frame since the event. While it was clear that it had affected her deeply, her descriptions were largely factual and offered with a minimum of affect. She seemed to be suppressing her feelings most of the time. But she was adamant that she wanted to proceed with the therapy.

The issue she wanted to work on was defined as follows:

I want to accept the way Tom died and stop envisioning it all the time.

The <u>target</u> was when she had cut him down and he was lying on the floor. She had to pick up his head to give him CPR, but the rope was embedded in his neck so tightly that she could not tilt his head. She had to cut the rope. She saw that his nose had burst and there was blood and mucous on his face. She had to give him CPR. She said: "His face was so close and he was so cold. I couldn't help or get him to answer. I had to stick my finger in his mouth and it was *so cold.*" This was the most distressing moment for her.

It was not easy for Thea to identify her feelings and locate them in specific parts of her body. We worked on this together for some time. Such suppression and containment of feelings may serve as a coping strategy or defense mechanism, particularly in instances of acute recent trauma. It is as if a curtain closes in the mind and only opens periodically as it did for Thea first thing in the morning. Helping clients to access their feelings without their becoming overwhelmed or retraumatized is a delicate art.

The <u>feelings</u> she identified were:

> helplessness that she located in her chest,
> shock that she located in her head,
> loneliness/despair that she located in her stomach,
> fear that she located in her back,
> horror that she located in her neck,
> anger that she located in her shoulders,
> sadness that she located in her heart,
> confusion that she located in her arms.

Her <u>negative cognition</u> was:

> I should have been able to see this coming and have
> stopped it.

Her <u>positive cognition</u> was:

> There was no way I could have seen this coming or
> stopped it.

The <u>VOC</u> (Validity of Cognition) was a three. She could intellectualize that it was not her fault or her responsibility, but she could not feel it as true at this point.

The <u>SUDS</u> (Subjective Units of Distress Scale) was an eight. She explained that it still seemed somewhat fake or unreal to her. I believe this is how the unconscious mind protects us – with the curtain of unreality mentioned above.

Resources

1. For nurturing and support, she chose:
   - her mother who she described as "really kind and giving and nurturing,"
   - and her grandmother who, she said, is "really sweet and so much fun. She should get a grandmother award."

2. For strength, she chose:
- her godmother who "has been through a lot and always remains positive. But she's not afraid to talk about the negative, too."

3. For wisdom, she chose:
- her Dad who is "the smartest person I've ever met and he's not afraid to tell it like it is."

The quality she chose that would be most helpful in resolving this issue was "clarity of faith." She could not own this quality herself, but identified her godmother as the person who best exemplified it. "She knows people are okay once they've passed and are dealing with what they need to. She has clarity about this. To her, it is fact."

Her safe place was the back porch of her parent's house in Colorado some years before. She would be lying on a chaise longue in the afternoon sun looking at the aspen trees and horses grazing in the distance. She could hear leaves rustling in the wind and smell the grass below the deck. She felt calm and at peace. Her repeating word was "beautiful."

Processing Session (2 hours)

She began the session with a SUDS of nine.

= [12]I just feel so bad that I didn't help him after I cut him down.

= I really couldn't help him. The police told me I couldn't help him.

---

[12] = Indicates Bilateral Stimulation

[Knowing her negative cognition, I asked her: "Do you believe this?" She said: "Yes." But I felt this assurance might be premature.]

= His eyes were open. His head was turned away from me, and it was cold. The window was open. I was sitting there shocked.
= The rope was so far into his neck, there was a huge dent in it like it was broken.
= I'm thinking it's so weird that he's not here and how he would like to be here. It's strange to do things without him.
= I just think he made a really bad decision. I feel like this decision doesn't make sense to me.

[I asked if she would like to talk to him about it.]

= I feel he's out of pain and that he just couldn't battle his addictions anymore.

[While I invite her to let Tom speak, she does not take up this suggestion, but offers her own conclusions.]

= He was so much in pain and so sad about life.

[I wonder if she might find it easier to talk to him if we go back in time, but she rejects this suggestion too. Instead, she proposes that his mother might be willing to speak for him.]

= She thinks he was upset about not having a job and got really depressed.

[I follow up on her idea that it was a really bad decision and ask if *he* feels he made a bad decision.]

= No.

[Apparently, it was not a bad decision for him.]

= What about the rest of us? Was it a bad decision for us?

= He thinks everybody would be better off without him. But I don't agree. His nephew idealizes him. How could he be better off? I know he won't be. I feel such sadness for him and all of us.

[I invite her to tell Tom directly.]

= I told him, but he thought his nephew would be okay and so will everybody. He just couldn't do it anymore. He just couldn't handle life.

= No one will be the same. I've become more jaded and selfish. I'm not wanting to share with anybody ever again in my life. You left me! What's the next guy going to do? Am I so easy to leave?

[I see that she is at risk of internalizing this event as a reflection on her value, so I want to address this. I ask: "Is this about who you were as a partner?"]

= Maybe he thought I could handle it. He thought my parents would help me. He knew they were staying longer than planned. Was this why he chose to do it then?

= I'm pissed. It's an awful thing to do to someone. He could have just left ... but then, I'd have been worried so I'm thankful for this. He must have known I would have done something to try to help. I had complained about the Xanex they were giving him. I think he really wanted out and was really tired. Maybe he left life, not me?

[I ask her to repeat the last statement.]

= *He left life, not me!* He told me how much he loved me. He loved his mother and his friends.

[I asked her to repeat the statement "He left life, not me" over and over as we did a Body Scan. Every part of her body was relaxed except her stomach and her back. She said she felt lonely (stomach) and afraid of "everything" (back).

We went back to the target and the SUDS was a ten.

[I believe this escalation was probably because she was finally addressing, rather than suppressing her feelings.]

= I feel fear. Was he afraid? Did it hurt?

[I suggest she could ask a doctor or the coroner.]

= The coroner says it hurts, but not for long. And he really wanted this. It's something I would never do. No matter how bad things are, I would never consider taking my life. And I would never want him to do that either.

= I don't think he really thought about all the crap I would have to deal with. I'm angry.

[I validate her anger. She responds to this.]

= I'm pissed off and I'm allowed to be pissed off about this.

[We do a Body Scan. Her SUDS is a six. Clearly, she has more work do to, but the time is up. We leave her anger in the place she selects – the Utah desert – and agree to come back to it in the follow-up session.]

This is one of the rare cases I have worked with where the work does not complete in the processing session. Once she has begun to see that she has no responsibility or fault in the situation, she begins to feel her anger at her partner for what he has put her through. Even if it was the right decision for him, it has been a horror for her and he didn't consider that. She has a need to be angry.

Follow-up Session

Thea reported that she had been feeling weepy and crying more out of anger and frustration. She wanted to protest to Tom: "Why did you do this? Why? Why?"

She recalled that just a few weeks before, she had told him how proud of him she was for his not drinking. "We're going to be okay," she had said.

When she went back to the target, her SUDS was a seven.

= The cop said he was gone. "Why can't you help him?" Thea wondered. The EMT came in and went to ask. They were laughing in my kitchen. I was pissed. The cop said: "There's nothing else we can do."

= I was mad inside, not outwardly. *I know I did everything I could.*

> [I had her repeat the last statement doing a Body Scan. Every part of her body was relaxed.]

= I don't want to get mad at Tom for fear of lowering his self-esteem.

> [This comment may seem irrational given that the man is dead. However, it is not unusual for people to believe they must maintain in my office the patterns they have adopted in life. I explain that no one outside the room would be directly affected by any of their expressions of anger or fantasies of revenge. But it can be very healing to them.]

Then, she continues:

= His mother is very guarded and private. She cuts people off if they let her down. But I let everybody into my world, even with their problems. I don't like confrontation and will avoid it at any cost.

> [She identifies the pattern that is holding her back. I continue to encourage her to express her anger at Tom.]

= He did it in our living room knowing I'd be coming home and would find him. It's hard to get mad at him. (She's struggling ... then she finds a link.) I'm mad at him for drinking because he couldn't do *anything* when he was drinking. He was useless. Then I did get pissed at him and yell at him. He'd feel so terrible.

[I ask if there is a memory that comes up.]

= I remember driving him to Rehab and he was drunk. I stopped the car and yanked him out and screamed at him.

[I encourage her to get in touch with her anger and what she wants to do with it.]

= I want to push him. I want to smack him across the face. (She stops cold for a moment. I encourage her to continue.)
= Why would you want to hurt me so much? I want to shake him and yell: "What the hell were you thinking?"
= Maybe he thought I was strong enough. But no one can be strong enough for something like that. That was really fucked up and truly mean – the only mean thing he ever did. It makes me question his state of mind.
= He was on painkillers. I'm mad at the guy who gave them to him. I'm going to throw him in his wheelchair into traffic. He's hit by a car.

[She's really getting angry now and I encourage her to express all of her anger toward Tom.]

= I'm shaking him and tossing him over the balcony. He falls on the gate and is hanging. I go down and kick him in the legs. He's saying he's sorry. "How *dare* you do this?" He says he's sorry, sorry ... I'm kicking him in the balls; then, punching him in the face. I'm throwing him down on the ground. "Why did you do this to me? How could you be so mean to me?"

= I do forgive him, but I'm still pissed off. At my ex-husband! At my father! He said he was so fucking sorry this happened after two years of him not talking to me. I'm angry at his stupid friends who had a memorial for him without us. They weren't his real friends.

> [After this venting of anger, I ask for her level of disturbance. Her SUDS is a five. Then I inquire: "What keeps it from being a zero?"]

= I'm confused, she replies. What the hell happened? You did it that quick? The first time he took a bunch of pills, but he told me to take him to the hospital. He said it was a cry for help. We got him on the right track. Suicide is completely foreign to me. I can't understand why anyone would want to do that.

> [I try to offer some understanding of the state of mind he might have been in, feeling that life was just too painful to bear. I suggest that she ask him if this is true.]

= Yes. He was worn out. He was at the bottom. He couldn't handle it anymore. But I still don't believe it.

> [I suggest she go through the steps that will make it real for her.]

= He's in the bag. Then, in the fridge for three days. Then, to the funeral home where they prepare the body. Then, they burn him. They put him in a box and send him to his mother's house.

= I'd rather just think it was a mistake. I have to remind myself that it really happened. *Tom is dead.*

> [We do a Body Scan while she takes in the reality of his death. Her level of disturbance is at a two. In response to the question: "What prevents it from being a zero?" she sums it up by saying: "It's icky."]

There is nothing that EMDR work can do to change the inherent quality of the traumatic event. If it was something horrible, it will not become something okay. Even though the level of disturbance goes down for the client, an event like this *is*, undeniably, "icky."

Postscript

I saw Thea only one more time. It was four days later.

She said she was feeling "okay." She had been uncontrollably weepy for one day after our work and then she felt better. Her energy had returned and she was eating again.

I was concerned that she might need ongoing support, but she disagreed. She said she felt finished and she wanted to get on with her life. Apparently, that's exactly what she did.

Clinical Comments

This case presents the steps of the recovery process in a remarkably clear and courageous way – from guilt and self-recrimination that somehow she should have done something to prevent this tragedy to the indisputable knowledge that it was beyond her control; from the pain of feeling that her partner had turned against her to the understanding that he had turned his back not on her, but on life itself; and from the anger that he had put her through an experience of hell to a compassionate awareness that the point of desperation he had reached offered him no way out. Each of these inordinately difficult steps was met and processed by my client with a level of honesty and integrity that I felt in her presence, but find it difficult to convey in words. It was a trial of the human spirit. There is very little I need to add in the way of explanation or interpretation because, in essence, this case study speaks for itself. It is a rare precious gem that would be sullied by a stream of analytic verbiage. To be a companion on her journey was both an ordeal and an honor. As we finished up, I was busily worrying about her like a clucking mother hen, while she was calmly and firmly reassuring me that she was going to be okay. I do believe she was right.

As a therapist, a case like this can be painful not only during the therapy work itself, but afterward as well. I had images of her dead partner replete with gory details when I lay in bed at night. I kept thinking of her coming home expecting to eat pizza with her lover and finding him hanging instead. I felt outraged and angry at him for allowing her to face a shock like this. Couldn't he have warned her or done it some other way? I kept imagining what a nightmare it must have been for her to have to cut him down and give him CPR. My mind fixated on the blood and mucous close to her face and the horrid coldness of his body as she administered CPR. I wondered if I would have been capable of doing the same. I felt righteous indignation at the police and ambulance attendants who were less than compassionate and sensitive to her plight. My feelings went from disgust to rage to sympathy and round and around again.

In this way, Post Traumatic Stress Disorder can be an issue for us as EMDR therapists as well as for the clients we are working with. I once, only half-jokingly, created a diagnosis for myself called "Compulsive Empathy Disorder." To the extent that we as therapists are experiencing empathy with our clients, to that extent we will inevitably be experiencing the same trauma the client has experienced. Hence, it is important to be aware of the potential for therapist traumatization and be prepared to take appropriate steps to resolve such trauma by association. Those of us who are EMDR therapists will likely benefit from a support network of other EMDR therapists to help us manage this work. Facing the brutality of life and death is not for the feint of heart.

CHAPTER TWO

Profound Depression:

Fighting the Darkness

Case of Sam

As therapists, we spend a lot of our time dealing with depression. It is one of the most prevalent presenting problems in our clientele. It is also one of the most resistant to change. It is not unusual to spend months, even years, watching a client mired in depression. We suffer with them and for them, often feeling hopeless and despairing ourselves.

I am reminded of a depressed client I worked with a number of years ago. She was smart, beautiful and had been severely depressed for as long as she could remember. She had spent fourteen years on anti-depressant medication and in weekly therapy with a psychiatrist. She had been institutionalized for extended periods on two separate occasions during the time of her therapy. She had a good relationship with her therapist who, no doubt, was well trained and proficient in her skills. Yet this client made no progress at all. She came to me saying she was just as depressed as she had been at the start. We tried all the methods I could think of – including cognitive behavioral, art therapy, Gestalt therapy, and hypnotherapy – all without significant improvement. Finally, she agreed to try EMDR. In the session, she released a storm of anger she must have suppressed for years. She chopped her mother into pieces and fried her in a frying pan. However outrageous this may sound, this woman came away feeling happy for the first time.

Perhaps this dramatic experience was somewhere in the back of my mind when I agreed to work with the case at hand. There was certainly no obvious reason on the surface to believe that our work would be successful. This man had a history of long-term chronic depression and, despite a good relationship with his therapist, he was getting steadily worse. He was understandably cynical and had no faith in the process. Admittedly, this would not be my most impressive case to include if I simply wanted to prove a point. I actually thought it was my first EMDR flop. In the end, while I have some criticisms of the work I did, the results went beyond anything I had anticipated.

Background Information.

The client in this case is a sixty-one-year-old white male who had worked as an operations manager for the same company for ten years. We'll call him Sam.

Sam was married to his first wife for thirty years and had three children with her. They were separated about five years earlier and were divorced two years prior. His ex-wife and children are strong evangelists who definitely did not approve of the divorce. He remarried five months before our work together and was living with his new wife, Lynn, and her fourteen-year-old son.

His current therapist referred Sam for EMDR because he was stuck and was not progressing. In fact, he was going down-hill. He had been seeing this therapist for over a year and had a good relationship with her. He attended CODA[13] and ACOA[14] meetings regularly. However, his state had pro-gressively deteriorated.

Sam had had a major depressive disorder for many years with recurrent bouts of depression and feelings of self-loathing. He had been to a number of therapists in the past (whom he called "useless"). He tried various psychotropic medications that he subsequently stopped because of the adverse side effects. He was currently in treatment with a psychiatrist who reported that he was on a stable medication regimen. Nonetheless, he went from bad to worse.

---

[13] Codependents Anonymous
[14] Adult Children of Alcoholic and Dysfunctional Families

In November of 2009, his depression got so bad it immobilized him. He became unable to perform his job out of a paralyzing fear of making a mistake. He went on disability from December until May of 2010 and was just attempting to return to work on a half-time basis when I met him.

Sam described his depression as a weight he named "the darkness." It was a state of utter hopelessness and irritability in which, he reported, he would start cursing and raging as if, he said, he had Tourette's. In the extreme, he would become what he called "catatonic" and was unable to engage or respond at all, as if he were "in shock." He reported feeling fundamentally flawed and beyond repair, with a deep fear that he couldn't do *anything* right.

When asked about the origin of his depression, he said he had been emotionally abused by his father, an Evangelical minister, whom he called "a rager and a sex addict" with "darkness" in him. His mother had watched the abuse without intervening on her son's behalf. Sam explained that his recent therapy had opened up the frozen feelings he had overridden in the past and now he didn't know what to do with them. He rushed everywhere, he said, trying to avoid the relentless messages from the angry voice inside his head. He recognized that he was still carrying his abusive father within.

Preparation Session

The <u>issue</u> that Sam identified as the goal of his EMDR therapy was:

> I want to take in stride times when I make a mistake or face a task in which I might fall short of perfect.

For Sam, the most disturbing example of the issue he wanted to work on was an experience he had at six years old when he was sitting with his two sisters in the back seat of the car and his father was driving with his mother in the front. Sam was drumming his fingers on the armrest of the car door. His father turned around, taking his eyes off the road, and screamed at his young son: "I thought I asked you to stop that! What is wrong with you?" His face was contorted with rage, Sam remembered, and his eyes were full of hate. "If you don't stop," his father screamed at him, "I'll run the car off the road!"

Sam reported that he felt like he had been shot or like a grenade had gone off in front of him. He was in shock – "like something had been ripped out of me and that something was my soul." It was silent in the car and Sam felt stunned and immobilized. He had an overwhelming sense of shame as if he were very small, utterly worthless, incompetent, and "fundamentally irredeemably flawed." This was the worst moment of the experience for Sam and formed the target for our work.

The feelings Sam identified as associated with his disturbing experience were:

>   shock that he located in his upper chest,
>   fear that he located in his gut,
>   hurt that he located in his heart,
>   shame that he located all over his body,
>   despair that he located in his shoulders,
>   hopelessness that he located in his head.

As his <u>negative cognition</u>, Sam suggested the following possible options:

> I am bad;
> I am incompetent;
> I am irredeemably flawed;
> I can't do anything right;
> I am worthless.

He chose as his negative cognition:

> I am worthless.

Sam's <u>SUDS</u> was ten, the highest level of disturbance on the scale.

Sam's <u>positive cognition</u> was:

> I am a good man.

Sam's <u>VOC </u>was one (completely false).

After establishing the protocol, we then created a set of resources.

Sam's resources were as follows:
1. For nurturance and support, he chose:
- his new wife
- and his grandmother;

2. For strength, he chose:
- Jesus
- and Arnold Schwartzenegger in his *Terminator II* role;

3. For wisdom, he chose:
- Obe Wan Kanobe who "had vast experience fighting the dark side"
- and King Solomon.

The quality he felt he needed to possess to resolve his issue was self-esteem.

He brought up a recent example driving home with his new wife and the kids when he had been what he regarded as "a catalyst for such a good time because of who I was – funny, loving and free."

I realized that I had not had time to establish a safe place in the preparation session, so it was introduced in the follow-up session. This could have been a problem, but, fortunately, was not in this case. I did make it clear to him, as I do with all clients, that they can stop the process at any time if they are confused or disturbed or have a question, simply by signaling to me.

Processing Session

Prior to our starting the processing, Sam reported that he had been getting increasingly impatient and angry the last couple of days. His tone was rather hostile and gloomy. The SUDS he reported was a six, down from the ten he had reported in the preparation session.

Sam begins:

= All I want is to sleep. I feel hopeless, stuck. I'll never get it.

> [He actually closed his eyes and lay back in the chair. It looked like he was going to sleep. It was obvious that he was *not* into the process. The voice of his resistance is his depression speaking.]

= I'm feeling that I'm always going to be like this.
= I'm heading for self-destruction. It will be slow. I will isolate and use drugs again and go downhill.
= I'll be very lonely and it won't work for me. I'll be trapped between two worlds with no way out and no relief. I'll be in a hell of misery.
= I'm standing in front of myself going back and forth like the "beep, beep" of the scanner.

> [Note the dual focus between self and observer that the client makes explicit here.]

= The observer sees the other part on fire, melting, saying: "Help me!"
= I've been trying for years. The observer reaches out and grabs me, but he falls away. He slips away. He can't help me.

> [Sam is feeling hopeless that he can find a way out. He spends some time stuck and complaining. This is the pattern of depression, circling in place, with only negative feelings and blocked options. We call this stuckness typical of dysfunctional thought process "looping." It is a closed system. After letting him circle in this negative space for a while, I then ask if there is

a resource that might be able to help him here. He chooses Jesus, one of his two resources for strength.]

= Jesus says: "I love you." Sam says: "Bullshit!" Then he adds: "I flash back to a traumatic event in my childhood where my Dad is raging and cursing and then, he leaves us. I feel betrayed by God."

[Jesus was a resource he chose for strength, but I had not checked for ambivalence. This turned out to be a mistake on my part. Sam felt that Jesus had abandoned him when he was a child by allowing his father to leave the family. I wonder if we might repair this rupture and so I ask if he wants to tell Jesus how angry he is at Him.]

There is a period of silence. He does not verbalize his anger. He looks frozen and deadpan. Then, he reports back:

= Jesus is non-responsive. His eyes are blinking. I'm about ready to walk. He's just my projection, not my real higher power. Just a facade, not a real person to connect with.

[I realize that his alienation from God is a separate, bigger issue that will take us away from the issue at hand, so I choose not to pursue this now.]

Sam continues:

= There's no one who could help me.

He remains stuck in his depressive thought pattern. (There is a long pause.) Then he says:

= Except maybe Schwarzenegger – I mean the guy he was in the *Terminator II* movie. Yes. He's come from another dimension to help me.

[This is the first rapid shift we observe in this process. Suddenly, the bilateral stimulation moves him past his depressive belief system that there is no possible help available to embrace another option. What I regularly observe is that there is a deep and powerful energy for change that gets harnessed in this work.]

= The Terminator asks what I need. I tell him: "I need to be released from prison." He opens the bars and I walk out.

Sam continues:
= Let's go break the hyperlink in the car.

[He is referring to the target.]

= I point at my Dad and the Terminator steps in. He interrupts my Dad and tells him to stop yelling, drive the car and cool down, and then apologize to his son. "That's no way to talk to a little boy," Schwarzenegger scolds him.
= Dad is shocked into silence. He didn't expect an advocate for me and it stops his cascade of anger. He is even grateful. He stops and thinks and now he sees what is happening. He stops the car and tells me he is sorry.

[Again, we see a rapid shift in the client's prior belief system. He moves past his anger and allows his father to emerge as a caring human being. Given the depth of the client's depression, it is remarkable that he is able to make such a rapid transition. It does not always happen as quickly as it did in this case.]

I ask: "What does your father say to little Sam?"
= He says: "I'm sorry, Sammy, please forgive me. I just made a horrid mistake." Sam says: I feel relief and this fear is lifting.

> [Here again, the client expresses an immediate willing-
> ness to integrate this new picture. It is most likely
> because he is hearing what he needed and wanted to
> hear as a child.]

He continues with his father's apology:

= "You haven't done anything wrong. You're a good kid." Sam
says: "I accept this."

> [I hear from the client's feedback that, cognitively and
> emotionally, he is taking in this new information,
> but I want to be sure. I do a Body Scan to check this
> acceptance. The way I do a Body Scan is very specific
> and focused. It involves going back to each part of
> the body that was identified with the feelings raised
> by the target. We look to see if each individual part is
> contracted or relaxed.]

Body Scan:
- upper chest is relaxed (site of his shock reaction),
- gut is relaxed (site of his fear),
- head is relaxed (site of his hopelessness).

But there is tension in his shoulders (the site of despair).

> [I ask him what comes up when he is in touch with his
> shoulders.]

= He says: "This isn't the first or the last time he treated me
badly."

> [I suggest he talk to his Dad about these other times.
> I direct him to look at his Dad and make sure that his

Dad is looking back at him and listening to what he has to say.]

= His Dad says: "What other times?" Sam says: "Fuck you!"

[At this point I would have expected to go into anger processing regarding other abusive situations with his Dad, but the client comes up with a different option.]

= The Terminator steps in on my side. He mentions other times - like the fights with Mom, the time I didn't put his tools back, the walking on eggs all the time around him.
= Dad says "Oh." The client adds: "He's conflicted between his pride and what he knows to be true. "
= Dad says: "I see what you mean. I've been a real jerk and not a good father. It's true."

[At this point, we go back to check the client's shoulders. They are looser.]

= Dad says: "We both know you can't count on me. It's too far gone." (Client looks sad and sounds resigned as he reports this.)

[Seeing that his father cannot be a support for the child, I ask if his adult self might be there for the child. I ask: "Do you want to offer yourself as a support to the child you were?"]

= I can try, but I'm not perfect, and I haven't always been available. But I'm open to learn.

There is a pause while he looks dubious. Then he says with more conviction:

= Lynn (his new wife) could do it. She likes him and he likes her.

> [Again the client spontaneously presents a solution when the way seems blocked. It is evident to him, as well as to me, that he will need to work on his relationship with the child he was, but in the meantime, his wife can be a resource for them both.]

= His wife says: "I can be here for both of you and I will do whatever I can."

> [We check his shoulders again. They are relaxed. But his heart is a little tense (site of his hurt). I ask him to get in touch with his heart.]

= We've done so much and tried so hard. The child is not happy with me, but he is good with Lynn.

Then, the client adds, speaking from his adult self:

= I'm willing to learn and work on taking care of you.

> [We go back and check his heart. It is relaxed now. Since the Body Scan is complete, I direct him to go back to the target and notice the level of distress that it has for him now. To my surprise, the SUDS he reported was a five. Remember, he started at a six. I'm thinking something has gone very wrong if it's still a five and I am confused by this. I decide to ask him about his positive cognition. It was: "I am a good man."]

= "I have doubt," he says. "It seems half black and half white."

[Now I am convinced that something has gone wrong. The SUDS and the PC are both problematic.]

(There is a pause.)
= Wait! Now the white is eclipsing the black! I feel hopeful.

[He has an excited tone and a smile when he says this. Remembering that he began in a place of no hope, I feel a little better too.]

= What is true for me is: "I *want* to be a good man."

[As a positive cognition, "I am a good man" does not feel quite right for him, but "I want to be a good man" does. As mentioned earlier, sometimes the PC needs to be modified based on what happens in the processing work.]

We do a Body Scan and install the new positive cognition.

He is visibly relaxed. He seems to have made his peace with his father's limitations and is trusting his wife to spearhead a new relationship with the child within. He is aware that he needs to work on his own relationship with his child and trusts himself to pursue that goal. That ends our processing session.

I go away thinking that we will need to work on a repair of his relationship to his child self. We may also need a separate processing of his fractured relationship to God. We plan a one-and-a-half-hour follow-up session.

Follow-up session

The client came in smiling and reported that he had "turned a corner." He had a fun weekend with his wife and kids. He was elated.

We went to the target and he said the level of disturbance was a zero. Now I could be elated too.

When I inquired about the five he had reported at the end of the previous session, it turned out to be a misunderstanding on his part. He thought the SUDS was an evaluation of what had occurred – that is, of his father's behavior – not of his own level of disturbance as he recalled the troubling events of the past. With this confusion clarified, he stated with conviction that his distress level had been a zero in the past session and still was a zero.

For the follow-up, I did a hypnotherapy session with him in order to establish his safe place and install his resources there. Then, I utilized a method from Laurel Parnell known as "tapping in."[15] This method is not EMDR processing per se, but it uses bilateral stimulation to anchor positive thoughts and experiences. I wanted to see if it could help him repair his relationship with his child.

I asked him to recall an experience of loving somebody and he chose his cat. Then I directed him to notice, in turn, what he saw, heard, felt in his body and felt inside as he thought about loving his cat. He reported that his chest swelled up and he felt warm. He saw himself with a big grin on his face and heard himself talking in a playful voice. As his cat's energy went up, so did his. "It's like an exchange of energy," he said, "like a circle. I feel completeness. It's a bonding experience."

At this point, I asked him to visualize loving his child and

---

[15] Laurel Parnell, *Tapping In: A Step by Step Guide to Activating Your Healing Resources Through Bilateral Stimulation*, (Boulder: Sounds True, 2008).

see if it was possible to have the same bonding experience, the same exchange of energy with the child, as he had with his cat.

The child responded negatively at first. "You fake! You're full of it! I don't trust you at all!" It was a natural reaction given that the client had been so distanced and unsupportive of himself for years.

Then, Sam suggested they look at photos together, including some of himself and his new wife. "He sees I'm different now with Lynn beside me. He's smiling and allowing it." We installed this new experience with the bilateral stimulation. Sam went out feeling hopeful.

He began practicing self-hypnosis on a daily basis. He went to his safe place and his child self was there. So was Jesus. Jesus wore a business suit and a hat with a crown of thorns.

At first, there was a great distance between them. Jesus sat behind a large desk. The desk got smaller and smaller each day until Jesus came out from behind it. Then the desk was gone. They got closer and closer each day until they were sitting together, all three of them. Big Sam and little Sammy were happy with the connection between them and ready to address their relationship with God.

Shortly thereafter, Sam reported that he had been feeling shame one morning and he asked God what He saw when He looked at him. God did not answer, but Sam felt seen in his essence. Then he looked at himself through God's eyes and erased the shame. He saw that what mattered was not his performance rating or the mistakes he had made but his "hanging in." It was not the pluses and minuses but his spirit, his divine spark, that gave him value. "He's so proud of me," Sam announced, glowing with pride.

From a man who felt he could do nothing right, he had become aware of his intrinsic value independent of his mistakes or accomplishments. From a man who was unable to function due to shaming messages from his abusive father, he became capable of loving and supporting himself. It is a goal that is fundamental to many different approaches to therapy. What is unique to EMDR is the time frame in which it has been achieved.

Clinical Comments

I have observed that some clients seem to process easily. The starting gun goes off at the moment the scanner is turned on and they are "off to the races." The necessary solutions seem to arise spontaneously with little effort on their parts or mine. Powered by the bilateral stimulation, the steps to change seem to simply flow out of them as new connections are made in the brain. We see this fluid process in the case of Sam.

Other clients are a different story. For various reasons, they are unable to proceed without continual assistance and guidance from the therapist, sometimes at every step of the way. It might be because they habitually avoid or suppress their feelings and need suggestions to help them become aware of their feelings in the moment. It might be because, although aware of their feelings, they are not comfortable expressing feelings to another person. Some clients need validation that it is okay to feel what they feel. Others need encouragement to say what they feel out loud or tell it to another person. Frequently, they need permission to act out their feelings in fantasy because of years of holding back their emotional responses. They would rather implode and do damage to themselves than risk upsetting a person who is important to them. We will see this in the next case, the case of Trevor.

EMDR theory contains within it two mutually opposing themes. One is the idea that EMDR therapy is a self-directed process. We let the client follow whatever comes up in their minds, trusting that they will go where they need to go. However long it takes, however blocked they are, the therapist's responsibility is to "hold" the process until the client finds a solution, their own unique way out of the maze of their stuckness.

The other theme is implicit in the notion of cognitive interweaves.

Francine Shapiro says:

> The interventions I developed are strategies to "jump-start" blocked processing by introducing certain material rather than depending on the client to provide all of it. The term *interweave* refers to the fact that this strategy calls for the clinician to offer statements that therapeutically weave together the appropriate neuro networks and associations.[16]

If a client is stuck and "looping," the therapist can challenge the blocking beliefs that hold them back or bring up questions that point to another alternative. This implies that the therapist can make interventions that move the process forward. Of course, the client has to accept these interventions. They are not forced upon them by the therapist. But the therapist does not have to wait, perhaps interminably, for the client to discover them on his or her own.

How does an EMDR therapist resolve this apparent dilemma? I suggest that it will depend on the client and their

---

[16] Shapiro, *Eye Movement Desensitization and Reprocessing*, 244. Dr. Shapiro suggests the cognitive interweave as a strategy for "highly disturbed clients" or those with "particularly complicated pathologies." Perhaps, as I believe, it has broader applicability.

process. When the processing is moving forward with its own energy, I step out of the way and allow it to flow. When the client is blocked, if I see a possible way out, I will raise it and see how the client responds. I will neither hold it back, nor insist upon it. I am aiming for that middle ground which allows me to engage and share options with the client, while they remain the authority on what fits for them.

Perhaps each EMDR therapist needs to decide this issue for themselves. Personally, I am less at ease with a non-directive approach and am more inclined to be an interactive type of therapist. The next case study will be an obvious case in point. Unlike Sam, Trevor needed active continual participation on my part. It almost devolved into a regular counseling session with bilateral stimulation in the background. However, in the end, it allowed the client to move in the direction he wanted to go.

If I see a way out of the maze, I will propose it. It is up to the client if they want to go that way.

CHAPTER THREE

Rage Attacks:

The Dilemma of Clark Kent

Case of Trevor

Trevor was a mild-mannered man. He spoke softly and his affect was generally flat. That is the reason he reminded me of Clark Kent, the mild-mannered, geeky journalist for the Daily Planet who acted as the front for Superman. Except that in Trevor's case, it was not a hero for social justice who lay hidden behind his quiet and pleasant facade. It was, instead, a man of seething resentment who erupted, apparently without warning, with explosions of rage and anger. These outbursts were deeply disconcerting to his wife and, no less so, to Trevor himself. Trevor came for therapy because he could not understand what he was so angry about.

Background Information

Trevor described himself as a "geek Dad." He had worked in technical services for some years, but was now "retired" and stayed at home to care for his four-year-old adopted daughter while his wife went out to work. Trevor was forty-four years old.

Trevor reported that he had had "lifelong" depression and anxiety. His doctor reported that he had chronic hypertension. Trevor was on a regimen of Lexpro for depression and Ambien for insomnia prescribed by a psychiatrist he had been seeing on and off for ten years. His wife (whom we'll call Amy) questioned the effectiveness of this treatment. While Trevor agreed that his psychiatrist was "pretty passive," he himself liked this quality about him - perhaps because he and the psychiatrist had this trait of passivity in common. He likely would have continued with the same therapy indefinitely.

The catalyst for his coming for EMDR therapy was Trevor's rage. Both he and his wife were concerned about the future impact on their daughter if the rage attacks continued unabated. According to Trevor, the episodes seemed to be triggered by situations that were not planned or chosen by him. For example, one time his wife's sister decided spontaneously to spend the night at their home with her kids. Trevor was enraged. Another recent incident was during a barbecue they were hosting at their house. Trevor said: "I don't like parties anyway, and I always have to do all the work." He became surly and irritated and was not polite to his guests. The issue, he concluded, was "control."

Growing up, Trevor had always been a "good boy." He was in the honors society at school and never got into any trouble. Apparently, his sister got into enough trouble for them both with her stealing, drug trafficking and drug abuse that sent her in and out of rehab and jail. He was very close to his mother whom he described as warm, caring and nurturing. His father was the Food Services Director at a university and an entrepreneur on the side. Trevor said: "He worked all the time." He referred to his father as "a piece of work" and "an asshole in some ways" – i.e. arrogant and intimidating – because of his verbal authoritarianism and self-importance. "I can hear his voice when I discipline my daughter."

According to Trevor, neither of his parents was strict or gave him much direction. In his senior year, he dropped out of college and worked instead. He felt this was a big disappointment to his father. When he later tried to go back to school, he missed the exam and never completed his courses. As a result, he never got a degree. "I was smart enough but just didn't do it," he said. Trevor lived with his parents until after college when he left home to move in with his wife.

Trevor and Amy tried for three years to have a child despite the fact that he was "not really big on having a kid." "It was Amy's wish, not my choice," Trevor admitted. When their attempts to conceive were unsuccessful, they decided to adopt a child from a foreign country. "I was very reluctant to adopt and still have times when I resent it," Trevor said. It was decided that Amy would continue in her job and Trevor would be a stay-at-home Dad. "She's the one who wanted the child and *I* get to deal with her."

Unfortunately for Trevor, his wife's job involved some travel, so he was left as the sole parental figure for periods of time. He expressed feeling "abandoned, over-burdened and overwhelmed" when she was out of town. He had a deep despair and anger at the unfairness of his role. When his wife gave him "grief" about not working, he was deeply resentful since, he argued: "She needs me at home to go on her trips." Then he repeated a comment his daughter had made that obviously struck a nerve: "My mommy goes to work and my daddy cleans the house." The stigma of this role reversal deeply affected him. Trevor was stuck in a martyr position.

Preparation Session

We faced a choice about how to proceed. Trevor's anger was causing problems in his relationships, but his anger had a message for him about the life he was leading. Did he want to address the anger or the *message* of the anger? He chose to look at his expression of anger first. I recommended that he consider couple counseling to deal with the consequences of his EMDR work.

The issue Trevor chose to work on was:

> I would like to remain calm and reasonable in stressful and overwhelming situations.

The most disturbing example of this issue was a recent party he and Amy were throwing for old friends (and no family) at their new house. Trevor spent days getting ready for the party – cleaning the house, shopping, and preparing food. For most of the party, he was either in the kitchen cooking or outside barbecuing. He remarked, not surprisingly, that he really did not enjoy the parties they had. He "popped off" to several guests with impatience and impoliteness - thereby becoming "old man me" - i.e. cranky and crabby. He didn't remember all the incidents that irritated him, but he knew that what he was feeling was *rage*. A little kid was relentlessly ringing the doorbell; another went pee in his daughter's bedroom; and Amy was dogging him about opening a very good bottle of wine. Trevor went into their bedroom to get a moment of solitude and Amy came after him. He told her to "back off and fucking leave me alone." This was the most disturbing moment and formed the <u>target</u> for our work.

The <u>feelings</u> that came up when he recalled the worst moment in the bedroom were:

> rage that he located in his temples,
>
> overwhelm that he located in his stomach,
>
> agitation that he located in his fists,
>
> hopelessness that he located behind his eyes,
>
> frustration that he located in his shoulders ("I worked so hard and didn't even want the party"),
>
> resentment that he located in his upper jaw and cheeks (at his wife for making him do it),
>
> self-pity that he located in his heart ("I am Cinderfella"),
>
> feeling "fed up and sick of taking care of other people's needs" that he located in his diaphragm.

The <u>negative belief</u> he had about himself in response to this situation was:

> Nothing I do will ever be enough.

The <u>SUDS</u> he reported was an eight.

The <u>positive cognition</u> – i.e. what he would like to believe if the work was successful was:

> I'm doing the best that I can.

His <u>VOC</u> or <u>Validity of Cognition</u> was a three.

Trevor's Resources were:

1. For nurturing and support, he chose:
   - his grandmother on his Dad's side who really cared about him,
   - and one of his longest closest friends, Lisa, who "really gets me."

2. For strength, he chose:
   - Superman because he is powerful and invincible. [I had forgotten this when I described him as Clark Kent.]

3. For wisdom, he chose:
   - Obama who had to overcome so many obstacles to be where he is today,
   - and another friend, Joshua, who is "the smartest guy you'll ever meet" and gives great advice.

The quality he felt he needed was inner peace and tranquility.

He recalled the time he had to give a speech in court in front of officials in a foreign country to convince them to grant their request to adopt their daughter. "Normally I'd be flustered and anxious but, instead, I was calm, tranquil, confident and self-possessed."

He chose as his safe place a log cabin in a remote setting in Canada. He is sitting with his feet up and nothing he needs to do. He feels "indulged" and "away."

It is evident that this safe place is the polar opposite of his "Cinderfella" life.

Processing Session

For this session, I took both handwritten notes and an audio recording. I have condensed the transcript of the audio recording in minor ways, but essentially it is complete. Clinical comments added after processing statements are indicated in parentheses.

When Trevor was ready to begin the work, the SUDS he reported was an eight.

Rachel: I'm going to review with you everything that we set up in advance as our protocol. I'm going go back through it to remind you and, then, I'm going to tell you what I want you to focus on. Okay?

Trevor: Okay.

Rachel: So, I have two statements of the issue. I think it's the second, but you can tell me. The first one was: "I would like to manage my anger more effectively" and the second one was:

"I would like to remain calm and reasonable in stressful and overwhelming situations." It's the second one?

Trevor: Yeah.

Rachel: Right, that's what I thought. Okay. Now, the target comes out of an experience you had at a party you were throwing for old friends (and no family) at your new house. You spent *days* getting ready for the party: cleaning the house, shopping, preparing food. And there you were in the kitchen, cooking for part of the time and then outside barbequing for the rest of the party. You said you don't really enjoy parties and that you "popped off", using your terminology, to several people and weren't patient or polite. The mask came down and you became "*old man me*", crabby and cranky. A little kid was relentlessly ringing the doorbell and you told him to knock it off, and the mother didn't like the way you talked to her son, Amy told you. She thought you were being rude to her. And some other aggravating things were when a friend's daughter went pee in your daughter's bedroom and you got mad about that. So, of all of those annoying things – the amount of work you were doing, the kid ringing the bell and his mother thinking you were rude, and the fact that some little kid went and peed in the bedroom – there was a lot about the party that was bothering you. But the most disturbing thing that happened was when Amy followed you into the bedroom and was dogging you about opening a really good bottle of wine and you disagreed.

Trevor: Yeah … Although I think there was even more. I think there was a shaking. When that was happening, I was just trying to get away from everything.

Rachel: You were trying to get some solitude. That was when you were in the bedroom, sitting on your side of the bed, and you told Amy to "back off and leave you fucking alone!"

You were enraged. You were trying to get some time to yourself and she was bugging you.

Trevor: Yeah, I was just trying to cool down.

Rachel: Okay. So now, take yourself to that moment where all of these annoying things are bugging you and you finally get into the bedroom to try to get a break and Amy is in there, bugging you. You're REALLY angry and annoyed at that point.

Trevor: Mhmm.

Rachel: And the feelings that come up that you identified were *rage* that you located in your temples, a sense of being *overwhelmed* that you located in your stomach, *agitation* that you located in your fists, *hopelessness* that you located behind your eyes, *frustration* (that you worked so hard and didn't even want to be having a party) that you located in your shoulders, and *resentment* at Amy for making you do it. It was her idea, it was her party and you were doing all the work. And that resentment you located in your upper jaw and cheeks. There was *self-pity* (you described yourself as "Cinderfella") that you located in your heart – you were feeling sorry for yourself. And you were pretty much *fed-up* and *sick* of taking care of other people's needs – and that you located in your diaphragm. The negative belief that you hold about yourself when you recall the target, that moment in the midst of this party was: "Nothing I do will EVER be good enough." Does everything that I've said so far feel pretty right and right on and accurate, Trevor?

Trevor: Yes.

Rachel: Okay. So, what I'd like you to do now is to hold three things in your mind at once: the target situation – going back to that moment sitting on the *bed of rage,* the feelings that I have just listed as the responses you had to that target, and the negative cognition or negative belief that NOTHING that you do will ever be enough. Hold those three things in your mind. Focus on them and ramp up the disturbance until it is as high as you can make it at this moment in time. And when you get to that point, just tell me a number from zero to ten where ten would represent the most disturbance that you can imagine, and zero would represent neutral, flat, no charge at all. When I hear that number, I will start the scanner and you will witness and observe what happens in your mind when the scanner goes on.

(Long pause)

Trevor: So, I'm sorry; you're needing a number from me?

Rachel: Yeah. What you're going to do is hold those three things that I just described and tell me when they get to the highest level of disturbance that you can produce at the moment, and what that number is.

(Long pause)

Trevor: Um, it's eight.

Rachel: Okay. So, I'd like you to go back to the target and visualize yourself at the party. And you're in that state of rage because so much has been bugging you, and you've been working so hard, and you're trying to get some time alone, and Amy is there insisting on this wine and so on. Just go back there and notice what comes up.

(Long pause)

Trevor: Yeah, I just wanted to be left alone.

Rachel: Okay. And how did it feel? Is there anything else that goes with that? Is there a feeling of: "I just want to be left alone!" (childish aggravated voice) or is it a calm quiet feeling: "I just want to be left alone"?

Trevor: It's a little bit of both, actually.

Rachel: Okay, so stay with that: "I just want to be left alone."

(Long pause)

Rachel: And what's happening now?

Trevor: I'm still on the side of the bed. Um. I don't know, I guess part of it is that I'm not that angry right now. I'm trying to get into that moment, but I'm just kind of worn out on the side of the bed.

> [The client is unable to get in touch with his anger. He is imploding in the session just as he does in his life. I go with what he is able to feel.]

Rachel: So, just get in touch with how worn out you feel. You spent days preparing; it's been so hard. You have so much to do. You're running in; you're running out; you're cooking in both places. You're just drained with trying to do everything for other people.

(Long pause)

Trevor: I just wanted them to leave, and I wanted to watch TV by myself.

Rachel: Yeah.

Trevor: I'm also thinking, as I'm sitting on the bed, how much work is going to be involved in cleaning up everything after the fact too.

Rachel: Absolutely.

Trevor: I just don't want that party smell in my house afterwards. You wake up the next morning and it smells like old appetizers and stuff.

Rachel: So, you want to watch TV, but you're also realizing that there's going to be all this clean up.

Trevor: Yeah, the road ahead … from that point.

Rachel: So, I'm gathering you're not feeling too excited about that prospect?

[I'm noticing that he talks about his thoughts, but avoids identifying his feelings.]

Trevor: No. I'm going to be cleaning it pretty much by myself.

Rachel: And you'll be doing it by yourself?

Trevor: Pretty much.

Rachel: And how is that for you?

[I'm trying to steer him toward expressing his feelings.]

Trevor: A lot of work … but I'm also kind of a perfectionist.

[He slips away from feelings and remains centered on his cognitive concerns.]

Rachel: You mean, you make it harder than it needs to be?

Trevor: Probably. I don't accept as much help from Amy as I probably should.

[I see an opening to his martyr script here.]

Rachel: Ah. So, doing it by yourself is partly your choice?

Trevor: In some ways, yeah.

Rachel: "In some ways." Would you actually *like* to have more help from her?

Trevor: Yeah.

Rachel: Do you tell her that?

Trevor: Um, yeah. That usually gets thrown back as: "I work really hard at my job too."

Rachel: Okay. I'd like you to imagine right now that Amy's there and you're going to ask her for help. You're worn out and tired and you've been doing all this work and you'd like her to help clean up. Visualize Amy. Can you look at her? Can you see her looking at you? Can you get her attention? Is she listening?

> [I'd like to make the interaction less cognitive and more experiential.]

Trevor: Mhmm.

Rachel: Okay. So, tell her how you feel. You can do that silently or you can do it out loud. The only thing is, if you do it silently, I don't know when you're finished.

Trevor: I'm finished.

Rachel: And what did you say?

Trevor: I just said: "Can you please help me?"

Rachel: And what does she say in response? Just *notice*. Don't remember, but pay attention to what comes up *now* as you listen to her response.

> [It is not his old scripts in his head that we want to access, but his experience in the moment with the scanner on.]

Trevor: She says: "I will."

Rachel: Ah, so she said she *would* help you?

Trevor: Yes.

Rachel: Is that a surprise for you?

Trevor: No. Whether it happens enough is going to be the next issue.

Rachel: Okay. So she says she will. When you ask, she says she will. When you started, you were assuming that you'd be doing it all by yourself, and the first thing that was different is that is that you actually did choose to ask her for help and she said "okay." We don't know yet how that's going to play out, but we know that if you didn't ask, you'd be very sure you'd be doing it by yourself, right?

[I'm drawing out the learning from this so it won't be missed.]

Trevor: Mhmm.

Rachel: So, there's asking. She said "I will." Okay. Let the drama continue and see what happens. You could say something like: "Let's start then. Let's get this damned thing done! I'm tired and let's get it over" or whatever you would say. So maybe if you could watch what happens?

Trevor: Well, no one ever taught her how to load a dishwasher correctly. So I usually have go in and redo whatever she's put in there. Whenever she says she will help, it's not necessarily helpful; it's just lateral help.

[Notice how he goes back into his past experience with her. We also see how he maintains his victim role. Either he doesn't ask for help or he doesn't accept the help she offers because it isn't good enough for him. In either case, he remains stuck with the responsibility that he deeply resents.]

Rachel: Well, if you have to redo it, then it's not helpful at all.

[I begin by validating him. However, I know that this approach has kept him stuck in the victim role.]

Trevor: No.

Rachel: So, how is it that you allow her to do something that you already know she's *not* going to do properly by your standards? There's a whole bunch of jobs to be done, isn't there?

[With this intervention, I am inviting him to reassess his approach.]

Trevor: Yeah.

Rachel: So, what comes up for you when I ask you that?

Trevor: Have her do other things to help.

Rachel: Does that feel like a useful idea?

Trevor: On paper.

Rachel: Okay. Again there's distrust; there's skepticism. Let's play it out. So you say: "You know what? Instead of the dishwasher, how about today you do …" and you pick whatever else you want her to do. What did you pick?

Trevor: Um, just picking up stuff.

Rachel: Okay. Watch and see what happens when you assign her the job of picking up stuff. I take it you mean like dishes and …

Trevor: Yeah, you know, just garbage, the stuff that's around the house, bottles and trash and stuff.

Rachel: So, how's she's doing? Just observe and notice.

[The client has negative experience in the past and negative expectations for the future. I'm encouraging him to stay with the process in the moment, knowing that the bilateral stimulation may open up new possibilities.]

Trevor: She's doing okay.

Rachel: She's doing okay. So that part she *can* be helpful with?

Trevor: Mhmm.

Rachel: Does she bring the dishes in and then allow you to load the dishwasher?

[I'm hoping for a cooperative model of working with his wife.]

Trevor: Yeah, although at that point, the dishwasher was pretty much already full and ready to just be loaded. I guess I don't know how to completely address that. Yeah, it was more like bringing the dishes over and having them ready for the next batch.

[He's not yet ready for a new model, but he doesn't reject it out of hand either.]

Rachel: Okay. So she's bringing the dishes in, and maybe you're rinsing them off or whatever you do before you stick them in the dishwasher or maybe scraping off the food or whatever ... Okay, so how is that feeling? Are you getting help? Is it working?

Trevor: Yeah, it's better.

Rachel: It's better? Okay. Is there some way it can be even better? Even better still? Check in and notice if there's *anything* that's a little annoying, a little frustrating, or that you have a little bit of resentment about. Because this is a new situation for you where you're actually getting the sense that Amy is helping *helpfully*, if you get what I mean.

Trevor: Mhmm.

(Long pause)

[He's struggling to integrate this new picture.]

Trevor: She's … um … she's trying.

Rachel: It's important that you realize that. Does it help you feel better?

Trevor: Yeah.

Rachel: Okay, good. Is there anything else she could try to do, or do better that would be even more helpful for you?

Trevor: Less socializing.

Rachel: Is there anyone left at the party?

Trevor: Well, no. I mean that as in: "Let's not have as many things at our house."

Rachel: Oh, I see. Less socializing meaning less parties period.

Trevor: Right.

Rachel: Ah.

Trevor: But, in that moment? Is that what you're asking me?

Rachel: In the moment of your cleaning up, she's doing a better job than you expected, right? You thought you were going to have to do it all by yourself, but you asked her, and you asked her to do something that she could do properly, that you would not feel you had to redo, and that made a big difference. Because my sense is that you're describing feeling like you're in a partnership right now. Is that correct?

Trevor: Yes.

Rachel: Okay. But the fact that there is a party at all has not been addressed. That's still to be addressed. Do you want to deal with that now?

Trevor: Sure.

Rachel: Okay, so how do you want to deal with that? Do you want to sit down and talk with her? Or you want to do it while you're cleaning up the mess? How do you want to do it?

Trevor: Mhmm …. I'm thinking the next day.

Rachel: Okay, so flip forward in time to the next day, and tell me how you're going to choose a time.

Trevor: Well, when I wake up.

Rachel: Okay, so when you wake up, what happens?

Trevor: I ask her for help cleaning up and not having as many parties or social events at our house.

Rachel: Did she hear you?

Trevor: Yeah.

Rachel: Do you know she was listening? Can you see her?

Trevor: Yeah.

Rachel: And what do you see? What expression is on her face? Where is she in relationship to you?

(Long pause)

Trevor: She's um … kind of sad.

Rachel: She looks sad? And what happens for you when she looks sad?

Trevor: She's worried about me.

Rachel: And what is she worried about? Does she tell you?

Trevor: She's worried about how angry I get.

Rachel: Okay, and how do you feel about that?

Trevor: Confused.

Rachel: Confused? What's confusing for you?

Trevor: I still don't know why it goes from zero to eight when I get mad. She doesn't know either. So we are both just kind of stuck with this random rage that we both have to deal with.

Rachel: So, I didn't hear her answer your request about the parties. Did she duck that? Or did she answer you?

Trevor: She said: "We will try to not have so many parties in the near future."

Rachel: Ah. She agreed. Okay. But she's sad because of the anger?

Trevor: Yes.

Rachel: And you feel confused because you don't know what's going on with the anger either?

Trevor: Uh-huh.

Rachel: So, let's go to that anger place. Can you bring yourself back to a moment of rage, Trevor? Can you take yourself back into the rage that you felt? And what moment is it?

Trevor: I'm sort of hyperventilating.

Rachel: In your memory or in the moment?

Trevor: In my memory, just prior to going back into the bedroom to try and calm down. Preceding that was almost like a point of hyperventilation.

Rachel: Okay, so get into that moment. When you say "hyperventilating," what that means to me is your breathing is really hard and fast?

Trevor: Yeah.

Rachel: Do that for a minute, just to get back into the state. [He breathes heavily.] And what is that about for you? See if you can grasp that moment of "grrrrr" and make noises like I am if that helps you get a sense of what's going on for you.

[With the breathing, the sounds and the imagery, I'm trying to help him get in touch with what he is feeling. He has studiously avoided going there until now.]

Trevor: Okay. It's um … a fight or flight, caveman thing.

Rachel: So, even if it may seem crazy and irrational, what would be the kinds of feelings and thoughts you would have? "I CANT STAND THIS!" "I'M GOING TO DIE!" "THIS IS HORRIBLE!" or whatever is going on for you.

[Again, feeding him sentences to give him permission to own his angry feelings]

Trevor: I feel like I'm holding back violence.

Rachel: Okay. Let's imagine the violence you are holding back, realizing that, in fact, you're sitting in a chair in my office and you're not going to hurt anybody. We want to go there in fantasy. Imagine the violence. Imagine what would happen if you let it go and didn't hold it back. What would happen? What's your image? What's your feeling? What's your picture?

[For many clients, reminding them that no one will be hurt by their expressions of anger or rage in the therapy session is necessary to release their inhibitions and reverse the implosion that is habitual for them.]

Trevor: I'm punching Amy.

Rachel: Okay. Let yourself imagine that, knowing you're not hurting her in reality, but you need to work this through here. So, you're punching Amy. In the face? In the body? Where are you punching her?

Trevor: Yeah, it's physical; it's with my fist. But I feel horrible.

Rachel: Just let yourself remember that this is not hurting her and see if you can give yourself permission to go with what you normally would *not* do. So, let yourself punch her. Go for it. Where are you hitting her?

Trevor: In the cheek.

Rachel: Okay, so punch her. Feel your fist connect with her cheek and keep on punching her as long as you need to, getting that feeling out. And see if there are words or thoughts that go with it. "*You* wanted to have this party! I didn't want to have this party! I have to do all this work!" Whatever it is, let it out, Trevor.

(There is a pause. He is silent.) Can you put those words out?

Trevor: I just want to disappear.

[His anger is so imploded that, initially, he cannot face it in himself without wanting to run away or disappear.]

Rachel: I think that's avoidance of the violence you feel rather than what the violence itself is saying. Is that true or am I wrong?

Trevor: Hold on, I'm getting too worked up. (He chuckles.)

Rachel: Get worked up! I'd like to see you worked up because I don't see it right now. I see you holding back.

Trevor: Uh-huh.

Rachel: Now, what would happen if you gave yourself permission in fantasy to go with what you don't let yourself go with in reality? What would happen? Kick her, punch her, throw her on the ground, scream and yell, or whatever it is you would do if you were not civilized in the way you are.

(Long pause)

Rachel: What's happening, Trevor?

Trevor: Well, I'm hitting but, besides being angry, I'm feeling remorseful and I'm trying to find a calm spot. Um … like the violence is just kind of a temporary outlet, but it's not the real solution.

Rachel: Well, I'm not sure you're letting yourself go into the violence and I'm really encouraging you to go with it. Go with it for now, for this work, and see where it goes for you. So, stomp on her, crush her, break her up into little pieces, and grind her up in a grinder, whatever you need to do, whatever that violent impulse is, do it right now, if you are willing to give yourself that permission. And see what happens.

So, what is happening right now? What are you doing?

(Long pause)

Trevor: There's this seething, horrifically angry person.

Rachel: Uh-huh; yes, there is.

Trevor: With no skin.

Rachel: Is this you?

Trevor: Pure rage.

Rachel: Okay.

Trevor: Covered in blood.

Rachel: And what is he doing to Amy? Kicking? Screaming? Shouting? Punching? What is he doing? Let him out.

Trevor: He's pummeled so hard on her face that she's … just … I knocked her out. She's out.

Rachel: Okay, she's lying on the ground. Is her face bloody? Bruised? What do you see?

Trevor: Yeah, I cracked her skull, and I feel horrible.

Rachel: Okay, remember you haven't hurt her in reality, but let's just go with it. You cracked her skull, you knocked her out and there's still rage. There's still more you need to do. Yes?

Trevor: No, I just killed my life partner.

Rachel: You killed something that was making you crazy. Can you see what it is that made you want to pummel her to death? And say that to her, lying there in whatever state she is. "You drive me crazy!" "You make me do all these things I don't want to do!" That's what I'm imagining, but put it in your own words.

Trevor: I'm not really mad at her.

Rachel: Aha? Really? No? Who are you really mad at?

Trevor: Me.

[He'd rather turn the anger inward against himself than face the anger at his spouse.]

Rachel: Are you sure?

Trevor: I'd say it's equal. There's just as much rage directed to myself as there is to her. I was going to say I was angry at her for nagging me to do more with my life. And I'm realizing that I'm complaining about that, yet I really feel like I need to do that more and I'm really disappointed in myself.

Rachel: Uh-huh. And you don't like her nagging you – especially if she's right. That's *really* annoying. You can nag yourself enough; you don't need her to do it. Could you tell her in whatever state she's in, with her cracked jaw or whatever, that you don't want her nagging you anymore and mean it? Can you say those words?

Trevor: Stop fucking nagging me.

Rachel: That was a good start, but it still sounded a little weak. Could you say it just a little bit more convincingly, with a little more energy?

Trevor: Stop fucking bugging me!

Rachel: Good. Again. STOP FUCKING BUGGING ME!

Trevor: STOP FUCKING BUGGING ME!

Rachel: Does it feel like you can get in touch with that? There's probably a zillion times you wanted to say that to her.

Trevor: Yeah.

Rachel: And maybe there's a picture of some of those times that can – like a kind of serial that goes by your mind as you think about it – think about three or four times you would have *loved* to have said: "STOP FUCKING BUGGING ME!" What times?

(There is a pause and he says nothing.) "I don't want to have parties!" for example.

Trevor: Choosing when I had my doctor's appointment, recently.

Rachel: "I WANT TO DECIDE!" Put it into your own words with the same force.

Trevor: I wanted to decide when I was going to go see my doctor. Um, not have her, you know, pick it for me. That's *my* life.

Rachel: Yep. What else?

Trevor: She tends to treat me like her mom treats her dad, and he has a little bit of dementia.

Rachel: Ah. That's insulting.

Trevor: I know.

Rachel: "Stop treating me like I have dementia!" or whatever words fit for you.

Trevor: It's Alzheimer's. Part of it is that I see that pattern of nagging being passed from a mother to a daughter and I don't want that.

Rachel: Tell her.

Trevor: I don't want to be treated like your dad.

Rachel: Tell her: "STOP TREATING ME LIKE I HAVE DEMENTIA, LIKE YOUR DAD!"

Trevor: I can take care of myself.

Rachel: It sounded a little shaky.

Trevor: I can take care of myself!

Rachel: Again.

Trevor: I CAN TAKE CARE OF MYSELF!!

Rachel: Say it so that Amy can hear you and you can hear you.

Trevor: I take care of everyone; I can take care of myself!

Rachel: Good. What else would you like to take care of that she doesn't let you take care of?

Trevor: Obviously, our party situations.

Rachel: Tell her.

Trevor: I want to be able to plan parties on my timeline.

Rachel: Okay. And that would be a lot less frequently from what I understand. Is that right?

Trevor: Yes.

Rachel: And when you have a party – *if* you decide you want to have a party, if *you* decide – how would it be different than from the parties you've been having based on Amy's decision-making?

Trevor: Oh, it would be cheaper, less production. We're not putting on a seminar for plastic surgeons which, unfortunately, is what she does now.

Rachel: Okay, so: "MY TIMELINE and MY STYLE!"

Trevor: Numb. These fingers are numb.

[He has been holding the sensors more tightly than he realized.]

Rachel: You're grasping harder than you realized. Okay. What else? This is your chance. Lay it out there. All the things that have been bugging you for years need to come out now. You've got your chance. Tell her.

Trevor: Clean the litter box.

Rachel: Do you like the cat?

Trevor: Oh yeah, he's mine. (He chuckles.)

Rachel: Ok, so it's not about having a cat?

Trevor: Well, it's her cat; she wanted the cat. I didn't, but of course I love him. He's like my little buddy.

Rachel: "I DIDN'T EVEN WANT A CAT TO BEGIN WITH!"

Trevor: No, I didn't. And I didn't want a baby either.

Rachel: Okay, tell her that.

(Long pause)

That's a harder one, huh?

Trevor: Yeah, she knows.

Rachel: But you need to express it, even if she knows. You need to get it out there, Trevor.

Trevor: I didn't want to be a dad! I didn't want to have to raise a child, especially with my template.

Rachel: With your template? Meaning ...?

Trevor: What I had to offer based on my personal experience and who I am.

Rachel: So, there you are; you got a cat you didn't want and a child you didn't want. What is it that you want from her now? It's really hard to get rid of the child. How could it be better for you now?

(Long pause)

How about the fact that you're the one doing most of the work to raise the child?

Trevor: Yeah.

Rachel: Yeah. Not only did you not want the child and not want to be a dad, but you're a stay-at-home dad now ...

Trevor: Yeah.

Rachel: Do you want to be a stay-at-home dad?

Trevor: Not really.

Rachel: Well, then, could you tell the truth to her?

Trevor: The problem is, I don't know what else I would do.

Rachel: Well, let's not go there just yet. The first thing is to recognize the feelings that you're having and what you are blocking which comes out in these rage attacks. Do you see that? It's under the surface and the "small thing" – what may look like a small thing – just sucks back down into the underground volcano of rage and the whole thing comes up from a zero to an eight in a second because a little kid was ringing the doorbell? No, it's because of all these other things that you've been holding back. You don't want her to decide your life. That's what it comes down to. "Don't decide when I go to the doctor;" "Stop treating me like I'm your dad;" " I can take care of myself;" "I want to plan parties on my timeline and in my style" – meaning: cheaper and less production. "I want you to clean the litter box." "I didn't want a cat to begin with and now I've got one." "I didn't want a child and now I've got one." "I don't want to be a stay-at-home dad." What else?

Trevor: I don't want a dog.

Rachel: Oh, you have a dog too?

Trevor: No, we don't.

Rachel: You don't want one?

Trevor: No. 'Cause I know that's what's going to happen.

Rachel: Yep.

Trevor: It's just going to be another thing to worry about.

Rachel: You know, what would happen if it was the way it's been up until now – that you would be taking care of the dog.

Trevor: Yep.

Rachel: What else? Let yourself have this opportunity to get through the whole (pardon the metaphor) litter box of complaints that have been buried under this "I'm going to be a nice guy," "I'm going to be a good husband," "I'm going to be a good father." Underneath, you're blasting with resentment. What else?

Trevor: Well, part of it is really sad. I don't want my daughter to feel that she … um … she loves me so much …

Rachel: Wouldn't your daughter be so much happier with a happy dad?

Trevor: Yeah.

Rachel: Instead of this martyr dad? Sorry to use the expression, but it fits, doesn't it?

Trevor: Yeah.

Rachel: Imagine that you really told Amy *all* of how you feel and how this simply isn't working for you. What happens as you imagine yourself clearing this? Clearing the slate and letting her know what's going on inside, Trevor?

Trevor: Nothing changes. There's not really much we can do about her job. I mean, she's got to be gone; she has to travel. It's part of the job. Which means I have to stay behind and take care of Mika.

Rachel: So, you're saying there is no solution other than the one you've got? The only possible way this situation could be fixed is for you to carry on in your martyr role? Is that true?

Trevor: Well, yeah. That's kind of practically … how it has to be.

[This belief that there is *no* way out of his situation underlies his depression and his rage.]

Rachel: Well … I have trouble seeing the force of that necessity. Maybe there would have to be some pretty big adjustments. Maybe she couldn't do that job. Maybe someone else would have to stay home with your daughter. Maybe you would have to divide it up differently. Maybe she would have to be in a preschool. I don't know the answers, but are there other possibilities? Interesting that you don't see anything else as possible.

Trevor: No, she's in preschool now. Again, yeah, I *am* a martyr because she is taken care of … um …

Rachel: What if you were not a martyr? How would it be different if you were not the martyr that you've been?

Trevor: I guess I would be proud of what I have accomplished. I don't always feel that I've accomplished *anything*.

Rachel: What would you like to be proud of? If we had a magic wand and could find a way for you to accomplish what you want and be proud of that, what would it look like? Can you visualize that?

Trevor: Yeah.

Rachel: And what comes up?

Trevor: It's a state of mind that I would find myself in when I was trying to figure out something electronically. It's like everything sort of disappeared around me and all I would have is my brain and the solution. That would give me a sense of purpose and also a sense of accomplishment if I could connect and figure out why things weren't working.

Rachel: So, it's not that you're saying you want to be an electronics genius. You're saying you want to see an option that has that click, that rightness about it, like the solution that you might get to an electronic problem.

Trevor: Yeah, like displacing the water in a bathtub.

Rachel: Okay, Archimedes, do you know how that would feel if you could find something that would fit? Do you have any images that come up as you just sit receptively with the possible click of a lifestyle that would fit better than what you're in right now?

(Long pause)

You don't have to analyze or criticize, just notice what comes up. What do you get?

Trevor: I want to work. I want to do something besides take care of a house and a baby – a four-and-a-half-year-old, almost five-year-old – and I *can't.*

Rachel: And you want to go out to work? Or work at home? But just not do the babying stuff?

Trevor: No. I'd probably be going back to what I was doing before – which was helping people with their problems. I stepped out of that because I wanted to fix my own. They are not fixed, but I need to go out and do something else.

Rachel: You were helping people with their problems in what way?

Trevor: Um, electronics.

Rachel: Okay, and that was satisfying for you?

Trevor: Yes.

Rachel: And you felt a sense of accomplishment? Yes? And it did involve your leaving the house?

Trevor: Yes, yes it did. I liked using my brain. I'm really smart and I'm just stagnating.

Rachel: Yeah. "Housewife Syndrome." I don't mean that as a put down. I think there is a state of mind that some people who stay at home care-giving kids can get into – especially if they are very smart – where they just feel like their brain is rotting.

Trevor: Yeah.

Rachel: Yeah. And your brain feels like that for you. You need to use it. And the best way you can think of would be doing the kind of work you did before? Is that right?

Trevor: What I'm doing now is trying to shut it down. I can see that.

Rachel: Okay. Your brain needs to be alive and working and vibrant and you need to use it. You have a good brain. I'm imagining you saying to your brain: "I'm sorry. I've deserted you. I realize I owe you an opportunity." Is this too far out for you? Do you see what I'm getting at? Would you be willing to make that connection with your brain that is atrophying back there? Could you even make a promise to your brain?

Trevor: That I would use it more often.

Rachel: That you will find a way to use it more often. Yes?

Trevor: Yes.

Rachel: So, say that now.

Trevor: I want to find a way to use my brain more often.

Rachel: And how does it feel as you say that?

Trevor: I'm noticing the way I said the word "often." Um, how am I feeling?

Rachel: Does it feel good to think that?

Trevor: It's a little scary.

Rachel: Yes, it is. Scary and exciting.

Trevor: Yeah.

Rachel: Do you want to speak about the fear part of it?

Trevor: Well, you know the fear is there if there is something that I have to do – that I really have to do – for *money*. I've never been depended upon for money.

Rachel: Okay, so you're saying it's scary because you have to do it for money, or is it that you want to do it for money so that you're not dependent on someone else?

Trevor: A little of both. Yeah. I've never had to be self-sufficient on a financial basis other than just living poorly.

Rachel: So, you're saying you want to learn how to be self-sufficient financially? You've never had to be?

Trevor: No.

Rachel: Okay. So, it's something that would make you feel good about yourself and you'd like to find a way to do that. But it's a little bit scary because you're not sure how that's going to work out?

Trevor: Yeah.

Rachel: That's understandable. But, as you try it on, how does it feel in your body as you imagine being able to earn money using your brain, your good brain? And being able to help people and earn money at the same time? How does that prospect feel for you, Trevor?

Trevor: It feels good.

Rachel: Could you tell Amy what you are discovering about yourself right now?

Trevor: Amy, I want to use my brain.

Rachel: Good.

Trevor: I'm way smarter than you.

Rachel: Maybe.

Trevor: No, I am. (He chuckles.)

Rachel: I believe you.

Trevor: (chuckles) In some ways … But she does astound me. She really astounds me talking to doctors or on conference calls at home.

Rachel: Okay. Will you tell her: "I will astound you, Amy, when you see how smart I really am and when you see how I can use my brain"? Can you say that?

Trevor: Amy, I will astound you when you see how well I can use my brain?" … I shouldn't say that with a question mark. I didn't remember the whole sentence.

Rachel: And how smart I really am …

Trevor: How smart I am.

Rachel: Yeah.

Trevor: How good my short term memory is.

[The return of his sense of humor is a good sign of renewed hopefulness.]

Rachel: Ha ha. That's okay. You got it; you got the gist. I feel that there's a hesitant pride in you. It's like you almost don't let yourself go to the feelings of pride and self-value that come up when you say that. It's as if you're reaching for it, but you're almost afraid to touch it.

Trevor: I'm afraid to create more problems.

Rachel: What's the fear? More of what problems?

Trevor: One of the reasons that I stopped taking clients was that I couldn't handle dealing with all their problems and mine. I had to let one client just go 'cause I was just so tired of having to deal with all these little problems - even though I would charge him, I just didn't want to deal with it. And he had a big scary dog that, I guess, I was worried about.

Rachel: So, to use your brain means you also have to be very selective in the kind of work that you do so that it does not overwhelm you or put you in a position where you're being a martyr again.

Trevor: Yeah.

Rachel: I think that you might have a tendency to go that route - even in your work - where you start doing things for other people that are not good for you, and you feel overwhelmed, and then the resentment builds, and you just want to explode. That's a possibility you do *not* want to recreate. So, it would be important to be aware of that. Can you visualize yourself doing work that enhances you, helps others, and *doesn't* overwhelm you or create problems? Can you imagine that possibility? Maybe you'll have to have less clients. Maybe you'll have to reject some clients. Maybe you'll have to form a different angle on the work. Maybe you'll have to say "no" - which is just not your strong suite, but it's a teachable skill. Can you see yourself walking down that road?

Trevor: Yeah.

Rachel: Do you think you could earn as much or more than Amy does?

Trevor: No, but she's miserable.

Rachel: So you would have less money, but she would actually be relieved if she didn't have to do this job that she's been doing?

Trevor: Yeah.

Rachel: Ah. I didn't know that. Actually she might be very grateful for you to use your brain.

Trevor: Yeah, she would be. But that's a seat change I don't think I'm ready for.

Rachel: What do you think readiness would look like?

Trevor: Well, of me being the primary breadwinner. My problem up to now is I don't have as marketable skills for a client or for a business and my resume is nothing that makes sense … (that probably didn't make sense).

Rachel: It's a process of getting yourself situated with the kinds of skills and experience that will allow you to command the salary you would like, and it's not going to happen overnight. But can you see a path in which that would be a possibility? Even if it doesn't happen in one step. Even if it requires several steps. That you could be working outside the house, feeling better about yourself, and Amy might be doing a different job or less of this job, so both of you were contributing to the household for a while, at least. And neither she having to put up with a job she's miserable with, nor you putting up with being a stay-at-home dad that you're miserable with. That both of you could be happier doing something else.

Trevor: (chuckles) Yeah.

Rachel: And maybe you'd have to make a little less money for a while for that to happen. And I'm not sure the implications of that, but seems like it's do-able. Maybe you'd have to move to a different town; maybe you'd have to get a smaller house; maybe you'd have to supplement your income somehow. But you'd be proud of yourself. Do you think that it could be enough? That what you could do as we look forward in time could be enough? If you really were doing the best that you can?

Trevor: Yeah. I think we would be happier.

Rachel: Aha. I'd like you to hold that image of the future. I don't mean the distant future. I mean more a process starting now in which you're moving towards using your brain, feeling good about yourself, being congruent with the things you want and the choices you're making, and feeling like you can take care of yourself. And that you and Amy are in a partnership in which you respect yourself and feel respected by her for the person you really are. And, as you hold that vision, I'd like you to pay attention to the way it feels in your body. I'm going to focus on each of the parts that reacted prior. I'd like you to let me know if they are relaxed or contracted. Notice your temples. Relaxed or contracted, as you visualize this new vision of your future?

Trevor: The temples are processing and scrutinizing.

Rachel: Okay. Get in touch with your temples and what would allow them to be relaxed? What do they need?

Trevor: The other problem is: now I'm conscious of the right and left brain with my eyes going back and forth – creative and logical – so my temples are relaxed – but I'm just noticing a lot more activity in my head.

Rachel: Okay, they are relaxed?

Trevor: Relaxed.

Rachel: Okay, go to your stomach. Relaxed or contracted?

Trevor: Relaxed.

Rachel: Go to your fists.

Trevor: My fists are better; they are pulsing.

Rachel: What about behind your eyes?

Trevor: There's still sadness.

Rachel: What's the sadness? That was the site of your hopelessness.

Trevor: A little bit of resentment. I realize that I lash out at Amy and Mika because I resent them, sometimes.

Rachel: Perhaps you resent them when you are not being who you really are, Trevor. That's the martyr part.

Trevor: Yeah.

Rachel: If you were not trying to be this martyr that does all the things you think you should do, but doesn't really want to do, can you imagine the resentment melting? Shrinking? Maybe even disappearing? You would make your own doctor's appointments, and you would be using your brain, and you would be working outside the home, and you wouldn't be having parties all the time, and you wouldn't be "Cinderfella." Could you imagine that? And when you imagine that, what happens to the area behind your eyes?

Trevor: I'm seeing almost like a sunrise.

Rachel: Wow, cool. What about your shoulders? Relaxed or tense?

Trevor: Tense.

Rachel: Tense. Okay, let's ask your shoulders what they need. When you get in touch with your shoulders, what comes up?

Trevor: (Sighs)

Rachel: That was the site of your frustration.

Trevor: Oh, I just have a lot of work left to do before we leave on this trip. And it's a trip I didn't want to go on.

Rachel: Here's the old pattern. Pay attention to how it feels to go according to your old pattern. "Not a trip I wanted to take." "Lots of work I have to do." This is the pattern. This is the martyr pattern.

Trevor: Yeah.

Rachel: So, maybe this could be your last experience of doing it that way, and maybe your shoulders are screaming: "I don't want to!"

Trevor: Yeah.

Rachel: What about your upper jaw and cheeks? Remember, we're visualizing a future in which you're getting to do what you want to do that fits with who you are as a man.

Trevor: Yeah, the jaw has loosened.

Rachel: Good. What about your heart space? (Site of his self-pity.)

Trevor: The heart's still a little tight.

Rachel: Still feeling a little sorry for yourself?

Trevor: Mhmm.

Rachel: Okay. Part of it is that you haven't convinced yourself yet that you are actually going to follow a new pattern. You have to see it in reality. You have to see it playing out to trust that you're actually going to follow this new opportunity that is opening up. Would that be true? You've been a martyr for quite some time and it's going to be a bit of a challenge to let go.

Trevor: Yeah.

Rachel: And what about your diaphragm? Think you can give up taking care of other people's needs all the time?

Trevor: I can try.

Rachel: "I can try." What would the statement be that represents the learning of this experience? The one you had picked was: "I'm doing the best that I can", but maybe that needs to be amended a little, like "I will do the best I can to honor myself going forward" or something like that. Am I on the wrong track?

Trevor: No, that's good.

Rachel: Okay, you tell me what you would want to say now.

Trevor: Um, I wanted … ah, actually I would phrase it differently. I would say: "I want to use my brain." Um. It's starting to *entropy*.

Rachel: It's starting to – sorry – atrophy?

Trevor: Atrophy. I was thinking of the word "entropy" and mixed them up.

Rachel: Yeah, well, they fit together. "I want to use my brain …"

Trevor: Um … While it's still there …

Rachel: "And make choices that fit for who I am." I think we need something like that.

Trevor: Yeah. "I want to use my brain and make some of my own choices."

Rachel: Uh-huh. Okay. That's good. I want you to say that a couple of times with conviction and notice how your body feels and if there's any protest or resistance coming from any part of your body. "I want to use my brain and make some of my own choices for my life."

Trevor: "I want to use my brain and make some of my own choices in life."

Rachel: How does that feel?

Trevor: Better.

 Rachel: Say it again.

Trevor: "I want to use my brain and I want to make choices, make my own choices, some of my own choices."

Rachel: Okay. Now, as a last step for this piece, go back to the target. You're sitting on the bed. You've just felt like you're going to absolutely explode. You're sitting on the bed trying to get a little bit of solitude and Amy's in there bugging you. How disturbing is that image for you at this moment in time?

Trevor: Six.

Rachel: It's a six. What prevents it from being a zero?

Trevor: I don't know. I'm just happy it went down. It diminished in significance. I mean the stuff I was worried about or mad about seems really stupid now.

Rachel: Uh-huh. A six suggests that it still has a pretty high level of disturbance for you?

Trevor: No, just a little bit. It's a six, but it's more fixable. That's just kind of the way I see it.

[There is a marked discrepancy between the explanation he gives and the number he reports, possibly indicative of his hesitation to accept this new picture of his life. I want to see what happens as he lives with it for a little while.]

Rachel: Okay. Well, let's see what happens with that between now and when we meet for the follow-up next week. Just hold that space for now.

And the last thing you want to think about is: "I want to use my brain and make choices - some of my *own* choices - for my life."

Follow-up Session

With all my EMDR clients, I recommend that they schedule the time after the processing session as free time for them - i.e. they have no obligations or commitments and can do whatever feels right to them at the time. Some clients want to sleep, some want to be alone, and some want to be with other people. In Trevor's case, I specifically recommended that he arrange to have Amy look after their daughter so he could have a "free pass" for the rest of the day or, at least, for a few hours after the processing.

Trevor reported that after the session, he had to get ready for a trip they were taking the next day to celebrate a family anniversary. It was a trip he did *not* want to take. Nonetheless, he had taken on the responsibility of preparing for it and had agreed to go. This was an obvious example of the victim/martyr pattern that had been habitual for him.

While normally the designated driver for social events, on this occasion Trevor chose to drink and take a cab instead. He and Amy got into "the worst fight they had ever had," according to Trevor. They had very different perceptions of each other and he felt ashamed of the way she perceived him. He ended up sobbing hysterically, repeating over and over: "I can't do this anymore." He threatened to leave the marriage.

The next day, they apologized to each other, and Trevor said he felt more vindicated in his wife's perception of him. He also saw how distressed she was about her job. Together they recognized that they needed to make some new decisions for their life.

When asked about the target, Trevor reported it was a three. He said the incident at the party was "the catalyst that brought me here and gave me the insight and power to express it to her." The memory was not at all distressing to him anymore. It had empowered him to take a stand and not let his wife tell him what to do.

When asked what prevented it from being a zero, Trevor remarked: "I see zero as null, but this is still needing to be resolved." A three, rather than a zero, made sense in this situation. There were decisions that needed to be made to address the discontent that had surfaced in the work. This would take time. It would also take time and practice for him to get used to speaking up for himself and what he needed.

Then he added emphatically: "it would be hard to get a zero out of me." Could this be a stand he was taking with me? With due respect for his newly found power, I happily conceded that a zero would not be required.

Clinical Comments

In my book, *Journey to Home: Quintessential Therapy and Beyond,*[17] I describe two coping stances in response to stress: compliance and defiance. These two possible stances come about as a direct result of a decision we make early on about how to handle our dependence on others.

In the first case, we fear losing the other we depend upon so we try to please. We do whatever they want in the hope that they will not abandon us and withdraw their love. In the second case, we deny our dependence on others and strike a fiercely independent stance. We act as if we didn't need anybody, as if we didn't have needs at all.

The case of Trevor is a clear example of the compliant position:

> (T)he compliant posture presupposes an implicit acceptance of our neediness. It is grounded in the recognition of our deep-seated and inescapable needs for physical and emotional caretaking. It is, in effect, a decision to regard these needs as primary ...The inclination of compliant people to be accommodating to others is, therefore, a direct consequence of acknowledging our dependence on them ...

---

[17] Rachel B. Aarons, *Journey to Home: Quintessential Therapy and Beyond,* (Santa Barbara: Journey Press, 2009).

> In view of this dependence, we do not wish to do any-
> thing that might incite withdrawal or rejection by the
> object of our need. It is a short step from this position
> to the avoidance of anger altogether, either other peo-
> ple's or our own. [18]

Trevor loved his wife and wanted her to be happy. There is
nothing inherently wrong with that. But his entire life was
structured on pleasing her at the expense of his own needs.
This is what led to problems for him. His "inexplicable" rage
attacks were coming from the discontent he had suppressed in
order to accommodate her. Although he tried to deny his anger,
it gained force beneath the surface and leaked out against his
conscious intentions.

Thus, as is evident in this example, anger represents the
shadow side of compliance, the part we deny and disown:

> The effort to suppress our anger creates an underlying
> strain and tension in us. We appear "forced" or rigidly
> mechanical. Our pleasantness has a hollow ring. All our
> emotions seem muted and colorless. Not only to others
> but also to ourselves, there appears to be something
> "missing," something flat or stale about our lives. [19]

Trevor's mild-mannered demeanor was, at least in part, due
to "implosion" – i.e. the pulling in of our emotional responses so
that, not only other people, but even we ourselves may be
unaware of them. Blocking so-called negative emotions tends to
block all our emotions, including the more positive ones. This is
why we may seem flat or colorless across the board. We can't
just repress anger and still have a joyous and vibrant life.

---

[18] Aarons, *Journey to Home*, Chapter 4, "Wrestling with the Shadow – Anger," 103-104.
[19] Aarons, *Journey to Home*, 104.

Moreover, anger does not simply disappear. It breeds resentment that can suddenly erupt in rage attacks as it did in Trevor's case.

> (O)ur pattern might be to go along agreeably until, one day, we just explode. We have a fit of anger, then feel guilty, and hastily return to our customary submissiveness. We try to make amends until, inevitably as time passes, the explosion erupts again.[20]

It is only when the compliant owns his anger that he or she can move out of this dysfunctional pattern. We have seen this truth in action in Trevor's EMDR processing session. It is when he embraces his anger at his wife that he is able to get clear about what his needs are and become empowered to present them to his partner. His anger is not an unfortunate by-product but an essential catalyst of the change.

Ongoing individual therapy with Trevor should be focused on helping him become more assertive in his communication with his wife. Couples therapy, which is strongly recommended in this case, should be used to address the issues that Trevor presented and to provide a forum to search for a compromise satisfactory to both Trevor and his wife. However, Trevor had come for EMDR treatment only. Once the traumatic issue was resolved, he returned to his own therapist to continue his work. This is one of the intrinsic features of EMDR when it is used as an adjunct therapy. We are left hanging about what happened in his life after EMDR therapy.

Hopefully, the combination of the insights he obtained in his EMDR work as well as the release of stored up anger and resentment made it possible for him to develop a life style more honoring of his needs as a person and as a man.

---

[20] Aarons, *Journey to Home,* 105.

CHAPTER FOUR

Self-Sabotage in Business:

Real Women Can't Do Math

Case of Taffy

If we carry a negative image of ourselves from our family of origin or from our significant other, we will carry this picture into our professional lives. It will hamper our ability to perform at our best and to accomplish the career goals we have set for ourselves. Convinced that we will fail, we find ourselves acting out this conviction, despite ourselves. The negative belief operates like a self-fulfilling prophecy and brings about precisely what we fear and dread. Forced to confront our incompetence and failure, we end up with the meager satisfaction of proving we were right.

No one wants this tragic outcome, but it happens all too frequently. That voice in our head – the voice that I call "the superego"[21] – is the carrier of these negative messages from the past. If it remains unquestioned and unchallenged, it will ensure that we fulfill our worst fears and enact our most dire predictions. In this way, the superego operates on us like a voice of doom.

If we want to be personally and professionally successful in life, it is essential that we learn to recognize and fight the superego. The next case study will show how one woman was able to override the messages that kept her stuck in a dependent role and develop confidence to pursue her business career.

Background Information

Taffy was a fifty-nine-year-old real estate agent who came to see me because of the extreme anxiety she was experiencing in her work situation. While she was an intelligent and capable

---

[21] Aarons, *Journey to Home,* Part 3, "Silencing the Superego", 69-100. The term "superego" was coined by Freud, but the concept I use comes out of Diamond Heart training and is akin to the Firestone concept of the Voice as the anti-self. (See Bibliography)

sales agent, she lived in perpetual fear of humiliating herself in front of peers or clients by saying or doing something stupid. Her worst nightmare was dealing with the mathematical calculations that were a central component of real estate transactions. She would procrastinate, freeze, and go into panic when numbers were involved. Recently on her own after years of marriage, this presented a major obstacle, not only to her self-esteem in the business world, but also to her ability to support herself financially. She was terrified that she would not be able to make it on her own.

I learned that Taffy was born and raised in a tiny town in Missouri. Her mother had grown up in this same town where her family had lived for generations. It was a truck stop in a farming area of about three hundred plus inhabitants. Taffy's grandfather ran the produce shop and her father was the mayor. Taffy reported that her mother was "very curious about the world but she never got to travel." Instead, she remained at home raising five children of her own as well as her oldest daughter's daughter. Taffy was determined that, unlike her mother, she would get out of that town and see the world.

In her senior year, circumstances conspired to create that chance for her. On Prom night, she had gone out with "the bad boy" in town – a boy she wasn't supposed to date – and got pregnant the first and only time they had sex. The boy wanted nothing to do with a child and Taffy refused to get married, so she was "hidden away" at her brother's while she was pregnant. Her parents offered to raise the child, but Taffy refused. She did not want to be stuck at home mothering in that truck stop town the way her mother and sister were. "I knew I didn't belong there," she said with conviction. Taffy gave birth to a little girl and gave her up for adoption in defiance of the prevailing view in her culture that adoption was simply "unacceptable." We see the spunk in this girl as she is able to resist following the approved path of her predecessors.

Shortly thereafter, she met a man from Iran (Kabir) who was "totally different" from the redneck boys she was used to. He had left his own country at seventeen years of age. While her previous boyfriend had dropped her when she got pregnant and advised Kabir to do likewise, Kabir was very supportive of her. They married a year later and moved away a year after that. She was free – or so it seemed.

Taffy described Kabir as "worldly" and "a take charge kind of guy." She never had to make a decision. She put herself in his hands. He was her "security," she said. If she bought clothes for herself at the store, they had to meet with his approval; otherwise they were returned. Although she did the finances for the family, he had to recheck all her figures; otherwise her work would not be accepted. While he was generous with gifts, he controlled when they came – and it was never on special occasions such as Christmas or her birthday. While he bought whatever he wanted for himself, she had no money of her own, and he would complain about whatever she spent. She suggested he pay her for her work, but he refused.

Nonetheless, Taffy accepted all this for thirty-seven years. While she found him "very controlling" and "a little narcissistic," he was, in her eyes, "a good man – honest and loyal." What she admired about her husband was: "He was a workhorse and he took care of everything." What she could *not* accept was his anger that grew over the years and became more and more directed at her. No one could reach his perfectionist standards, least of all her. "I became his whipping boy," she said. "I could never do anything right for him."

She accepted this abuse for so many years because, she said, she was afraid to be alone. She had no confidence in her ability to support herself, despite being trained as a nurse and licensed as a real estate agent. The last straw was when a young Iranian boy of nineteen disrespected her in front of Kabir and her husband would not do anything in her defense. She gave him an ultimatum. In her words: "I said it was him or me ... so I left." Presumably, he did not choose her. That marked the end of their thirty-seven-year marriage.

Is it any wonder that, after almost forty years of living in this relationship, she doubted herself as a competent business-woman? That she agonized over decisions because she had no trust in her decision-making ability? Or that she lived in perpetual fear that she'd appear stupid in front of her colleagues or clients? Although numerical calculations were a regular part of her work as a real estate agent, she experienced high levels of anxiety in dealing with numbers. She felt compelled to have another staff member recheck her figures – just as her husband had done. She was always afraid that what-ever she had done would not be done right. His voice of constant criticism had taken up residence in her head.

Preparation Session

Taffy wanted to focus on her anxiety dealing with numbers since it was such a central part of her work as a real estate agent.

Her <u>issue</u> was:

I want to address my anxiety dealing with numbers.

At first, the target was going to be her childhood experience of dealing with numbers in Grade three or four. She vividly remembered that her grade school math teacher was very scary and intimidating. "She had long red fingernails and she would hit you on the head if you made a mistake and sit you in the hall if you didn't understand something." The worst part of that experience for Taffy was the thought of being humiliated in front of the whole class.

Interestingly, I myself had a similar experience as a child with a Grade three math teacher, Miss Robb. She would point at a number on the times table and you were expected to pop up from your seat and give the correct answer immediately and in full volume. If you made a mistake, she would crack her ruler down hard on the desk and make deprecating comments about your intelligence. The pressure was intense. I believe that my serious dislike of mathematics began in that classroom – and it probably was not limited to me. How many students, particularly females, have been traumatized by tyrannical teachers like this?

However, in Taffy's case, we decided to focus on the anxiety she was experiencing currently in her real estate work. This had a higher level of disturbance for her than her child-hood experience. Moreover, this choice left it open for the processing to determine the relevant source(s) of her anxiety.

Taffy reported that whenever she had to write up a real estate deal, she felt terrified that she would not do it right. She had to get a step-by-step list of instructions and check each step with an associate. Despite her years of experience in the field, she did not trust herself to do it on her own. Even that was not enough for her. She then felt compelled to go to her broker to double-check her figures. This was painfully embar-rassing to her and formed the target for our work.

The feelings that accompanied the target were:

> embarrassment (feeling exposed as stupid) that she located in her throat,
> fear (her heart beating) that she located in her chest,
> anger at herself that she located in her jaw (grit teeth),

hopelessness and dread ("because this is my profession") that she located in her solar plexus,
overwhelm that she located in her lungs (needing air),
agitation and shakiness that she located in her arms.

Her <u>negative cognition</u> was:

I am stupid.

Her <u>positive cognition</u> was:

I am capable.

The <u>VOC</u> was a two or three.

Her <u>SUDS</u> was a seven or eight.

Even planning the session was anxiety producing for Taffy. She was not only fearful about her performance as a real estate agent. She was also afraid she would not do the processing "right."
We then created a set of resources for the work.

1. For nurturing and support, she chose:
   • two friends who were supportive – one who believed in her abilities,
   • and one who would listen and be there for her.

2. For strength, she chose:
   • her father who was very protective of her,
   • and her son who did not compromise his beliefs, but was always true to himself.

3. For wisdom, she chose:
- her brother who was very intelligent
- and his wife who was liberal and open-minded, non-judgmental of people, and helpful in working through problems.

The quality she felt she needed was confidence. She recalled the day her husband had put a finger in her face and she had replied: "You're not going to do this to me anymore! Get your fucking finger out of my face –I'm not going to live this way anymore." Then she had grabbed a few things and left, saying to him: "I'll be in touch."

Her safe place was the loft she had moved to when she left the marriage. She imagined herself standing in the kitchen looking at the ocean, hearing the sounds of people laughing and children playing in the park across from her place, smelling the sea and fires on the beach at night. She felt calm and safe. The word that came up to describe this experience was "content."

Processing Session

Taffy came in to the session reporting that she had just spent time trying to explain to her sister what she had learned in our work about being in the victim position.[22] She felt that her sister was repeating the mistakes she herself had made in her marriage. To her dismay, her sister would not listen to her. She came away frustrated.

The SUDS she reported was a seven or eight.
= I'm frustrated with myself. It's embarrassing to let someone else know that I need help.

---

[22] See Aarons, *Journey to Home*, Part 2, "Emotional Abuse: Breaking the Spell," 35-65.

= I feel like I'm a fraud. I can't really do this work. I wish the numbers would get clearer in my mind.

= I know I can do this to some extent because I ran my husband's business and I always did the numbers. He always double-checked them.

= Why can't I have this security? Is it because he didn't trust me or because I didn't trust myself?

= I think it's the latter. It's my insecurity … but maybe it's because of him too.

= I don't know exactly where it stems from, but I know that he is not a trusting person and he didn't trust me to do *anything* right!

= It sucks! You try and try and it's never good enough for him.

= I feel angry that he never gave me the benefit of the doubt and I was always having to prove myself to him.

= I wish I could do something to prove myself to him.

[This suggests that she is still trying to be good enough for him. I ask: "Did you mess up *everything*?"]

= No. I *could* do it, but he wouldn't let me go ahead without checking everything. He didn't trust the computer either.

[I ask: "Whose problem is this? Yours or his?"]

= I know it's his problem, not mine. But I can't change him.

[I ask: "So, do you wear it or 'return to sender'?"[23]]

---

[23] This phrase "return to sender" refers to a comment made by a former client that I often repeat to convey the message that we can choose not to take on what other people think or believe, especially about us.

= I have to "return to sender" and remove it from myself.

= I have to release myself from the feeling that I'm not capable. He left saying that I would never be able to manage on my own.

> [I direct her to talk to her husband about the messages he gave her about her capabilities.]

= I'm angry that you took out all your angst on me! You beat down my self-esteem so I can't trust myself anymore. Your negativity and anger poisoned us and me. When I'd try to reason with you, you'd just get louder until I gave up and shut up.

= I'm *so* angry at you for beating on me until I became a puddle. *I am not your whipping boy!* You didn't need to check! It was your problem, not mine.

= I need to learn to trust myself.

> [I ask pointedly: "Have you managed on your own the last two and a half years? Have you dealt with numbers adequately?"]

= I *can* do numbers on my own! I will not let myself doubt my abilities because I *have* proven myself.

> [I ask her to go back to the target and see what level of disturbance it has for her at this moment. She reports a five. I ask: "What prevents it from being a zero?" She says: "I want to know how I will be in the future." I turn to future template work at this point.[24] We begin with the next day.]

---

[24] Shapiro, *Eye Movement Desensitization and Reprocessing*, 206-210.

= I'm smiling and feeling confident, without any dread.

[I do a Body Scan on each part of her body identified earlier and each part is relaxed.]

Then, we look at a year from now. Each part is very relaxed. Then, we look at five years from now. Each part is relaxed.]

= "I'm putting money in the bank," she says, smiling.

[I ask if she might like to tell this to her husband.]

= "I made it through all that doubt and anxiety and I'm able to make it on my own. I'm capable."

[This was her positive cognition. So I ask her to repeat it.]

= "I'm capable. I know I'm capable," she says confidently.

[Her VOC was a seven. We do a Body Scan and install the PC. Her target was a zero.]

This ends the processing session.

Follow-Up Session

Taffy reported feeling "good" and "clear." She had no anxiety when thinking about numbers.

She shared that she was less focused on Kabir and thinking much less about him. "I could never live with him again," she said. "Even as a date, he's so negative; all he does is complain."

Her focus was on her career and where it was headed. "I'm still afraid to be financially independent," she admitted, "because I've always been dependent on him." She was considering other options besides real estate, but was worried that, whatever choice she made, she might not make enough to survive.

I suggested we do some superego work[25] to ensure that she was able to override any negative messages that might still be in her head from the many long years she had lived with Kabir. She came back saying she could not do the superego homework because: "I don't beat myself up anymore."

Postscript

I talked to Taffy about a year later. She wanted me to know that she was still in real estate and had just made a two-million-dollar sale.

Clinical Comments

It is not unusual to have a female client with low self-confidence and a poor self-image. It is truly unfortunate just how common this presenting problem is.

I have worked with countless women over the years who are overworked and underpaid because they are afraid to ask for a raise. Many of them are in dead end jobs because they don't feel capable of anything better. Many others remain at

---

[25] Aarons, *Journey to Home*, Part Three, "Silencing the Superego," 80-90.

home in the security of the homemaking role rather than face the challenges of the work world.[26] It is, I believe, a reflection of the dubious status of women in our culture. Despite the efforts of the women's movement and the years that have passed since Betty Friedan identified "the disease without a name,"[27] the situation of women does not appear to be all that different than it was in the fifties. There are exceptions, of course, but in the therapy room, the laments of women are very similar to those of our predecessors in Friedan's world.

One might be inclined to conclude from the Case of Taffy that the problem is a direct result of a traditional marriage in which the husband is the breadwinner and the woman is economically dependent on him. The economic power differential may be carried over into their interpersonal dynamic in such a way that the woman feels inferior to him. She cannot press for her rights as a human being because, after all, he pays the bills and how could she manage on her own?

While this is, no doubt, true more often than we might like to think, it is not the whole answer to the problem of women's self-esteem. In the next case study, we will see that the wife is the primary breadwinner and she has been professionally employed for many years. Unlike Taffy, she has confidence in her abilities as a businesswoman and is very assertive in the work world. However, when she gets home and has to deal with her husband, it is a very different story. She feels herself reduced to an obedient child who is unable to speak up for herself.

---

[26] I am not speaking about women for whom homemaking is their preferred choice and they are satisfied in this role. Nor would I want, in any way, to deprecate this role. On the contrary, it will be abundantly clear from several of the case studies in this book just how vitally important the mother role is. For example, see Chapters Six and Eight.

[27] Betty Friedan, *The Feminine Mystique*, (New York: Penguin, 1963).

CHAPTER FIVE

Submissiveness:

Love Without Garter Belts

Case of Danielle

Background Information

Danielle and Nils had been married for seven years at the time of her EMDR therapy. It was the third marriage for her and the second for him. Nils had been a dentist in Minnesota and then developed a business selling medical supplies in California. He had left his first wife of many years because she was alcoholic. He had two (now adult) children with her.

Nils was twenty-four years older than Danielle "if," she added, "we believe that he is the age he says he is." She herself was forty-nine years old. Previously, she had done therapy regarding her relationship with her father, particularly the sexualized nature of his behavior with her. He walked around the house naked until she was twelve or thirteen years of age. He commented on her tight jeans and, she said, "creeped me out by looking me up and down."

Danielle was a striking woman. She had auburn wavy hair and a pretty face. But what one noticed most about her was her height, set off by her long shapely legs and well-proportioned butt. No doubt, that was what her husband, Nils, noticed about her too. He loved to see her dressed up in slinky outfits when they went out together. He enjoyed seeing the envious looks of other, less fortunate, men who were not out with her – so long, that is, as she paid attention only to him. He definitely did not appreciate her being even casually friendly to other men. At home, he pressed her to dress up in sexy attire and parade in front of him. She said he particularly liked it when she put on stockings with a garter belt, stiletto heels, and no panties. It was a constant turn-on for him.

Danielle complained that Nils wanted sex all the time. He resented it when she had work-related meetings or social plans with friends on weekday evenings or at any time during the weekends. He wanted her to give *all* her spare time to him. And most of it he wanted to spend in bed. He had a notebook where he kept track of her orgasms and rated them for quality and intensity. He would sulk for days and give her "the silent treatment" if she took any time away from him, so it often seemed easier to her just to go along with his demands. Or he would tease her mercilessly, knowing she was not comfortable being teased. Despite her angry protests, he would persist, seeing from her reaction that it really got under her skin. She believed that he did it in order to punish her.

Every Friday night was date night and Danielle would drink, frequently to excess, to "get in the mood." She felt enormous pressure to be sexually responsive and innovative with him. She both loved the sexual attention and hated feeling reduced to a sexual object. Clearly, she was in conflict about this.

While she loved her husband, he was a source of perpetual frustration to her. As his business declined, she became the primary breadwinner of their family. Yet he resented the fact that she had to work. And she, in turn, resented the fact that he would not take any steps to get out of his business and find alternative work. He spent most of his time at home, but he resented helping with housework. He would commit to do tasks in their household and then not do them. Although he had been at home all day while she was working, she would come home day after day to find they still had not been done. Nor would he allow her to hire someone to do them. Although she made most of the money in the relationship, it appeared that he got to decide how the money was to be spent.

According to Danielle, Nils would resist changing virtually *anything* that bothered her – from the crumbs on the kitchen counter to racist jokes in social settings. It was particularly upsetting to her that he watched so much pornography online and that, to make matters worse, he would leave it on the computer used by his kids. He seemed to believe that cooperating with her would be the same thing as being controlled by her. And he wasn't going to let himself be controlled. Thus the only possible ending to a conflict would be if she gave in. Eventually, she would have to appease him, she felt, because being in conflict wore her down. She wanted to stay in her marriage without having to submit to his rule and lose her sense of self.

The irony in this case was that this woman was somewhat of a business dynamo. She seemed to have no trouble asserting herself in the professional world. In fact, she had at times been characterized as "forceful" or even aggressive, and she could be perceived as intimidating in her outspokenness. More than once, she found herself the target of harsh criticism from other staff members and from superiors. She had strong opinions and had to learn discretion in how and to whom she stated them. We spent many hours in therapy figuring out how she could manage the political in's and out's of the non-profit world she moved in. One would certainly not have guessed that this tailored woman in a business suit by day would, at night, be prancing in stiletto heels and garter belt to please her sexually demanding husband.

Preparation Session

Danielle explained that she was very frustrated and concerned about her marriage. "Nils was an only child who was spoiled by his mother. He still wants to be the center of attention and he still wants to be spoiled. He's so high maintenance!"

She went on: "I don't want to be his project. I don't want to be 'improved' by him. It's so much work to do anything he doesn't want. I have to be someone I'm not with him."

The <u>issue</u> she wanted to work on was:

> I want to be stronger in my relationship with Nils – to realize and express my true feelings about what happens.

The incident she chose to focus on was a time when she was getting dressed to go out to dinner in a dress Nils wanted her to wear with a garter belt and nylon stockings. She was hot getting out of the shower and it was "*so annoying* putting them on," she said with obvious vexation. Then, she looked in the mirror and she did *not* like what she saw. "My legs looked fat and my thighs were hanging out! It did not make me feel sexy, but I wore it anyway. I felt annoyed and off-kilter the whole night. I was so pissed!"

The <u>target</u> was the moment she looked in the mirror and hated what she saw.

The <u>feelings</u> that came up for her as she recalled this moment were:

> anger that she located in her jaw and fists,
> fear (of not looking good) that she located in her chest,
> sadness that she placed in her forehead and eyes,
> anxiety that she felt in her stomach,
> frustration (with herself) that she located in her throat,
> despair and hopelessness that she felt in her shoulders.

As her <u>negative cognition</u> she considered :

> I am weak;
>
> I am unattractive.

She finally chose:

> I have to do what he wants in order to get love and approval.

Her <u>positive cognition</u> was:

> I can recognize what's true for me and act on it with a man I love.

Her <u>SUDS</u> was an eight.

The quality she felt she needed was courage. She recalled a time when she had expressed what she thought and felt about her boss to board members of her agency – at the risk of losing her job.

Her safe place was a setting from the *Narnia Chronicles:* a high plateau with green grass where she sat at the base of a tree with a deep feeling of being accepted and loved for who she was.

Danielle chose the following as her resources:

1. For nurturing and support, she chose:
   - Asland from the *Narnia Chronicles,*
   - and Disneyland's *Fantasyland* which is "clean and innocent and sweet."

2. For strength, she chose:

- Dagny Taggart from Ayn Rand's *Atlas Shrugged* who "has no qualms about saying what she wants and speaking the truth because she doesn't care at all what people think;"
- and Dara Taurez, an Olympic medal winner over forty years of age who persevered in competition even after she had a baby.

3. for wisdom she chose:

- Queen Elizabeth who thought things through in order to rule the country through fifty years of conflict;
- and Einstein who was humble and wise and had an amazing perspective on life.

Even when resources are not actively utilized in the processing, I believe it may be comforting to clients to have them in the background as potential figures of support.

Processing Session

Rachel: I'm going to review what we set up and then I'll give you instructions from there.

Danielle: Okay.

Rachel: And from this point on, you can forget your perfect social skills.

You don't even have to look at me. If I speak to you, you'll answer me, but both of us are going to be inside your process. We're not really here in the room, if you know what I mean. We're really connecting with what's going on in your inner experience.

Danielle: Okay.

Rachel: So, your issue is: "I want to be stronger in my relation-ship with Nils to realize and express - or to become aware and articulate - my true feelings about what happens."

And the memory that you wanted to use was a time when you were getting dressed to go out to dinner in a dress that Nils wanted you to wear with a garter belt and nylons. And you were hot. You were getting out of the shower and it was really annoying for you to put on those stockings and the garter belt. And you looked in the mirror and, in your perception, your legs looked fat and your thighs were hanging out. You did not like how you looked. It did not make you feel sexy at all. But you wore it anyway. You felt annoyed and out of kilter the whole night and you were really pissed. Really pissed at the decision that you made to wear something that was so uncomfortable and unappealing to you. The moment in this experience that was the most distressing - the target -was the moment that you looked in the mirror and saw your image in the mirror and you didn't like how you looked.

The feelings the target brought up for you were: *anger* that you located in your jaw and your fists, *fear* of not looking good that you located in your chest, *sadness* that you located in your forehead and your eyes, a kind of *nervousness* or *anxiety* that you felt in your stomach, *frustration* with yourself that you located in your throat, a sense of *despair* or *hopelessness* that you placed in your shoulders.

The negative belief that you had about yourself was:

> "I have to do what he wants. I have to do what Nils wants in order to get love and approval."

What you would like to believe about yourself - the posi-tive cognition - is that you can recognize what's true for you and act on it with him or with any man that you love. At this point in time I'm going to ask you to hold three things in your mind. First, the target. The target is that moment when you looked in the mirror and saw yourself. Second, the feelings that come up now as you recall that target and which I just listed – the anger, fear, sadness, anxiety, frustration and hopelessness. And, third, the negative belief: "I have to do what he wants in order to get love and approval."

Hold all three things in your mind and ramp up the level of disturbance until it is as high as you can make it at this moment in time. And when you are at that point, you're going to give me a number between zero and ten that represents your level of disturbance. When I hear that number, I will turn on the scanner and you will be observing in detail what comes up in your mind when the scanner is on. Is that clear?

Danielle: Yeah… Seven.

Rachel: Notice what comes up.

Danielle: Well, my stomach feels nervous … and I feel like crying. My throat is choked. Just, you know, the same feelings. Angry. Angry at him. Angry that I've been doing that.

Rachel: Angry at him and angry at yourself – that you're doing that. Okay. Stay with the anger.

Danielle: I guess the thought that came up was: "Why do I always do that?" I let myself acquiesce without even thinking.

Rachel: When you think about your acquiescing without even thinking, what comes up for you? Are there examples or memories?

Danielle: I mean, a lot of the things that I've done with Nils come up all the time. I mean, all these Friday night date nights. They're all like a big blur.

Rachel: Can you let them focus or do you want to keep them as a blur?

Danielle: Well, I think they're a blur because I was drinking.

Rachel: Is there anything, any specific detail that comes up or any specific occasion?

Danielle: Yeah. The thing that just came to my mind was walking in to see Nils on the computer looking at pornography, or looking at pictures of women in lingerie. He has this picture in his bathroom of a former lover actually, standing out on some terrace in Paris with the Eiffel Tower in the background. She's got on a fur coat that she's opening up and she just has lingerie on and there's the garter belts and the stockings. And it makes me feel … I question myself. I start going: "Oh, what's wrong with me? Why are these other women okay with it and I'm not?"

Rachel: I see. So you feel that because they were okay with it, you should be too?

Danielle: In some ways, I feel like there's something wrong with me. Even though, I mean, superficially I know that's not true, but somehow … I mean, Nils always says that he's trying to fix me.

Rachel: To liberate you?

Danielle: Yeah. Exactly. That I have this … that I'm just repressed or something.

Rachel: Do you agree with that?

Danielle: No, I don't.

Rachel: Are you sure?

Danielle: Yeah. I'm pretty sure. I do a lot of things sexually. It's just that I don't like wearing these things. I think what really comes up is that I get so angry, because he's never satisfied. That's when I feel like I'm choking again. Like no matter what I do, it's never going to be good enough for him. But I keep trying. Instead of just being myself and being okay with his not being happy. I don't like it when he's not happy and showing me he's not happy.

Rachel: So, you need him to be happy.

Danielle: Yeah. I guess I do.

Rachel: And is he happy most of the time?

Danielle: As long as he's getting his way. Which isn't entirely true. I mean, he doesn't get his way with everything, but ...

Rachel: But you can be sure he'd be happy if he got his way.

Danielle: Yeah. That's for sure.

Rachel: And what about when he doesn't get his way?

Danielle: He gives me a hard time, teases me. Mostly what he does is tease me and everything is a joke. I can't even have a serious conversation with him. Sometimes I can, but only if I really push the issue and I'm so upset that I have to.

Rachel: So, what's it like for you when he won't be serious?

Danielle: It's really annoying and frustrating and I get really angry. It's like the movie with Cher when she slaps Nick Cage and says: "Snap out of it!" That's how I feel sometimes. because I just feel invisible. And I know it sounds weird, because I know that he doesn't feel that way, but that's how I feel.

> [If a person does not share their true thoughts and feelings he or she will feel invisible. Notice that it is even hard for her to affirm this feeling of invisibility because he does not validate that feeling.]

(She continues:) It's just so hard. I mean, the other day, I was in the living room and we were watching Jeopardy. We always watch Jeopardy. He had been cooking dinner and we paused it about ten minutes after seven and I said: "Well, how long has it been cooking?" and he said: "About an hour." I said: "I've never cooked this before, but that's probably enough. Then we can have it after Jeopardy." So, we watched Jeopardy and then he goes in the kitchen and I went back on the computer.

I always ask him if he wants help, but he never wants help, so I'm on the computer. Then I make a phone call. Then about a half hour later, I come out and he had already eaten dinner and he didn't tell me it was ready or anything. I said: "Why didn't you tell me it was ready?" He said: "Well, I thought you knew." I said, "How could I know?" So we spent twenty minutes arguing about whether or not he should have told me dinner was ready or not. It's just so frustrating. We have an apartment. It's so small. I don't know why he can't just say: "Dinner's ready." And then the fact that he has to argue with me about why that would be necessary.

[This is such a telling example of the dynamics in their relationship and of the kind of power struggles couples get into when they operate from insecurity and low self esteem.]

It's just one example of so many things that happen with him. I have to fight with him – I mean, not physically, but I have to really say: "Sit down. I need you to understand where I'm coming from. It just doesn't make sense. I didn't see you go and open the oven and, even so, what's the harm in you telling me dinner's ready? I don't understand why this is so complicated." So it's just exhausting. That's why, a lot of times, I don't say what I want or how I feel because it ends up being so exhausting. I'm getting frustrated right now just even thinking about that.

Rachel: Good. Stay with the frustration.

[I see the angry look on her face and the tension in her body.]

That's right. That's good. Stay with the frustration, because this is the feeling you get a lot in this relationship. And if you were to do what you feel like doing when you're frustrated – which you won't do when you're with him because you don't want to hurt him and you don't want to upset him and blah, blah, blah …

[Meaning all the reasons she gives herself for holding back and not expressing how she really feels.]

But here, he doesn't feel it. He's not going to know and I'm not going to tell him. What does that frustration want to do? What do you feel like doing now?

[As in the case of Trevor, anger lies beneath the compliant posture and needs to be released for the person to recover their sense of self.]

Danielle: Well, it's like the other time, when I took him home from the hospital and he again began smashing ants with his fists on the kitchen counter and rubbing them on his pants, and I asked him not to do it and then I started to do it, but I didn't. I controlled myself. But I wanted to jump up and down and be like a little kid with a tantrum. Just screaming at him saying: "You're driving me crazy!"

Rachel: Okay. So, can you give yourself permission to do here what you could not do there? Visualize yourself jumping up and down, screaming and having a tantrum like a little kid and saying what it is you'd like to say when you're doing that.

Danielle: I want to just say: "Just listen to me. Hear what I'm saying. Hear how I feel."

Rachel: I'm wondering if you could say that a little bit more powerfully, forcibly and maybe even louder. "Just listen to me! Listen to me!"

Danielle: Just listen to me! Listen to me! LISTEN!

Rachel: Yes. Like that. Say it a few more times. Really get into that.

Danielle: JUST LISTEN! LISTEN TO ME!

Rachel: Okay. Good. Now, when you're saying that, look at Nils. Is he, in fact, turned toward you? Is he listening? Is he there?

Danielle: Yeah. He's there. He is listening.

Rachel: Okay. He is listening. Now is your chance to tell him what you want to tell him.

Danielle: You're a pain in the ass!

Rachel: Good. You tell him.

Danielle: You are a pain. And you're making my life miserable because, no matter what I do or say, I feel like I'm invisible. It doesn't matter how I feel or what I think, you're just going to keep doing what you want to do, no matter.

> [Thus invisibility means to her not just covering up her feelings, but also feeling powerless to affect the other's behavior.]

How would you feel if I did that? Maybe we should live for a month like that and see how you feel.

Rachel: Okay. When you tell him that, just be quiet and receptive for a moment to see what his response is. Maybe he just stares at you. Maybe he yells. Maybe he says something back. Just notice.

Danielle: He'd argue with me.

Rachel: What's he saying?

Danielle: He'd say: "I don't always get my way. I don't always get my way. I acquiesce to you all the time." I'd say: "Like, well, like, with what?" "Well, I cook you dinner." I'd say: "Well, that's not acquiescing. That's doing something that you voluntarily want to do. I don't ask you to cook me dinner every night."

Rachel: What are you asking him to do?

Danielle: I don't ask him to do anything – except when something happens that bothers me, I ask him to not do it. I ask him to not kill ants with his hands and wipe it on his pants. I ask him to wipe the counter off when he's done – when there's food on it. I ask him to not push the cutting board back into the drawer when there are breadcrumbs all over it.

Rachel: Okay. So, like the ants, like the cutting board, like the counter …

Danielle: I ask him to not say bigoted jokes in front of his grand-kids.

Rachel: So clearly, these are areas that seem reasonable to you. But Nils is stubborn and will not do what you ask.

Danielle: Exactly.

Rachel: Okay, you can yell at him and jump up and down. You can jump on his head. You can rip him to pieces. That's fine here. Not in the world. But what do you want to do with this situation? He's like a kid who will not obey. He will not coop-erate. He's just going to do his own thing. So, where does that leave you?

Danielle: Well, it leaves me, you know, kind of in a place where I have to understand that that's the way that he is. But I have to understand that it's not me. He would do that with every-body. So it's not that he's not listening to *me*. He would just do that with everyone.

[This is a crucial shift she is making in seeing that it's not about her. She can separate his behavior from her self-worth and not personalize his defiance.]

(She continues:) I have to come to an understanding - like a level of acceptance - so that it doesn't bother me so much, you know, so it doesn't get to me. I don't think he's doing it to me on purpose.

Rachel: Okay, good. You can see that it's not an attack on you. But if he will not do what you want, what will you do about the situations that bother you? You can accept that he won't do what you want. That's a starting point. What else can you do?

[I think she needs an action plan. Even if she can accept that his oppositionality is not directed at her, there are a number of areas of their life where she has indicated she wants concrete change.]

Danielle: Well, I can walk away.

Rachel: For example, leave the crumbs on the counter and leave the room.

Danielle: Yeah. I can leave them there. I don't have to pick up after him. I've done that for, you know, most of the time we're together. But sometimes it just gets to me.

Rachel: Think about one of those times when it just gets to you. And then, what would you like to do?

Danielle: I'd like to sock him.

[She still has anger that needs to be expressed and this may be blocking her from seeing other possibilities of action.]

Rachel: Oh, maybe you need to. Visualize yourself socking him. Do you feel like you could do that? In fantasy; I don't mean in reality.

Danielle: Yeah. I can do it.

Rachel: Okay. So sock him. Sock him like you've never let yourself sock him. Sock him really hard. And there may be words that go with this. "I am so frustrated with you! I have all these examples where you will not do what I want. I just want to sock you." Or maybe there aren't words.

Danielle: I don't think there are words. I want to punch him right in the stomach.

Rachel: Alright. Punch him right in the stomach. Okay. Keep on punching him in the stomach. Are you doing that?

Danielle: Yeah.

Rachel: Okay. And what else?

Danielle: I want to stomp on his toe.

Rachel: Okay. Good. You can have your tantrum right on top of him.

Danielle: Exactly.

Rachel: Stomp on his toe. What else? You're getting into it now. You've only just started.

Danielle: Pulling his hair.

Rachel: Yeah. Pulling his hair. What else?

Danielle: I've had dreams. So many dreams where I'm just pissed at him. He does things like he doesn't know I exist - like I'm invisible. I'm just realizing that I have this happen in my dreams a lot. I'll catch him, you know, cheating on me in a dream. He'll come back to where we're supposedly living –

our house – and I'll recognize it in the dream, but he just acts like I don't mean anything to him.

Rachel: So, it's not just invisible. It's unimportant.

Danielle: Exactly. It's like I don't make a difference. He knows what I want. It's not like he doesn't hear me or see me. He just doesn't care. And then, in my dreams I have these raging fits of just screaming at him. Saying: "How can you do this to me? I can't believe that you would do something like that!" It's like this overwhelming feeling of despair – but rage at the same time. It's kind of this terrible confluence.

Rachel: Well, it's the rage of not being able to impact him and the despair of feeling like you don't make a difference. You don't matter.

Danielle: It's also being out of control like this. Even when I do what he wants, it doesn't matter.

Rachel: Do you feel out of control yourself or are you saying that you don't have control over him?

Danielle: No control over him.

Rachel: That sounds like his modus operandi. That it's who he is. He will not allow you to influence him. He regards cooperating with you as being controlled by you.

Danielle: Yeah.

Rachel: And he will not go there. Do you see that?

Danielle: Yeah I see that. Because I look at it as cooperating and he looks at it as controlling.

Rachel: That's right.

Danielle: Like he has this oppositional defiant disorder.

Rachel: That's right. So, for him, cooperation is control. And where do you go with that recognition?

Danielle: Well, I kind of understand a little. I mean I feel it helps me to understand him a little bit better, I guess …

Rachel: That doesn't mean that you wouldn't still be raging.

Danielle: No. Of course not.

Rachel: And I'm not sure you've gotten your rage out.

Danielle: No. There's a ton of rage. I don't know what else I can do.

Rachel: You could destroy him right now. You could jump on him, rip him to pieces, fry him in a fry pan …?

Danielle: I'd rather just throw the kitchen.

Rachel: All right. Go for that.

Danielle: Okay. I'm throwing dishes; I'm breaking glasses; I'm turning over the little round glass table. There's this cabinet that he has with all his Danish plates in it. All of a sudden, I have a bat. Oh my!

Rachel: Good! Great!

Danielle: And I'm crashing into the plates. I'm tearing up all his fancy china. I'm smashing the pictures around on top of it and the candleholders. I'm going to go in the kitchen and I'm going to smash that damn yellow refrigerator that he won't get rid of. And the yellow sink. Oh.

Rachel: Go on. Go on.

Danielle: And then I'm going to smash all the Tupperware that just keeps getting messed up no matter how many times I straighten it up. And the old microwave that he won't get rid of. And the stupid old stove that the door's hanging off.

Rachel: That kitchen really pisses you off, doesn't it?

Danielle: It does! And I just renovated it as much as I possibly can except for buying new appliances. Oh … and he won't do it.

Rachel: He won't get new appliances.

Danielle: No.

Rachel: Look around. Your kitchen is just totally a mess. It's all debris. Notice how you feel. You still feel rage? You still feel anger and you need to let it out on him? You've done it with the kitchen. You're fed up with the kitchen, with the old microwave, the Tupperware, with the stupid stove, the yellow fridge. It's all yucky to you. You hate it!

Danielle: I hate it!

Rachel: You hate it.

Danielle: Well, I feel better. I feel like I'm heavy breathing over the bat in the corner of the kitchen. Kind of a relief to see everything.

Rachel: Well, you still have the bat in your hands. See if there's anything else you need to destroy or anybody else you need to destroy to act out the rage that you feel inside, remembering that nobody's getting hurt here.

Danielle: Well, I feel pretty good.

Rachel: Okay. Now, where do you go?

Danielle: I go into the living room, sit down on the couch and cry.

Rachel: Okay. Go with the crying. Why are you crying? What's the crying about? What are you feeling as you cry?

Danielle: Just hopelessness.

Rachel: Hopeless about what?

Danielle: Hopeless about trying to get my feelings heard.

Rachel: Okay. I think you're really talking about communicating with Nils and getting him to change the things he refuses to change. Is that right? Or is that wrong? You don't want to just tell him that you hate the yellow fridge; you want that fridge to be changed. You don't want to just tell him that you hate the crumbs on the counter; you want him to clean them up. Is that right? (She nods.) So, it's not just getting your feelings heard. It's getting him to do what you want.

Danielle: Yeah. Some kind of action to show that he's heard me.

Rachel: So tell him: "I want you to do what I want!"

Danielle: "I want you to do what I want."

Rachel: If you won't, then … what?

Danielle: I don't know what.

Rachel: Right. That's where you're stuck. He doesn't want to and he won't do what you want. So, if he won't – if that's just the bottom line and he cannot tolerate being cooperative because it makes him feel like a puppet on a string – then, what will you do with all this frustration and rage that you feel when he won't do what you want?

Danielle: I guess I'll leave.

Rachel: Okay. Well, that's one possibility.

Danielle: I mean, I can ask him to go to counseling. I can talk to him about it. But I've talked to him about it so many times.

Rachel: Well, let's imagine that he simply will not change and that's the bottom line. That's probably your best assumption here, right?

Danielle: Yeah.

Rachel: He won't do what you want. Now, what do you do? You mentioned one possibility is you'd leave.

Danielle: Yeah.

Rachel: Okay. Visualize that for a moment. You've decided this is hopeless. He's never going to listen to you. "I'm going to have to live with crumbs on the counter, and crumbs on the cutting board and cutting knife, and all these horrible things in the kitchen that I hate, and his refusal to listen to what bothers me, and I'm finally going to do something about it. I've had it. I'm out of here!" Do you want to tell him your decision before you go?

Danielle: Yeah.

 Rachel: Okay. Tell him now.

Danielle: Nils, you have been making me crazy for years. You never listen to what I say and what I want. You continue to do what you want no matter how I feel about it and I'm done. And so, I'm leaving.

[She needs to look over this abyss of possible separation to determine how important this relationship is to her.]

Rachel: And when you look at Nils, what do you see?

Danielle: I see him just crumbling.

Rachel: Oh. What exactly do you see? You mean he sort of falls onto the floor?

Danielle: No. Just his face. He starts … but he doesn't really crumble he just … in some way though, I'll be able to see him being upset.

Rachel: He's upset. Sure. All of a sudden you're doing something he doesn't want you to do. He's upset. Is that the same thing as crumbling? Or do you imagine that this man would crumble if you left?

Danielle: I guess I do imagine that he would crumble.

Rachel: You want to feel that you're that important? That if you left, he couldn't manage without you?

Danielle: You know, in some ways I feel like that's probably the case, but not from an emotional perspective – from a financial perspective.

Rachel: Well, either way. He is dependent on you.

Danielle: He is.

Rachel: Well, let yourself think that and know that. Let yourself take that in. That he is dependent on you. If you were to leave, his life would fall apart. Do you think he knows that?

Danielle: Yeah. He knows.

Rachel: And maybe that's part of why he doesn't want to cooperate with you. Maybe because he resents the fact that he's so totally dependent on you.

Danielle: Yeah. That's true.

Rachel: I don't know. That was a theory. Does that feel right?

Danielle: Yeah. I mean, I can imagine that would be very frustrating and emasculating for him. And so, the only thing that he gravitates towards, which makes him feel more like a man, is sex. So when he doesn't feel satisfied with that, he feels even more emasculated – like he doesn't matter.

Rachel: So, his need to feel like a man puts you in a position of having to tolerate crumbs on the counter and a whole bunch of other very annoying things ... unless you leave. Those are the only options you've seen so far.

Danielle: Yeah.

Rachel: What do you want to do? You see that it's hopeless. This man is never going to want to cooperate with you. That's how he's hanging on to his self-esteem and you don't want to live with this frustration anymore. That is your stuck place. Stay with that for a moment.

Danielle: Well, I think about his kids, you know? They've become my family, too.

Rachel: You couldn't have a relationship with them if you weren't living with him?

Danielle: I don't know how. I don't think that they would ever forgive me. They won't understand.

Rachel: You're afraid that they wouldn't forgive you.

Danielle: Yeah. I'd lose his whole family along with Nils.

Rachel: So, one of the reasons you stay has nothing to do with Nils, but has to do with his family and wanting to be part of that.

Danielle: Oh, absolutely. Even though they annoy me too sometimes. Maybe it's menopause. I'm just getting annoyed with everybody. Nils always makes jokes that he stays away from me because of my hormones. He has no idea how kind I have been.

Rachel: Do you think you're a raving maniac lady who's hormonally hysterical?

Danielle: I get close. I get close.

Rachel: Then you understand that that's his way of reducing you, of invalidating you …

Danielle: Yeah. I know. It's very insulting when he does that because I just look at him and say: "It's not that. You don't know what you're talking about."

Rachel: He annoys you sometimes *big* time and even his family annoys you sometimes too.

Danielle: Yup.

Rachel: Do you think there's a family that wouldn't annoy you sometimes?

Danielle: Ah … no.

Rachel: But there could be a man who would be less annoying than Nils.

Danielle: Oh, I'm sure there probably is.

Rachel: I think so too. So, you're going to stay with him because you want to be in his family. Because you want to be connected with his family?

Danielle: No. There are lots of parts of him that I love. I love a ton of things about him. But I need to be able to be heard and I need to have some sort of proof from him that I'm being heard. Whether it's in actions or words need to follow actions. I have to figure out what are those actions that I need from him. They need to happen. If they don't happen, then that's a deal breaker. I need to write it all down and then sit down with him and talk with him. And then I want to talk with him about this cooperation versus controlling. And I want to talk with him about how it must be emasculating to not have the income and be dependent on me.

Rachel: You're saying that you feel like you could talk to him and maybe it would make a difference. Do you think it would make a difference?

Danielle: I think it might. But I have to tell him that it's making me crazy to the point where I'm going to have to leave. Whenever I get mad, he always – he knows I'm uncomfortable being angry and so he has developed this way of smirking at me or looking at me like "You can't be angry with me. You can't be angry with me." And then I laugh, you know. But then it even feels worse afterwards. But even though I laugh, it's like (sighs) I feel … awful.

Rachel: Because you've abandoned yourself.

Danielle: Yeah. Exactly.

Rachel: Is there a way for you to tell him that you would not be disparaged or that you could work past the disparagement and still take yourself seriously?

Danielle: Well, I'm mad and he just feels like it's a joke. And again, I just feel like I don't matter.

Rachel: I hear you going back to wanting Nils to be the way you want him to be. But you had said earlier that you didn't think that was possible. So, it's back to you wanting (at least in his mind) to control him.

Danielle: Well, I don't know if it's possible to get anywhere without talking with him. I don't know. I don't know.

[She is going back and forth between unacceptable options - to leave him or get him to change. There is a need for a third alternative.]

Rachel: What else could you do if you didn't talk to him? Is there any other option that would be there for you that would make the point very loud and clear, but he wouldn't be able to pick on your words?

Danielle: Yeah. I could write him a letter. I could write him a letter.

[Obviously she is looping, circling in her stuckness. She can't see that writing to him would likely have the same problems as talking to this man.]

Rachel: Yes. You could write him a letter.

Danielle: I could tape a video.

Rachel: Oh, *you* could take action.

[I'm hinting that perhaps she has to become proactive.]

Danielle: Yeah, but I don't know what I would do - what I could do besides those things?

Rachel: Well, what would make things better for you, even if Nils wouldn't do them? What would you like to do that wouldn't put you in a position of being in a minefield of frustration?

Danielle: Well ... I have taken charge of doing the kitchen. I repainted all the cabinets. I repainted the wall. I just did it. He got real upset, but I just did it.

Rachel: How do you feel about that part of the kitchen?

Danielle: Well, that part's great!

Rachel: You're happier?

Danielle: Yeah!

Rachel: It made a difference for you?

Danielle: Oh, it made a huge difference! I wanted to do things in the house and it was just a matter of doing them, and not paying attention to what he thinks.

Rachel: Okay. That's what worked for you in that case.

Danielle: It did. It did.

Rachel: You just did them and didn't pay attention to his protests or what he wanted.

Danielle: Yup.

Rachel: And you felt good.

Danielle: Yeah. I try to cooperate. I try to make it something that we do together. But he doesn't want to do anything.

Rachel: So you did it yourself.

Danielle: Yeah.

Rachel: And it got done.

Danielle: Yeah, it did.

Rachel: And you didn't have to be frustrated. And you didn't have to feel like you weren't listened to, because his response was not essential.

Danielle: Right. Exactly.

Rachel: You did it anyway.

Danielle: Yeah. I can do it. I can do all of it. I mean, I can change out the green carpet. But I think most or more of my frustration is not things - it's not necessarily the things about the house that are frustrating me.

Rachel: Let's make sure we understand that. The house is not all, but it is part of the frustration.

Danielle: The house is part of it.

Rachel: And you could do something about that, even though it may take you time.

Danielle: Yes. It will take me time.

Rachel: Just for a moment, let us pause on what you could do and then we'll move on. I know this is not everything. Just let yourself go through in your mind what you could do if you give yourself time to do what you want. Just give me a short list of the things you want to do.

[Although this is not the whole solution, it is empowering for her to make explicit the steps she could take on her own to bring about changes that are important to her.]

Danielle: The carpet in the front room would be replaced. The whole front living room would be repainted. I would get sofa covers for the couches. I would put new flooring in the kitchen. I'd rip out the carpet in the hallway and have flooring go from the kitchen down the hallway. I'd probably put new carpet in all the rooms. I'd redesign our bedroom and redesign the guest room. I'd redesign the guest bathroom a little bit – repaint it, rip up the floor in the bathroom and the hallway.

Rachel: You've got projects that will keep you busy for quite a while.

Danielle: I want to beautify our home.

Rachel: I hear that.

Danielle: It's an apartment. We rent it, but …

Rachel: It's your home.

Danielle: Yeah, it's my home and he's been just so resistant. It's just – it wasn't our place. He lived there before and, to be quite honest, what I'd rather do is just move to a new place that's our place. I've thought about that a lot. It's just that we have really good rent and so we're kind of stuck, because it's such good rent.

Rachel: Yeah, that's hard to find.

Danielle: So, it's either improve it and make it new so it has my signature on it, or move to a new place that's really new for both of us.

Rachel: Will he move?

Danielle: I've talked to him about it and he just doesn't want to.

Rachel: Okay, so when it's something that requires his cooperation, you're dead in the water. You say you could move or you could redecorate.

Danielle: I could move. I could redecorate.

Rachel: But you can't make him move if he refuses.

Danielle: Right.

Rachel: You'd have to move without him.

Danielle: Right.

Rachel: And when you went there for a few minutes of imagining leaving, you said: "Well, but I like his family and there's a lot I like about him and I really love him." And you pulled back from that option, but it's there. It's out there. It's one possibility.

Danielle: Uh-huh. But I like being with him.

Rachel: Right now, it seems that he doesn't want to move. It sounds like the only option that's under your control would be redecorating, whether he likes it or not. You just do it.

Danielle: Right. Exactly.

Rachel: And you could have a plan. The plan that you just mentioned could take you a couple of years or more to do. But at least you'd know you were working on a plan. With each step, you would be getting closer and each little piece you do, you could be happy with.

Danielle: Exactly.

Rachel: That feels okay?

Danielle: Oh yeah, absolutely.

Rachel: Okay. But that's not the only problem. Let's go to the rest of the things that bug you – like having to wear the clothes that turn him on that you hate. Go back to the target. Remember that?

Danielle: Yeah.

Rachel: What could you do about that situation?

Danielle: Well, I haven't worn what he has wanted me to wear for a long time. I wear what I want to wear and what I feel like wearing. Sometimes I'll have a drink and then go: "Oh, okay, I'll go put on a short dress." Then, I'll go in there and put on a short dress and I'll look at how I look and I'll go "No." And I'll put back on what I was wearing before. So, I guess, part of me wishes that I looked good in that – which I don't think that I do – so then, I don't put it on. And he's still fine with it. I think that he has not complained. He just says: "I give up." Like it's such a sacrifice.

Rachel: Okay. Good. He found out that there was an area that he couldn't control you.

Danielle: Right.

Rachel: Just like you can't control him in a ton of things that you wish you could.

[Autonomy is a two-way street.]

Danielle: Exactly.

Rachel: And he "gave up." What that means is he's accepting that you made a different decision and that you don't have to do what he wants. You don't *have* to do what he wants. Do you?

[The point is driven home. She is her own person.]

Danielle: No. I don't.

Rachel: And does he still love you?

Danielle: Yes. He does. But there's just ... you know, he still loves me, but I feel like he's disappointed in me.

Rachel: Because you're not giving him everything he wants.

Danielle: Right. Exactly. And I don't like that. I don't like that he feels disappointed in me.

[She will have to choose between pleasing him and being her own person.]

Rachel: Because you had this need up till now to make him happy.

Danielle: Right.

Rachel: So, that means that he should never be disappointed.

Danielle: Right.

Rachel: Which is more important? Making yourself happy and wearing something you feel good in or making him happy and feeling weird and kinky all night?

Danielle: Making myself happy.

Rachel: Are you sure?

Danielle: Yeah. Absolutely. And being okay with him being disappointed. Just saying like he says: "Oh well." I'll say: "Oh well. We can't have exactly what we want sometimes."

Rachel: See how you feel when you imagine taking that stand.

Danielle: I guess I feel relieved. But it's funny how I just want to hold on to forcing him to agree - like there's something wrong with him for being disappointed with me. It's just frustrating for me I guess. And out of frustration, I start judging and wondering why he is like that. You know, I just don't understand why he can't be happy.

Rachel: Let me wonder for a moment, Danielle, if he might possibly have a similar response to some of the things you get upset about. "Why do you care if there are crumbs on the counter? Is that going to disappoint you? Is that going to make a difference? Why is it such a big deal that I don't clean off the knife? Why do you care? Why can't you be happy?" Do you see what I mean?

Danielle: Yeah, yeah, yeah.

Rachel: Does that help at all to think of it from the other point of view?

Danielle: Yeah, it does. It does.

Rachel: Maybe there are ways in which both of you feel like you don't get what you want sometimes. The other person won't give it to you. And you'll either do it yourself or you'll do without it. And maybe that's just the way it is.

Danielle: Yeah. I see that. That's good.

Rachel: Okay. When you think about the target now – that time that you were struggling with the stockings and the garter belt and trying to put them on to please him so he would be happy – then, you looked in the mirror and you hated what you saw. What level of disturbance does that have for you right now, at this moment in time?

Danielle: Well, when I first saw it just now, it was a two.

Rachel: Okay. What prevents it from being a zero? I'm just asking that question to see what comes up.

Danielle: Just because they're a pain to put on. Garter belts are so hard to put on – just the physical difficulty with them. Not the fact that I'm doing it because he wants me to. It's just that they're annoying.

Rachel: Okay. So, they still have a level of disturbance in that you don't want to wear them.

Danielle: Well, actually, earlier when we were just talking, I realized that, if my legs were long and lean and thinner and stronger, then I don't know if I would have the annoyance. I guess it's just that I'm not happy with the way my legs look.

Rachel: Oh. So you're saying that part of it is frustration with your own body.

Danielle: Exactly.

Rachel: Just notice that. It's a different issue, and it might get projected on Nils when, actually, it is your dissatisfaction or disappointment with yourself.

Danielle: Yup.

Rachel: It's good for you to become aware of that piece. But there are other things that you do or did up till now in order to get love and approval from Nils that, maybe, you aren't willing to do anymore. And what kinds of things might those be? Besides redecorating the house.

Danielle: I want to have more freedom when I'm at home.

Rachel: Okay. Tell me what that would mean.

Danielle: Not to be locked into being in the same room with him when I get home, because I've been working and he's been home alone and so I feel this obligation. He's always complained about how he never sees me, and we've tried to work out times where it's just us. We do have the whole weekend together, but during the weeknights, I have things that I'd like to do. You know, I have writing that I'd like to do and other projects that I want to work on. He doesn't say anything, but I know that if I go and just do work in the back room, he turns passive aggressive and starts being quiet and then doesn't say anything. Then, the next morning, I ask him what's wrong and he'll say: "Well, I don't know if you care. You were back in the room all night." Stuff like that. That's another thing that's frustrating, because I don't feel that his level of need to be together with me is matched with mine.

Rachel: Just like his response to the crumbs on the counter doesn't match with yours.

Danielle: Exactly.

Rachel: You're different human beings.

Danielle: We're different.

Rachel: You can't make him be the person you want him to be.

Danielle: No.

Rachel: And you've decided that doing what you want is important to you. So, what can you do in the situation where you come home on a weeknight, you have other things you want to do, and he wants you to sit with him? What action can you take?

Danielle: Well, this is what we tried to do before, but we just haven't been disciplined about it. Just setting up certain nights that are "us" nights and other nights that we can do whatever we want separately. And the only reason why it hasn't happened is because it's so crazy for me with this job and my other job. But I can set it up. It'd just have to keep my boundaries and be disciplined about it. But then sometimes I don't feel like … sometimes I'll come home and I'll just want to crash on the couch and watch TV, you know?

Rachel: It needs to be flexible.

Danielle: Right.

Rachel: There are times when what you want doesn't fit the schedule. You want to have freedom, you said.

Danielle: Right.

Rachel: You want to be able to say something like: "Hey, you know what? Let's cuddle and watch TV for a while; then, I've got some stuff I need to do." Or: "I'm going to go do some stuff and then I'd like to come back and spend some time with you." But what if he looks all downcast and dejected because he's not going to get you for the whole evening? Can you look at the difficulty you have disappointing Nils? Not giving him everything he wants? Because, obviously, he's not going to tie you up and keep you on the couch beside him. You can go and do what you want. The only thing that stops you is your concern about his response.

Danielle: Right. Exactly.

Rachel: Stay with that. Stay with that for a minute.

Danielle: I get nervous.

Rachel: Nervous. Okay. What's the nervousness?

Danielle: Well, I get worried in advance that he's just going to give me the silent treatment and then, I'm going to have to drag it out of him, and then, it'll finally come out days later. We'll have a little talk again about how I don't pay attention to him. Which isn't true. I guess that's what it is.

Rachel: Okay. You've gone down that road, it sounds like, a zillion times. And you know – you've got a script – you know how it's going to be. He's going to give you the silent treatment. That's his choice. His action. Yes?

Danielle: Yup.

Rachel: Then, yours is … you respond to that by: "I *have* to drag it out of him."

Danielle: I don't have to drag it out of him. I could just let him be silent.

Rachel. Yeah, you could. Have you tried that?

Danielle: I could ignore him.

Rachel: Just go about your business. Do what you do. Smile at him. Say …

Danielle: "Good morning."

Rachel: And, say he doesn't answer – just go on. Imagine that. What comes up for you?

Danielle: Well, I have this need to make things okay, you know. I don't like someone being upset with me. It's uncomfortable for me. I don't like it.

Rachel: You're saying that it's too uncomfortable for you to manage?

Danielle: No. I've done it lots of times. It's just that it's – I just feel like he's being such a baby. I don't know. Maybe I want to prove that I'm right and he's wrong. That he's being silly and ridiculous. But proving that and having him realize that – what difference does it make, you know?

Rachel: Apparently, it hasn't made any difference, from what you've said. You've walked down that road. So you try to drag it out of him. You try to explain and justify and rationalize and make new agreements, and it happens over and over and over again. You're banging your head against a brick wall. Can you see that?

Danielle: Yeah. Yeah, I do.

Rachel: So, what that is may be that you can't stand the fact that the man you live with isn't happy with you every minute of every hour of every day in every way.

Danielle: That sounds so ridiculous.

Rachel: So, if he looks askance and he looks downcast or crestfallen – if he's disappointed in some way – then you have to make it right. Where does this come from? When did that become your job in life?

Danielle: Well, that became my job a long time ago, I guess.

Rachel: Well, you want that job?

Danielle: No.

Rachel: Did it start with him or earlier?

Danielle: Oh no. It probably started with my Dad.

Rachel: With your Dad. Okay.

Danielle: And my Mom, too.

Rachel: So who's the baby? You called Nils a baby.

Danielle: Me.

Rachel: You're acting like a child that needs to be constantly pleasing Mommy and Daddy so that she'll be loved and approved of.

Danielle: Yup.

Rachel: Did it work?

Danielle: No …

Rachel: Are you sure?

Danielle: Well, they love me.

Rachel: Do you love you because you do whatever they ask?

Danielle: Well, no. They love me just for who I am.

Rachel: And do you think Nils would love you if you didn't do everything he asks? Would he?

Danielle: Yeah. Yeah. I'm sure. Absolutely sure.

Rachel: So, therefore ...

Danielle: It might not be comfortable for me because this past stuff, you know ... changing it is uncomfortable.

Rachel: Well, whenever we do something new, it's uncomfortable. Even if it's for the best. Because we're not familiar with it. Because it's not usual for us. So, I'd like you to imagine just not taking on this campaign that you have to make your daddy Nils happy every minute, in every respect. That if he's disappointed, he'll get over it or he has to grow up and deal with it That you don't have to keep him as a baby who is always fed and diapered and clean and never cries. Do you want to be living with a baby? Or do you want to be living with a man?

Danielle: I want to be living with a man.

Rachel: But you're treating him like a baby.

Danielle: I know. It's kind of this reciprocal thing, you know? He feels emasculated and I treat him like a little kid.

Rachel. Yup. Like a little spoiled kid. Not just a little kid, but a spoiled little kid.

Danielle: Well, he is a spoiled kid too, but he needs to grow up.

Rachel: How can he grow up if he's given everything he wants? If he's treated like a baby? So, tell Nils what you've just learned.

Danielle: Nils, I am not going to baby you. I am not your mother. You don't have to be happy with everything that I do. I am going to be okay if you're disappointed because it's inevitable, but I'm not going to try to make you happy all the time. You're going to have to grow up, and you're going to have to do some things for yourself, and that's just the way it's going to be.

Rachel: And could you say to yourself: "It's okay if this feels difficult sometimes, if I'm learning a different approach and I have some discomfort in making a change."

Danielle: Yeah. I can feel uncomfortable with Nils not being happy with me all the time. It's okay to be uncomfortable. It's okay for me just to watch my feelings, but I don't have to get something out of him or have him – I almost said forgive me…

Rachel: Yeah. That would be what I would have thought too.

Danielle: To say it's all okay and it's fine and we agree and kiss kiss, you know. It's not a fairy tale.

Rachel: So, what you're saying is you can recognize what's true for you and act on it with the man you love. Who is Nils.

[I'm reminding her of the positive cognition that was the goal of the work.]

Danielle: I can realize what I want and I can act on it with the man I love, who is Nils. And I do love him.

Rachel: So, I'm going to ask you first to think about the target when you were doing what you absolutely didn't want to do and then think about this new statement. As I run this statement by you, I'd like you to pay attention to each part of the body that you identified as having some disturbance earlier. The statement is: "I can recognize what I want for me and act on it with the man I love."

Danielle: "I can recognize what I want for me and act on what I want with the man I love, Nils."

Rachel: And what do you notice in your jaw? Is it relaxed?

Danielle: Yeah. That's right.

Rachel: What about your fists?

Danielle: Loose.

Rachel: Very good. Now say the same statement again.

Danielle: "I can realize what I want and act on it with Nils."

Rachel: And notice how you feel in your chest.

Danielle: I feel good. I feel relieved.

Rachel: Good. Say it one more time.

Danielle: "I can recognize what I want and act on it with Nils."

Rachel: Good. And pay attention to your forehead and your eyes. Do they feel contracted like you might want to cry?

Danielle: Nope.

Rachel: Very good. Say it one more time and pay attention to your stomach.

Danielle: "I can realize what I want and act on it with Nils." There's nothing.

Rachel: Stomach is relaxed?

Danielle: Yeah.

Rachel: Okay. Say it one more time and notice your throat.

Danielle: "I can realize what I want and act on it with Nils."

Rachel: It's relaxed?

Danielle: Yeah.

Rachel: And the last one is with your shoulders.

Danielle: "I can realize what I want and act on it with Nils." They're relaxed, except for needing a massage.

Rachel: Okay. Your body has now responded to this new belief system with relaxation and calm. And when you go back to the target now, what level of disturbance does it have? Where is it now?

Danielle: Nothing.

Rachel: It's a zero?

Danielle: Yes. I don't really care. Yeah, I mean, I wouldn't even be putting them on anyway.

Rachel: Probably not. Only if you wanted to compete with the lady in the fur coat. (I am smiling as I say this.)

Danielle: Only if I wanted to.

Follow-Up Session

Danielle reported that she had noticed "a huge reduction in anxiety and worry about what Nils thinks." In his typical fashion, he had repeated some of the patterns of behavior that were upsetting to her prior to her EMDR work. Following the work, she was able to recognize that his behavior was predictable and not get hooked.

In order to get more specific about how she would handle problematic situations in the future, I posed the question to her: "How do you see the relationship moving forward in terms of what you need to do to be more honoring of yourself with Nils?" We used the bilateral stimulation to enhance the processing.

Her first response to the question was to acknowledge that she needed to reflect on her needs and wants in the relationship on a regular basis. How could she hope to meet her needs if she were not aware of them? She decided to take time first thing each morning to journal and get connected with herself.

Then, she realized that, to ensure her privacy to reflect, she needed her own computer that she could take with her out of range of her husband. She made a decision to buy a laptop for herself.

Her biggest concern was his teasing and most of the session focused on that issue. She entertained the options of walking away if it disturbed her or telling him that it was not a good time and asking him to stop. She anticipated that he would respond by joking back. Sometimes she could tolerate his joking and maybe even tease him in return. Whether or not she could do that would depend on how she was feeling at the time. She surmised that he resorted to joking when she tried to be serious with him because he got defensive or was simply stubborn or refused to be accountable. In any of these cases, I asked her to consider: "What does that say about you?" This question prodded her to realize that his joking was not a reflection of her value as a person or an indication that she had done something wrong or was a bad wife. She came to the conclusion: "It's not about me. That's just Nils. That's how he is."

She now had three tools she could take forward in her marriage: first, checking in with her feelings in the moment; second, reminding herself that it was not about her; and third, accepting her partner's personality as independent of her. She saw that she could tolerate who he was as a person without changing her behavior to please him. Although she felt sad about some of the decisions he was making in his life, she needed to let him be responsible for his own choices. Just as she was responsible for hers.

The last step was for Danielle to decide to become proactive in meeting her own needs when Nils was unwilling to do so. I loved how she resolved the ongoing hassle of the coffee filter. His constant checking day after day to see if she had folded the filter paper in the coffee maker really irritated her. She went out and bought a permanent filter that did not require a paper. Problem solved.

By the same token, she decided that if Nils didn't want to help her redecorate their apartment, she would hire someone to help her. She got very excited about the changes she would make to improve their place, changes that were obviously very important to her, but not to him. They were separate people, each with their own thoughts, feelings and priorities. She did not need to give up her self to be loved by him. [28]

Clinical Comments

The case of Danielle is, in many ways, an abbreviated differentiation[29] process. One way of understanding differentiation is to think of it as the ability to tolerate the anxiety of disagreeing with someone who is vitally important to you. It means standing your ground in the face of conflict despite the fear of rejection by the other. It is a recognition of the ultimate separateness of people and their fundamental autonomy. This means that people are in relationship out of choice and have the freedom to leave. It is both terrifying and exhilarating to realize that love is not an obligation but a gift.

To manage this awareness requires a level of developmental maturity that would be best facilitated by fulfillment of early attachment needs or, in the absence of this positive attachment history, coming to terms with the areas of significant neglect or abuse. It is in the mirroring by the primary caregiver that the child develops a self-image, and in the attunement with the primary caregiver that the child learns to value him or herself. In the absence of such healthy attachment, one faces a much more difficult challenge. To be an adult when the child inside is still in need of connection with mother is a formidable task, as we shall see in next chapter, the case of Ryan.

---

[28] The transcript of this follow-up session has been included in Appendix A at the back of the book for those who wish to see the actual details of her processing.

[29] The concept of differentiation is central in the work of family therapist Murray Bowen, *Family Therapy in Clinical Practice* (New York: Aronson, 1978).

CHAPTER SIX

Despair:

The Ravages of Maternal Narcissism

Case of Ryan

Ryan usually arrived disheveled, as if he had just gotten out of bed. Sometimes that was exactly what had happened. Our appointments were frequently at noon and he would wake up and rush right over. Usually he was late and this upset him. We talked about various ways he might get there on time, but somehow there was always a reason why it didn't work out.

Perhaps the most telling example was when he took a back route to avoid the traffic – and therefore be on time – but he missed the turn-off. He had to go miles and miles past his destination on this old highway all the way to the next town because there was no alternate place to turn off. He arrived about twenty minutes late in a state of utter frustration and exasperation. It was an understandably annoying experience and would have been for anyone. However, for Ryan, it was proof positive that nothing he did in his life ever worked out. I saw it as an error anyone could have made and, in fact, I had made it myself in the past. We talked about where he needed to turn and how to recognize the turn-off should he take this same route in the future.

In the next session, Ryan was late again. This time he was absolutely furious with himself: he had missed the turn-off again! According to him, this showed indisputably that he was beyond hope, that there was something wrong with his brain, and that it was irremediable. He ranted and raved for quite a long time.

What emerged from his diatribe was the fact that, once he realized he had missed the turn, he had turned around and gone back. He had not continued on to the next town. To me, this represented a learning curve that was inherently hopeful. He had learned from his past error and had corrected his mistake. He was unlikely to miss the turn again and, if he did, he was able to make the necessary correction. Isn't this how most people learn? We don't always get it right the first time, but we are moving in the right direction. Clearly, he had benefitted from his past experience and made progress. In my mind, this should have been encouraging to him.

But Ryan was inconsolable. He adamantly refused to see anything positive or hopeful in his behavior. It was a foregone conclusion: he was doomed to failure. Nothing would *ever* work out for him. Sadly, this was Ryan's mind-set in all arenas of his life.

Background Information

Ryan was twenty-four years old and had graduated from university a year before we met. He had completed his Bachelor's degree in Theater Arts, but had been cut from the acting program in his sophomore year. He was very bitter and resentful toward his teachers and his fellow students in the program because he felt that he had been willing and capable of performing, but was not given sufficient guidance and support to succeed.

Ryan had also trained as an EMT and had only one written test left to complete his certification, but he had not done it. When asked why he didn't complete the last requirement, his response was: "What's the point?" He was currently employed in a dead end job that, he acknowledged, was below the level of his capacities. But he lacked the motivation to make a change.

His capacities were undeniably impressive based on an in-depth psychological assessment he shared with me. He was in the Very Superior range of intelligence with an IQ of 145, although inattention and anxiety may have diminished his performance. He told me that he wrote and rewrote all his papers because he was constantly judging himself by perfectionist standards. Even if other people regarded his work as acceptable, he would dismiss their opinions as without value. In the assessment report, he was diagnosed with Attention Deficit Disorder, Combined Type, as well as Generalized Anxiety Disorder and Dysthymic Disorder with occasional episodes of Major Depression.

Despite his being in the very superior range of intelligence, Ryan was convinced that his mind was "broken." He insisted that he could not do ordinary things, enjoy ordinary things, focus on what he wanted, or explain what he meant – things that ordinary people take for granted. No matter how hard he tried, he was certain that he would inevitably reach a state where learning would be blocked for him. His mind would be reduced to what he termed "a garbled mess of flashes and echoes." From Ryan's perspective, it was indisputable that he lacked the patience or the stamina to complete a task, he lacked the imagination and motivation to accomplish a goal, and his brain lacked the ability to learn. And all this, according to him, was simply and finally "irreparable."

As well as doubting his own mental functions, Ryan felt he was incapable of having a love relationship. He complained that he did not know how to be in a relationship because, he said, he did not like himself and did not know what he wanted. His relationship history was, admittedly, rather bleak. He reported only one romantic relationship with a woman that had lasted a week. Then, he felt he couldn't handle being in a relationship and that he had to get out of it. He said he had "never let anything go anywhere after that." There was a girl he was interested in, but he would not ask her out because, he told himself: "Even if she did say yes, I would ruin it somehow and then I would have messed up her plans."

Ryan had been in therapy since he was six years old. At the time of his parents' divorce when he was five years of age, he had made a suicidal threat which he now dismissed as merely "a bluff" to get attention. However, it prompted his mother to put him in therapy. He had spent many years in psychoanalysis with a Jungian therapist whom he still continued to have contact with. He commented that this therapy had helped him see the problems he faced, but had not helped him fix them. His mother had also been in psychoanalysis for over twenty years. Apparently, his mother's mother had committed suicide by "sticking a gun in her mouth" when his mother was eleven years of age. He threw out labels like "bipolar" and "borderline" for his mother, but could not be sure of their accuracy. What he knew for certain was that she had difficulty connecting with people and, in particular, with him.

He recalled a time in his early childhood when he had made a book in elementary school that he had shown to his mother. Clearly, she had not given it the interest he needed or desired. Her attention seemed so "hollow" to him that he had thrown the book in the trash. He characterized his mother as a person who was just "going through the motions" on a super-ficial level that did not permit genuine connection. There seemed to be "an unbridgeable gap" between them that, he claimed, was always blamed on him. He would be criticized by his mother's partner, Julie (whom he referred to as his "stepmother") for upsetting his mother if he tried to make himself heard by her. He said he really disliked this woman and was not inclined to respect her authority. He felt he had been emotionally abused by his stepmother while his mother "looked the other way."

Initially, he wanted to do his EMDR therapy in relation to his stepmother because she had been such a negative influ-ence in his life. At the last moment, he decided instead to focus on his relationship with his mother. The deeper issue that he was ambivalent about addressing was his inability to connect to his mother.

Preparation Session

Ryan came into the session feeling pleased about a recent experience of being validated by his uncle Carl for some work he had done years before that his uncle had remembered and genuinely appreciated. It brought home to Ryan how different it felt from the "fake" validation he got from his mother. He never felt that she was genuinely interested in his feelings or respected his concerns. To his dismay, it was "all about her" – her needs overrode everything else. She could not get outside herself to really hear or empathize with him. The "unbridgeable gap" that he sensed with his mother was her being trapped in her narcissism. This had become the template through which he saw all relationships, past and future, real and imagined, in his life. He was adamant in his belief that he would be as isolated and disconnected from everyone as he was from her.

The <u>issue</u> he wanted to work on was first stated as:

> I want to stop assuming that everyone will be as narcissistic as my mother.

It was then restated as:

> I want to feel comfortable with the connections I make with people and feel they are genuine.

The restatement allowed him to focus more on the positive goal he had for the work and how it might impact his life going forward.

The situation he wanted to address was a fight he had had with his mother about a year and a half earlier regarding his finishing his Bachelor's degree. Ryan had become deeply disheartened about school and saw no practical purpose to finishing his degree. Instead of the understanding and encouragement he needed from his mother, she had attacked him. According to Ryan, she refused to listen to what he had to say and demeaned his feelings, threatening to cut him off financially if he did not do what she wanted. She accused him of trying to dupe her and get money for nothing. Although he was crying in front of her, she gave him no comfort and would not yield an inch. He quoted her as saying: "Don't put your bullshit on me, you little fucker!" He felt she put all the blame on him and refused to look at herself. "I couldn't believe she could be so cold, closed and unsympathetic," Ryan said. Then he added: "I thought I'd end up just like her."

The <u>target</u> was the moment he was crying on the floor and she wouldn't yield an inch.

The <u>feelings</u> it brought up for him were:

> panic that he located in his throat,
> shock that he placed in his eyes,
> resignation that was in his face,
> helplessness and vulnerability that he located in his gut,
> desperation that he felt in his arms,
> anger or frustration that he placed in his jaw.

The negative beliefs he brought up when he reflected on the target were:

> No one cares about me;
> I have no worth;
> I'll never be able to connect with anyone;
> I have no emotional value;
> My feelings are worthless.

He chose as his <u>negative cognition:</u>

> I'll never be able to connect with anyone.

His <u>SUDS</u> was a ten.

His <u>positive cognition</u> was:

> I do have valuable human emotions that people can connect with.

His <u>VOC</u> was a one.

Ryan's resources were as follows:

1. For nurturing and support, he chose:
   - his uncle Carl who was a very accepting person – even if you disagreed on issues – and he didn't hold a grudge.

2. For strength, he chose:
   - Lieutenant Ripley from the movie *Alien* who got into seemingly hopeless situations and remained calm

and collected and did what needed to be done in a humane way.

3. For wisdom, he chose:
   - Yoda who always had something wise to say to help you discover what you needed to learn;
   - and Buddha who really understood suffering and had respect for people's autonomy. He never forced his views on anyone.

The quality Ryan felt he needed was faith in himself. He recalled a time in the desert on a backpacking trip when he had to convince the three leaders that they were going the wrong way. He knew he was right and had no doubts about himself.

Ryan's safe place was a beach at night on a different planet where he could see the stars, planets and galaxies all lit up and hear the waves rolling in on the sand. "It was wondrous," he said, and he felt safe and alone.

It is somehow apt that the only place Ryan could feel safe was on a different planet.

Processing Session

Rachel: I am going to review what we just set up, and this is the time when you can mention if you think something needs to be changed.

Ryan: Okay.

Rachel: What you're doing now is you're focusing inside; the rest of the world doesn't matter. In fact, you and I will be talking inside your process, almost like we are not in the room – or our being in the room is irrelevant; put it that way.

Ryan: Okay.

Rachel: The issue that you want to work on is: "I want to feel comfortable with the connections that I make with people and feel that they are genuine."

Ryan: Uh-huh.

Rachel: The target is an incident that occurred a year and a half ago when you got in a fight with your mom about your finishing your Bachelor's degree. You didn't care and you saw no real practical purpose to the degree at that time. You were genuinely disheartened and she needed you to finish it. She didn't care about your feelings, despite the fact that you were crying in front of her.

Ryan: Uh-huh.

Rachel: She kept trying to walk out. She said that what you were saying was "bullshit," that you were doing it just so you didn't have to work. She didn't encourage you as you needed, but *attacked* you instead. She wouldn't listen to what you had to say and demeaned your feelings. "Don't put your bullshit on me, you little fucker!" she said. She didn't give any credence to your concerns or your feelings. She blamed all the difficulty in communication on you and wouldn't look at herself at all. Even though you were crying, she wouldn't yield an inch. She gave you no comfort. She just wanted you to do what *she* wanted and your feelings had zero impact on her. She thought you were trying to dupe her and get money. You couldn't believe that she could be so closed, cold and unsympathetic. And you were thinking that you would end up like her.

The feelings that that event brings up for you now are *panic* which you located in your throat, *shock* which you located in your eyes – like being stunned or dazed, *resignation or a feeling of giving up* which you located in your face, *helplessness or vulnerability* which you located in your gut, *anger and frustration* which you located in your jaw, and *desperation* which you placed in your arms.

The negative belief or negative cognition that you had about yourself was: "I'll never be able to connect with anyone." What you would like to believe, if the work is successful, which is called your *positive cognition,* is: "I do have valuable human emotions that people can connect with." That seems false to you at this moment in time with a VOC of one. That means the level of truth is at its lowest.

Ryan: Mhmm.

Rachel: What I am going to ask you to do is hold in your mind the target, the negative belief that you have about yourself, and the feelings that the target brings up. Hold all three in your mind, ramp them up to the highest level of disturbance and then give me a number out of ten that represents the number that you are at – the level of disturbance you are at now. Once you tell me that number, which was a ten before our break, I will start the scanner. Your job is simply to be an observer and reporter of what comes up for you in your mind – *not* what you think and expect based on the past, but what is happening now as the scanner is on.

Ryan: Okay.

Rachel: I'll wait for the number.

(Long pause)

Ryan: Ten.

Rachel: Okay, good. When you are ready, just let me know what's coming up for you.

(Long pause)

Ryan: I'm finding it really hard to focus.

Rachel: Just notice what's in your mind – in your experience, thoughts, memories, feelings, bodily sensations – whatever is there.

Ryan: I kind of have like a panicked need to flee the experience.

Rachel: Uh-huh.

Ryan: And just a real need to isolate from my emotions and a need to kind of separate and like, it's hard for me to feel anything unless I'm looking at the incident from a third person perspective.

Rachel: You could do that.

Ryan: I feel like I just want to curl up in a ball …

Rachel: Uh-huh.

Ryan: And just kind of shrink up into a nothingness, like a singularity. I don't know, I feel kind of like I want to implode, I guess.

Rachel: Uh-huh. Almost disappear?

Ryan: Uh-huh.

Rachel: So, stay with that feeling, wanting to curl up in a ball, disappear.

(Long pause) And what's happening?

Ryan: I think I'm still finding it really hard to stick with the feeling.

Rachel: You said it would be helpful for you to be in the third person or second person.

Ryan: It's a lot easier to work with.

Rachel: Uh-huh.

Ryan: Sort of looking at … I mean, it's hard to kind of recreate the scenario from memory and put things as they were without trying to "soften" them, I guess. Or rewrite them as being not as extreme or intense. I guess I'm kind of belittling what happened. I'm trying to recreate it and diminish the experience.

Rachel: In some way, minimize it.

> [In the interaction between parent and child, typically, the child tends to undervalue his own feelings and abandon his own perspective in favor of the parent's position.[30]]

Ryan: I guess, yeah ... It's just sort of ... um, I guess kind of belittling what happened and trying to recreate it and sort of diminish the experience, I guess.

Rachel: "Not such a big deal as you thought, wasn't that bad" – that kind of thing.

Ryan: Yeah. Yeah.

Rachel: Allow yourself to see the part of you that is in the experience, crying and upset and obviously responding pretty strongly, and then, the part of you that is observing and watching. Let yourself have that dual focus. And just notice what comes up.

Ryan: I feel like I'm sort of safe to experience my emotions if I'm not in myself. I have to remove myself and sort of be like an invisible floating entity in order to feel safe in feeling my emotions.

Rachel: And what emotions do you feel when you are a little bit separated from them?

Ryan: Um ... I don't know. It's hard. I feel like ... It seems really hard to sort of stimulate my emotions to come back right

---

[30] See Aarons, *Journey to Home*. Principle six in the logic of the therapeutic journey states: "the child identifies with the parent and loses empathy with him or herself", 23.

now. It seems like they're sort of ... uh ... I don't know, disappearing into the woodwork.

Rachel: Sort of like you would like to disappear?

Ryan: I guess, yeah. I guess I sort of feel abandoned in a sense, not only by my mom, but by anything that would help me. I guess I'm aware that feeling my emotions in this situation would be helpful, and I sort of feel like they are abandoning me.

Rachel: So, let yourself be in that abandoned state. Abandoned by your mom or any possible resource that could help you. What's that like for you?

Ryan: I don't know, it just feels like ... empty or giving up. Just sort of ... I feel like the only option I have is to just turn on myself.

[This is remarkably insightful on his part. He sees that the primal source of his self-hatred and self-disparagement is the abandonment he feels in the relationship with his mother.]

Rachel: If you were to turn on yourself, what kinds of things would you say against yourself?

Ryan: I don't know. I'd call myself pathetic and disgusting and insignificant.

[Just the kind of statement that he is habitually making about himself.]

Rachel: And Ryan, have you done this? Is this familiar to you?

Ryan: Yeah.

Rachel: So, you have done this. You have turned on yourself rather than face the emptiness, the hopelessness that you feel in this type of situation with your mother.

Ryan: Yeah.

Rachel: Okay. Do you want to keep doing that?

Ryan: No.

Rachel: So, what about going to the place that you've been avoiding by turning on yourself and let yourself know what it feels like to be abandoned by your mom.

Ryan: It feels pretty bad.

Rachel: Say more about it.

Ryan: It feels like ... like I'm not there.

[When the parent is incapable of mirroring the child, the child feels invisible and has difficulty developing a sense of self.[31]]

Rachel: Uh-huh, right.

Ryan: Like, I'm losing myself. Like the world behind me has just completely fallen away, and that I'm sort of being written out of existence.

Rachel: Pretty awful feeling, huh?

Ryan: Yeah.

Rachel: Better to feel attacked and the pain of that than to feel the pain of feeling like you don't exist. Like you're being written out of existence.

Ryan: Yeah.

---

[31] Aarons, *Journey to Home.* Principle three in the logic states: "Self-image is the result of mirroring by the other," 12.

Rachel: So you can understand why you might have made have made that choice in the past.

[If he can not only understand, but also empathize with his traumatic abandonment in the past, he might be more open to making a different choice in the future.]

Ryan: Yeah.

Rachel: Do you exist, Ryan? Are you there? Are you real? Is there any part of you that responds to that question?

Ryan: The first thing is, there's a voice in my head that just says: *"Well, of course I'm real."*

Rachel: Uh-huh, yeah.

Ryan: But, I mean: *"what a stupid question"*…

Rachel: The feeling is of being obliterated and …

Ryan: I don't know, it feels very hollow … It seems like the kind of thing my mom would say – just sort of jump in and say for me. It doesn't feel like it's coming from me. It seems like it's coming from … I mean, I'm not letting the question hit me. I'm just sort of answering it without really being able to think about it so … Do I feel like I'm there? I don't know.

Rachel: Okay, let the question hit you, not necessarily by thinking about it so much as by letting it in, letting it register. Are you there? Is there anybody "to home"? Are you there, Ryan? Are you real? Have you been obliterated or written out of existence?

[I want him to begin to identify with the self inside that felt obliterated and let it speak the feelings that have been suppressed for years.]

Ryan: Yeah .... No.

Rachel: Yes? No?

Ryan: Am I there? Yes.

Rachel: Yes! Okay. And with that maybe very faint, maybe small part of you that knows "I am, I exist" – I'm wondering if you could speak from that part. And what would that part say?

Ryan: I don't know. It would say: "Leave me alone."

Rachel: Whom are you speaking to?

Ryan: Just everyone.

Rachel: Are you sure that's what you want? Do you want to be found?

Ryan: I feel like it's better than … I don't know … I just …

Rachel: It's better than being obliterated?

Ryan: I don't know.

Rachel: What's the struggle, Ryan?

Ryan: I want to just disappear.

[Connection with his inner child perspective has been habitually blocked by his self-deprecating defense pattern.]

Rachel: Are you sure that's what you want? You want to disappear?

Ryan: I don't what else to do. I don't know what other option there is.

Rachel: Well, maybe one option would be to let that voice, that self-assertion out, so you say to whomever - at this point it isn't clear - *"I'm here! I exist!"*

Ryan: I don't feel like there's anyone there listening.

Rachel: There's nobody listening …

Ryan: I feel like I'd just be talking to myself in an empty room.

[Obviously, I'm in the room and listening to him, but he is referring to the archaic template of trying unsuccessfully to be heard by his mother.]

Rachel: Well, I don't know whether you will be heard. But it seems to me that you do want to say something to your mother. From inside that small voice, there is a need to let her know that you are real. You exist. You have feelings. You are a person.

Ryan: I guess so … yeah.

Rachel: Is that true?

[He needs to find a way to recover his sense of self in the face of his mother's incapacity to acknowledge his presence. As he struggles with this possibility, he brings up a series of objections that represent rationalizations to maintain his habitual defense pattern.]

Ryan: Yeah, but I don't know what to say. I just …

Rachel: What would you say - if you were to speak?

Ryan: I just don't feel like she'd listen.

Rachel: I know you don't. But you can speak, nonetheless. If you were to say what you want to say, whether or not she's listening, what would you say?

Ryan: I don't know. It's just hard to feel like there'd be any point in saying anything.

Rachel: Well, you have given up on this. Do you want to continue?

Ryan: No, I just ... I mean, yeah, I want to continue, I just don't know what...

Rachel: I mean continue giving up.

Ryan: Oh. No, I don't.

Rachel: Well, then, maybe you'll be – what do they say? – "howling at the wind." But it seems to me that there is a howl there. And were you to express it, what would it be?

Ryan: I want to say: *"Fuck you!"*

> [This is a significant breakthrough for him. He is connecting with his anger at the annihilating treatment he has received. Anger often comes up first when feelings have been suppressed. Since anger is an energy for change, surfacing anger may potentially open up new possibilities for action.]

Rachel: Aha! That's good. I wonder if you would just say that.

Ryan: Well, I don't know what else I would say.

Rachel: Okay. Well, that's a good start.

Ryan: I'd say: *"Fuck you! Look at yourself! What are you doing? How can you treat me like this?"*

Rachel: Good. And as you say that, can you visualize your mother?

Ryan: Uh-huh.

Rachel: And rather than go by your past experience, simply notice in the moment what happens as you say: *"Fuck you! Look at yourself! How can you treat me like this?"* And see what happens with your mother. (Pause) What happens?

Ryan: I don't know. She doesn't seem to have much of a reaction.

Rachel: Mhmm. Does she …

Ryan: Well, at least I got her attention now.

Rachel: Oh, you did get her attention? Good. That's a start. So watch and see. Maybe you need to say more about how you feel. You've got her attention. What wants to come out?

Ryan: I don't know … "Look at me."

Rachel: "Look at me." That's a good one too.

Ryan: "Look at what you're doing to me."

Rachel: Uh-huh. Can you say it with a little more force? It feels like she could barely hear you.

Ryan: (Sighs)

Rachel: Can you or not? If it doesn't fit, that's fine, Ryan.

Ryan: I don't know … I just…

Rachel: *Look at me! Look at what you're doing to me!*

Ryan: (Heavy sigh)

Rachel: Maybe you need to tell her. Maybe she doesn't even get what you mean.

Ryan: I'm not sure she does.

Rachel: Yeah, me neither. So, tell her. Tell her what she's doing to you.

Ryan: "You're destroying me when you're supposed to be helping me. You're supposed to be there for me and you're… you're not just locking me out, you're stoning me."

Rachel: Yes, we have an expression "stonewalling".

Ryan: Yeah, but not just that, she's stoning me. I feel like I'm being, not just … not just being stonewalled, I feel like I'm having rocks hurled at me.

Rachel: Okay. Even more powerful. It's aggressive.

Ryan: Yeah. "You're not just denying me any sort of acceptance. You're kicking me while I'm on the ground."

Rachel: Mhmm.

Ryan: "You know, when I reach out for help, you smack my hand away."

[He is finally turning some of the anger he has turned inward against himself outward toward the person who has hurt him. The risk is that this may create a feeling of disloyalty that would sabotage his process.]

Rachel: Very powerful. So, you had her attention. Does she hear you? Do you hear what he's saying? This is her son saying to her: "*I reach out for help and you stone me to the ground.*"

Ryan: I don't know if she believes me.

Rachel: Well, that a different thing. Does she hear you and understand what you're saying?

Ryan: Yeah.

Rachel: Aha. Does she have anything to say? Or is she just staring at you?

Ryan: Um … (sighs) … No. I don't know.

Rachel: Just go into being receptive, passive, and watch, just look. Does she speak? No? Yes? She opens her mouth, she speaks, or she doesn't?

Ryan: She doesn't.

Rachel: She doesn't. This is pretty much your experience of her, right?

Ryan: Yeah.

Rachel: That's how she is. What comes up for you when she is non-responsive like this? What do you feel like you want to do? Remember, this is a fantasy.

[I want to encourage him to stay with his feelings and not abandon himself again. He is visibly vacillating between release and implosion.]

Ryan: I want to shake her.

Rachel: Me too. So maybe you can let yourself do that. Shake her.

Ryan: I just want to wake her up or something. You know, I want to slap her around, but not like I'm angry. I just want to get a response from her. But, the thing is, I don't want to, because I know that she's just going to put that in context of herself. If I do that, she's just going to see me as acting out.

[Dealing with a person locked into themselves is not only disempowering when they block you out and will not hear what you are saying. It is also exasperating when they reinterpret what they do hear in terms of their own preconceived notions. It feels like a closed system that you cannot penetrate.]

Rachel: So you're beginning to feel the impenetrability.

Ryan: I'm *f-r-rustrated*. I can't find a way to get through.

Rachel: Right.

Ryan: And it's … you know, I don't think It should be this hard, but I just want to grab her by the neck and make her look at the me that's crying, and balled up and, you know … bleeding.

[Below the anger is the hurt and pain.]

Rachel: Uh-huh. You can try that. See what happens ...And what happens? Grab her by the neck and try to force her to look at the you that is crying and bleeding, her son.

Ryan: I don't know I just can't believe that she ... I still can't believe that she sees what she's done.

[He does not *want* to see her as accountable. The child would rather blame himself than see the defects and limitations of the parent he depends upon for survival and love.[32]]

Rachel: What would convince you, one way or the other?

Ryan: I don't know if she ... if she could feel the despair I'm feeling, if she broke down and felt what I was feeling. I don't know how to do that without ... I don't know, doing the same to her, but I don't feel like that would work.

Rachel: Uh-huh.

Ryan: I just feel like then, I would ... then, I would be what she is.

Rachel: But you're not what she is, are you, Ryan?

Ryan: No.

Rachel: Look for a moment at the difference between you. Are you like her?

[He said previously that he was afraid he'd be just like his mother in his inability to connect with other

---

[32] Aarons, *Journey to Home*. Principle five states: "Each child wants to believe that his or her parents are okay," 19. "We cling to our abusers – or to our fantasy of them," 20.

people. And this is how he has been living his life up to this point. I want to help him differentiate himself from her so that he can perceive himself as someone capable of genuine connection and thereby move in the direction of his positive cognition.]

Ryan: No.

Rachel: What's the difference?

Ryan: That … that I have the awareness of myself enough to stop, and that I can accept fault within myself, somewhere, somehow, that I can … accept my mistakes.

Rachel: Uh-huh.

Ryan: That I realize the reciprocal nature of every relationship … that I can at least respect that, even if I don't necessarily feel it.

Rachel: And what's your mother like, by contrast?

Ryan: She doesn't need to see that. If she hurts me for my own good, the pain I'm feeling is simply my fault because I made her do it. Or, because I'm not giving her exactly what she wants, I deserve whatever I get because she's *right*. Because she knows best … that the ends she seeks justify whatever means she takes.

Rachel: Unassailable, huh?

Ryan: Yeah.

Rachel: It sounds like you are able to reach out for connection, and this woman is not able to reach outside herself to connect. Would that be right?

Ryan: I guess, yeah.

Rachel: Well, is it true?

Ryan: Yeah.

Rachel: And when you look at the difference between you and her, what comes up for you?

Ryan: I don't know, I feel kind of helpless too. I don't know, I guess I don't see that much difference.

[Given that he has just clearly articulated the difference between them, this step backward is not logical. It may be powered by guilt and a deep-seated fear of being separate from her.]

Rachel: You don't see the difference.

Ryan: Well, I just …

Rachel: So, does it seem true to you that you have a need and a desire and a capacity - a deep need and desire and capacity - to make a connection?

Ryan: I can't make her see that she needs this. I can't make her see that. Not only can I not make her connect, but I can't make her see that she can't connect. That by making her look at the damage she is causing, that even then, she won't - she can't - see that she is causing it.

Rachel: She's defended against seeing it.

Ryan: Right. She can't see why it's wrong, I guess.

Rachel: Uh-huh.

Ryan: She can't dissociate what she's done from what she is trying to attain. She's so fixated on what she wants that she can't see what she's doing, I guess.

Rachel: Especially if she's convinced that it's in your best interest, as you say.

Ryan: Right, and I'm also just sort of aware that it's a snowball thing, you know. Every bad thing she does in the name of her goals puts her farther and farther away from ever being able to see that it's just one more thing she has to blind herself to.

Rachel: So, this person is unresponsive. She can't speak, she won't speak, and she's blind. She doesn't see, she can't see. Think of that. So, what is your hope of getting through to her?

Ryan: That she'll be able to let go of what she doesn't already have and embrace what she does.

Rachel: Do you believe that's possible?

Ryan: I guess I have to. I mean … I *do* believe that's possible.

[Faced with the prospect of having to accept the futility of getting connection with his mother, Ryan chooses to hold out for the fantasy that, somehow. it will still be possible because this is what he thinks he "has" to believe. He is not ready to give up that primal longing yet.]

Rachel: Do you think anybody could help her? Anybody could get through to her? Anybody could help her see what's happening in her relationship with you?

Ryan: I don't know.

Rachel: Could Julia (her partner)? Could any of your resources?

Ryan: Could they? Maybe. But would they? I don't know.

Rachel: Well, you've only to ask. Who do you think you would like to ask?

Ryan: My uncle, I think.

Rachel: Uncle Carl?

Ryan: Uh-huh.

Rachel: Okay. Can you visualize Uncle Carl coming into the scene?

Ryan: Yeah.

Rachel: And he's going to try to get through to your mother about how much she's unaware, unresponsive, and unempathic to you. And what does he say?

Ryan: He focuses more on me – you know, huddled up – and he's sort of shocked at what she has done and can't believe what has happened.

Rachel: So, he's feeling the empathy that you wish that your mom would feel.

[By innuendo, I'm suggesting that Ryan might get what he wants from his mother somewhere else – i.e. from other supportive figures like his uncle in his life.]

Ryan: Yeah.

Rachel: And what does he do with the part of you that is all huddled and shocked and almost obliterated?

Ryan: I mean, he kind of leans over me in a defensive way and acts sort of protective at least.

Rachel: Uh-huh. Does he come over to your shell-shocked self?

Ryan: Yeah.

Rachel: And what does he do?

Ryan: He gets down and kind of tries to … I don't know …do what you do when you find someone huddled and bleeding and beaten? He has a blanket or something.

Rachel: Hmm, so he puts a blanket around you?

Ryan: That'd be nice.

Rachel: Uh-huh. Okay, and maybe he says some soothing words, maybe even hugs you. Would he do that?

Ryan: I can't tell … I don't know. I see him more as sort of looking to my mom and almost demanding an explanation.

Rachel: And what happens as your mother sees your uncle ministering to you and looking to her for an explanation? What does she do?

Ryan: She says something to the effect that I was asking for it.

Rachel: And what does Uncle Carl say about that?

Ryan: I don't know, he's kind of in disbelief, I guess, that … I don't know… It's almost like he can't understand what she means by that.

Rachel: Uh-huh.

Ryan: It just seems like a concept that he would never really be able to wrap his head around.

Rachel: Uh-huh. Can you take in that your uncle is there to comfort you? Can you feel that comfort?

> [I'm inviting him to accept support from a source other than his mother.]

Ryan: Yeah.

Rachel: Can you let it in? And if he were to speak, would he tell you that you were a pretty cool guy? That he really liked you and wanted to be there with you and believed in your value? Would he say something like that?

Ryan: Yeah. He'd say that he'd take care of me, help me.

Rachel: Mhmm.

Ryan: And that it wasn't my fault.

Rachel: Aha, that it wasn't your fault. Can you let that idea in? That maybe this man has a different point of view that may be important for you to hear? Can you let that in, Ryan?

Ryan: Uh-huh.

Rachel: Or are you struggling with that idea? Do you really get it?

Ryan: It's a little tricky.

Rachel: Uh-huh. What comes up? What's tricky?

Ryan: I don't know, it's just ... I mean it's helpful, but I want that from my mom.

[This is his bottom line: "*I want that from my mom.*" I need to normalize this desire at the same time as help him see that other connections are more hopeful and promising.]

Rachel: I know you do. And when you say that, what does Uncle Carl say about that wish, that need, that desire that any child would have?

Ryan: He tries to help me. He tries to make my mom see what she's done.

Rachel: Aha.

Ryan: Kind of advocates for me on my behalf.

Rachel: Uh-huh, and how does that go?

Ryan: I don't know, it seems like he's having trouble getting through to her.

Rachel: Hmm, probably. Just notice whether there is any change, any hopeful shift in your mother as Uncle Carl is trying to make her see what she has done to you.

Ryan: I don't know, she seems like she's .... I don't know ... She can't exactly stumble on. And while she is so insistent that it was my fault, she's at least ... She can't just shut him out. It's having an effect.

Rachel: So, there is a bit of an effect.

Ryan: Yeah, I mean, it's starting to work.

Rachel: Aha.

Ryan: She at least has to acknowledge that I'm in a pretty shitty state.

Rachel: Hmm, that's a start. And when she recognizes that you are in a really shitty state, what happens? Does she turn toward you? Does she do anything? Say anything?

[Can he visualize her having a genuinely caring and remorseful response?]

Ryan: I don't know. She's starting to cover parts of her face, and she's having trouble justifying herself, and she's trying to shut him out, but not really having much of an effect.

Rachel: So, something is getting through about the fact that her son is suffering.

Ryan: She's like … just doing what she does when she's got her face all scrunched up and she's screaming at him to stop.

[Her defenses are more powerful than any maternal instinct.]

Rachel: Oh, doesn't sound like a lot is going through then. What you need to see, then, is that your mother fights to maintain her point of view. It's almost a necessity for her. Can you see that?

[I imagine that the loss of her own mother in such a traumatic way would have had a deeply damaging effect on this woman. It's not about blaming her, but about recognizing an incapacity that is being passed along to her son.]

Ryan: Uh-huh.

Rachel: She's screaming at him to stop. So, it's not just you she can't let in. She can't let in your Uncle Carl either.

[If he can see the same thing happening with his uncle, then perhaps he can stop personalizing the problem and blaming himself.]

Ryan: Uh-huh.

Rachel: There's some deep need in her, a kind of wall of self-protection. Do you see that?

Ryan: Uh-huh.

Rachel: And, even though you may not understand it, it probably preceded you by many, many years.

Ryan: Oh, yeah.

Rachel: You seem to know something about this, Ryan?

Ryan: Uh-huh.

Rachel: What do you know?

Ryan: I just know that not even I have really seen past all of her defenses, and I've never really seen her truly vulnerable.

Rachel: It must have been necessary for her to construct one hell of a defense system.

Ryan: I mean, she's even made herself look almost completely insane in front of people to avoid having to come to terms with some stuff.

Rachel: Uh-huh. So, this is not essentially and certainly not exclusively about *you*.

Ryan: Uh-huh.

Rachel: This is your mother's need to survive.

Ryan: Uh-huh.

Rachel: And you might suspect that there is one very frightened, very panic-stricken child somewhere in the middle of all that structure of defense. Can you even grasp that possibility?

Ryan: I don't know.

Rachel: I guess, my point is simply that you need to see that it's something going on in your mother that has to do with *her* issues, *her* wounds.

Ryan: Uh-huh.

Rachel: And it sounds like it doesn't really have to do with you. You're just the recipient of that behavior.

Ryan: But, I mean, she just can't get over the fact that it's an attack on her.

Rachel: So, Uncle Carl was unsuccessful just in the same way that you've been unsuccessful all these years.

Ryan: I guess, but – I don't know how to say this – *so far* unsuccessful.

[Again he pulls back from the dreaded realization that connection with her may not be possible because of who she is, regardless of what he or anyone else might do to try to get through to her.]

Rachel: I'm sorry, you don't feel it's been completely unsuccessful?

Ryan: Well, I don't feel like he would stop trying just because she's trying to shut him out so hard.

Rachel: Okay. Well, maybe Uncle Carl is going to hang in then. Maybe he can try a different approach. Maybe there's still some hope there. Give him a chance. And what do you see happen?

[If the client needs to keep on trying, regardless of how futile it may seem to me, I will follow his lead until he is ready to take a different direction.]

Ryan: That would be tough. He's sort of shocked at how strongly she resists, how defiant she is to even hear the situation that I'm in - that I'm bleeding to death almost - and she won't even accept that she caused that. So he says it's more important to focus on me at the time and, I guess, maybe he does just give up on her.

Rachel: Aha. Is that okay with you? Or do you want him to keep on?

Ryan: I don't know. It seems that he simply can't. If he can't do it, it's fine.

[Now it is his decision. But we still check out other options so he can feel that we have pursued all possibilities.]

Rachel: Is there anyone else that you can think of who might?

Ryan: I think Julia could have an effect on my mom, but I don't know if I believe that she would ever turn that way. But, maybe if she saw me bleeding to death at my mom's hands, she might try to do something.

Rachel: Well, bring Julia in and see whether Julia is willing. You're there bleeding and feeling shattered. What does Julia do? Just watches that?

Ryan: She seems sort of shocked and confused, I guess.

Rachel: And what happens as the action continues?

Ryan: I don't know, she just... (pause) ... (sighs) ... (mumbles)

Rachel: Does she understand what's happened?

Ryan: I think she's having trouble understanding it.

Rachel: Could Uncle Carl help her?

Ryan: She'd listen to him.

Rachel: Okay. Imagine that Uncle Carl understands the situation and fills her in on what's happened in your experience with your mother. And imagine that she understands what she's heard.

Ryan: Now she comes over to me and sees if she can help.

Rachel: She really has a heart. She cares about you.

Ryan: She asks my mom if that's true.

Rachel: But she does come over to try to help and soothe you. It's important to know that. And she asks your mom. What happens then?

Ryan: She just says that I was asking for it, that she had no other choice.

Rachel: And what does Julia say to that?

Ryan: She says: "You had no other choice but to kill him? Rather than accept him, you had to kill him?" And she's sort of shocked into disbelief at the reasoning behind it.

Rachel: What does she do then?

Ryan: She says she can't deal with that right now and she has to focus on me, I guess. She and Carl are trying to get me some help.

Rachel: Now two people – Uncle Carl and Julia - are both seeing your pain and responding in a comforting and soothing way to you, Ryan. While your mother is shut down in her own fortress, two people have come to your aid. What does that tell you?

Ryan: It tells me what I already know – that I'm not wrong, that it's not my fault, that I don't deserve that.

Rachel: So, whose problem is it? Yours or your mother's?

Ryan: It's hers.

[This is said with a depth of feeling unusual for Ryan. It is a difficult admission for him.]

Rachel: Painful, isn't it?

Ryan: Yeah.

Rachel: But that seems to be the case.

Ryan: It's her problem that is keeping me from getting what I need.

Rachel: If you need to get it from her and her only. But there are other options, even in this situation.

[It is important for him to see that there are other people besides his mother who can meet his need for connection.]

Ryan: Uh … Uh … (He's struggling.)

Rachel: What's going on, Ryan? This is a very important moment.

[This is his critical therapeutic challenge: can he accept the limitations in his mother and turn to others for connection, or will he keep on insisting that he must continue to look to his mother for the connection he is missing?]

Ryan: I don't want to give up on trying to get from my mom what I need from her. And I just need for her to see what she's done. I need for her not just to look at it, but to really see it and really take it in and feel what she's made me feel. I need her to let me in – or to take me in.

Rachel: Yes, it's an understandable wish and desire. Very understandable. But possibly ...

Ryan: I don't know what she'd be willing to sacrifice to not have to do that.

Rachel: You're assuming that she has a choice, Ryan.

Ryan: It's true.

Rachel: What if she *can't*? What if she is simply not emotionally capable?

Ryan: I can't really imagine that. That she can't take in my needs. I guess, I find it hard to take in her need to keep that wall up.

Rachel: Perhaps because it runs so against your deepest need and desire, it's very hard for you to accept the possibility that this is simply not something she can do.

Ryan: I guess.

Rachel: And it's very painful. But I also want you to remember that, even in this situation, there are two other people that you brought in who are capable of giving you what you need. One of them you expected to be capable – Uncle Carl. But even Julia who has been constantly defending your mother and on her side and blaming you, in this situation, she is ministering to you and looking at your mother like she's out there in outer space. So there are other people who may be able to give you what your mother can't, if your mother can't. Can you let that in? Do you know other people in your life that could be responsive?

Ryan: I guess, my dad. But I've never really experienced him standing up to my mom or even being in a situation where he would defend me.

Rachel: Maybe the hope that he would defend you to her might not be the way to go. It might be more about getting him to listen or be supportive or responsive to the person you are. We're talking about connection. You want that connection desperately with your mom.

Ryan: He's not stonewalling me. But I just don't expect that he would be able to understand the damage that she does.

Rachel: No, but perhaps he could be there for your needs. Perhaps he could listen to you and appreciate who you are. Once you realize that this problem is not your problem but hers, you could start connecting as best you could with a number of other people who are available in ways that, right now, your mother isn't. And you mentioned your dad as one possibility. You might even connect more with Julia than you believe. And you certainly can connect with Uncle Carl.

What you could learn from this is that you *do* have the ability to connect and, in this way, you are blessed that you are not like your mom. Despite the fact that you may love her and want her always in your life, you may need to recognize that there are limitations she has that you do not.

[He will not need to feel so deeply incapacitated in relating to others if he can differentiate himself from his mother.]

Ryan: Uh-huh.

Rachel: What happens when you try on that picture?

Ryan: It's just … I'm not good at accepting impossibility.

Rachel: You and Don Quixote.

Ryan: If I give something up, I never accept that I can't achieve it. It's just that I can't figure it out. I feel like it's my own weakness or limitation. There's no wall that you can't get over or so thick that you can't get through it. Or what would it be walling off?

[It appears that the prospect of giving up connecting with his mother is simply not tolerable to him, so I look for some compromise that will be more acceptable.]

Rachel: Okay then, you can decide that you will not completely give up on your mom, that you will make efforts. And you can also recognize that you are a person who can make connections with other people much more easily than you can with your mom. That there is a richness of other options available, even if you don't connect with her.

You began by believing that you'd never be able to connect with anyone. Does that still feel true for you?

[This was his negative cognition.]

Ryan: No.

Rachel: What would be true for you right now? What would be the statement that fits for you, Ryan?

Ryan: That I know that I can connect with people, but I just don't have a lot of experience with it yet.

Rachel: So: "I know that I can connect with people and I need to have more experience of doing that." Is that right?

[This is his new positive cognition.]

Ryan: Yes.

Rachel: And is this a decision you're making to have more experience connecting with people?

Ryan: I guess, but I still feel like I have so much more experience *not* connecting with other people.

Rachel: That's true – up till now. So that's why you need to have more experience connecting with them. And there's nothing about you that prevents you from doing that. The sad thing is that what prevented the connection with your mom was in your mom, not in you, Ryan.

Ryan: Okay.

Rachel: So, when you go back to the target, and think about that horrible, painful, difficult experience, what level of disturbance does it have for you at this moment in time?

Ryan: A three. A three and a half.

Rachel: What prevents it from being a zero? Do you know?

Ryan: Well, I still care about my mom. And if it wasn't disturbing at all, it would be disturbing that I'm not at all upset that my mom can't step back and feel the same way.

[Here we see the fierce loyalty of the child. He also has a moral dilemma: he does not want to abandon her as she has abandoned him.]

Rachel: And that's the part of you that wants to keep trying because you do love her and care about her, recognizing that you also, for your own sake, need to go out and connect with other people who are more capable of that reciprocity you were talking about.

Ryan: Yeah.

[At this point it looks like he can accept the compromise solution.]

Rachel: So: "I know that I can connect with people and I need to have more experience doing that." Let's do a body scan and see if we can integrate that.

Notice your throat as you repeat the statement: "I know I can connect with people and I need to have more experience doing that."

Ryan: "I know that I can connect with people and I need to have more experience doing that."

Rachel: And how's your throat?

Ryan: I felt a little tinge of tension, but it's easing up. It's not getting stronger, but weaker.

Rachel: It's ebbing.

Ryan: Yeah.

Rachel: What about when you say that statement and pay attention to your eyes?

Ryan: Before they felt like a pull between them, disorienting. They're relaxed.

Rachel: What if you say that out loud and pay attention to your face?

Ryan: "I know I can connect with people and I need to have more experience doing so." There's residual tension, but it's ebbing.

Rachel: It's shifting, I hear. Now, say the statement and pay attention to your gut.

Ryan: (Repeats the statement) Also still ebbing and tension is fading.

Rachel: And what about when you pay attention to your arms?

Ryan: (Repeats the statement) They feel a lot more relaxed.

Rachel: Good. And the last one is your jaw.

Ryan: (Repeats the statement) I feel like I have to make an effort to clench it, rather than make an effort not to.

Rachel: That's really good. Okay, so I want you to say the statement one last time, and I want you to hear it and let it register.

Ryan: *I know I can connect with people and I need to have more experience doing so.*

This ends our processing session. I breathe a sigh of relief, thinking (unfortunately, prematurely) that we have found a solution that will allow Ryan to stop demonizing and isolating himself, but without forcing him to completely abandon his dream of connection with his mother.

Follow -Up Session

When Ryan came in to the follow-up session, he was in a markedly different frame of mind. He barely answered my questions. He had no feedback to give about the processing session. He refused to decide what he wanted to focus on in our follow-up session. When given the choice between addressing his future relationship with his mother or with other people in his life, he wanted me to make the choice for him, and only very reluctantly voiced a preference. He was unusually distant, non-committal and withholding. I sensed an anger under the surface and wondered how it would play out.

When we started the bilateral stimulation, Ryan was fiercely resistant. He complained that he could not focus at all. Then, he reverted to the kind of sweeping negative generalizations he had made when I first met him. He had never connected with anybody and obviously never would. Nobody had ever cared about him and nobody ever would. Nobody was to be trusted, even the resources that had come to his aid. Everyone without exception, Ryan insisted, had the same difficulty connecting with other people as his mother did. It was fruitless to imagine his life would ever be different.

Ryan's pessimism was global and entrenched. He was back in the dead end of despair he had started from, and he was not responsive to interventions of any sort that might have pointed a way out. He clung to his negativity like a grim security blanket.

What was keeping him anchored in his hopelessness? He could not move past the child need to protect his mother. He had to keep trying to get her love. Whatever obstacle there was, it had to be coming from him. He was responsible. It was his fault. There had to be something wrong with him. Whatever problem he could, even temporarily, glimpse in his mother ultimately had to be a problem in everyone. He could not give up his idealization of her, even at the expense of his happiness.

I am reminded of the striking example quoted by Stephen Levine:[33]

How often are we like the battered child on the front page of the Los Angeles Times, being carried gently from

---

[33] Stephen Levine, *Who Dies?*, (New York: Anchor Doubleday, 1982), 5.

the room by the compassionate matron, who reaches over the matron's shoulders shouting "Mama, Mama", to the woman in custody between the policemen on the other side of the room, arrested for burning the flesh and breaking the bones of this child.

In Ryan's case, it was not his bones, but his spirit that was broken. Nonetheless, he was not ready to give up on his mother and move on.

What this indicates is that EMDR processing can only take a person as far as they are ready and willing to go. It is not going to *force* a change, even if it seems to be clearly in the client's best interest. It offers choice, not compulsion. For a choice to be real, we have to be able to go either way – toward health or back to suffering. We are not compelled to heal. Unlike all the other case studies in the book, this client made the choice to turn back to embrace his pain rather than risk the perils of change. It demonstrates that we can and will maintain our stuckness if that is what we choose to do.

However, the potential for change is always there in the background. Because of the seeds that have been planted in this EMDR therapy, perhaps the next time an opportunity presents itself, a different choice will be made. [34]

---

[34] The transcript of the follow-up session with Ryan is located in Appendix B. It offers a live therapeutic example of working with strong resistance in a client.

CHAPTER SEVEN

Couples Therapy:

Interlocking Pathologies

Case of Stacy and Will

There is a saying that "when two people get into bed, it's a crowded place." That is because both sets of parents, as well as previous partners and significant other figures in their life histories, are there with the couple, exerting a hidden (and sometimes not so hidden) influence on how they think, feel and behave. The unfinished business that each member of the partnership has with one or both of their parents and/or other influential people in each of their past histories will very often be acted out in the couple relationship.

It may be at the selection stage. We may find ourselves attracted to a mate that is *like* one of our parents or, on the contrary, decidedly *unlike* one of our parents. This could be in terms of physical appearance or certain compelling personality traits. Or it may manifest in the dynamics of the couple relationship. It may be that their behavior calls up feelings and responses exactly like those we have to a parent or significant other, regardless of any perceived similarity between them. In the case that our partner does not readily fit the role we require, we may, often without conscious awareness, find ourselves provoking them to act out the part we need them to play. In these different ways, we ensure that we will have the opportunity to grapple with the unfinished business we are carrying from our family of origin or previous relationships. What is unfinished pushes for completion. The reenactment of unresolved issues in our relationship with parents or other significant figures from our past is an all-too-common theme in couples therapy.

Sometimes, the themes that are unconsciously reenacted by each person in the couple relationship interlock and fuel each other in a dramatic, potentially disastrous way. For example, suppose I need you to be the angry father I never came to terms with in my childhood. Hence, I prod and provoke you to the point that you become enraged and act out the angry father role. Then I have justification for becoming distant and withdrawing my love. At the same time, suppose you need me to be the withholding mother who always seemed distant and unavailable. Then, because you refuse to engage and address the issues I am complaining about, I will have reason to get angry and withdraw. Now I am acting out the rejecting mother you need me to be. Couples can play out this wrenching kind of drama for years.

If both members of the dramatic interplay were to work on the triggering issues that are unresolved for them, there would be hope that they may forge a new connection beyond the relentless reenactment of the past. Hence, EMDR can play a crucial role in helping each person defuse the trauma that compels their repetitive destructive behavior and, in this way, help to open up healthier options for relating in the present. To move past the projections we have forced upon each other and truly meet as the adults we have become is the beginning of a hope for connection.

Background Information

Stacy and Will were both engineers who worked for the same company. In fact, that was how they met. They had been friends at work before they started dating, and they had been dating for almost two years. Stacy was thirty-two years of age and Will was twenty-eight. Although they spent time at each other's apartments, they were not living together. They came into therapy to decide if they wanted to get married or not.

Stacy felt that time was running out for her. Her biological clock was ticking, and she wanted to have children before it was too late. Stacy's urgency was disturbing to Will and he responded by resisting her pressure to commit.

This was all too familiar to Stacy. She had spent seven years with a previous partner she was engaged to marry. As the wedding date approached, her fiancé seemed to display doubts and hesitation, so she broke off their engagement. She was understandably dismayed and deeply disappointed about this result. She made it clear from the start of our therapy that she did not want to "waste" more years in yet another relationship that might not lead to marriage. She was fearful that the same thing would happen with Will.

In his past history, Will had been deeply hurt in two serious relationships with women who had cheated on him with other men. He was concerned that Stacy still had feelings for her previous fiancé. His suspicion was exacerbated by the fact that Stacy had not told him the truth about the recent contact she was having with this man in regard to a house they owned together. Because Will was so adamantly opposed to there being any contact between them, Stacy had withheld this information from him. It came out that her ex-boyfriend had expressed deep regret at his former uncertainty and had asked her to come back and marry him. Will was fearful that he would end up rejected, yet again, in favor of another man. Because of his past experience with deception and the fact that she had withheld information from him, he did not trust that Stacy would be honest with him. Therefore, he held back from whole heartedly committing to her, just as her ex-boyfriend had done in the past.

It was a perfect set-up for reenactment. Each of them had histories that created an impasse of fear and distrust. They projected their pain from their past relationships on the relationship they were having in the present and could neither move forward nor walk away. They were stuck in indecision.

Further back in their histories, Will's father had been largely unavailable due to his having both a full time job and a school commitment. Will and his mother "butted heads," particularly during his teen years. In Will's view, his mother was a person who would not listen or empathize with him. There was no attunement with her. Regardless of what he said, she stuck to what she thought and was very opinionated. He experienced Stacy in much the same way. With his mother, he would be either passive aggressive, always having an excuse not to deliver what she wanted, or he would get flooded and erupt with rage – too often and too fast – just as he did with Stacy in their current relationship.

For her part, Stacy had anger issues with her father. She felt he had never been there for her and had treated her differently – and unfairly – because she was a girl. For example, he took her brother on camping trips, but would not allow her to come along. He would not listen to her protests about feeling unwanted and excluded. He would just shut down and ignore people when he didn't like what they had to say. Naturally, she had the same complaint about Will. He would put off discussing issues for days at a time. As her frustration mounted, she would confront him and he would feel cornered. Then, one or the other would blow up and that would be the end of the conversation. "We're both headstrong and stubborn people who have a hard time with criticism," they agreed.

Their ongoing relationship was riddled with conflict. They had terrible arguments on a regular basis. There was yelling and screaming. Hurtful accusations would be hurled at each other until someone would either storm out or be "thrown out" – and they would be forced apart.

The issues they fought about repeated endlessly and never got resolved. They fought over Stacy's having a relationship, real or imagined, with any males other than Will. Filled with distrust, Will would check her cell phone calls and email history looking for proof of her infidelity. The more he interrogated her, the more she recoiled from his unremitting jealousy.

They fought over the large debt load that Will carried that, for Stacy, represented an obstacle that stood in the way of their having kids. Fueled by her anxiety about time running out, she pressured him to be more proactive in reducing his debt. He responded like a teenager being coerced by his mother to do chores – he did nothing. She saw his resistance as proof of his lack of commitment to a permanent relationship with her.

They fought over spending time with each other's families of origin. Each of them was very involved socially with their parents and siblings. Stacy was uncomfortable with the amount of beer drinking in Will's family. She felt that Will avoided spending time with her family. Will had the same complaint about her. Each accused the other of not genuinely liking the other person's relatives and of, therefore, finding excuses not to go to their family events. They fought over who actually had spent more time with the other person's family.

Their fights would escalate quickly and quickly reach dead lock. They had an explosive quality that raised concerns about the potential for physical abuse in the future. Although there had been nothing beyond minor scuffles, the level of frustration was dangerously high. It forced them to fly apart in a storm of righteous indignation. There would be a period of separation until they came back together. Then, after a brief honeymoon period, the same fights would erupt again.

In the early phase of couple counseling, Stacy was in the pursuer position and Will was the distancer. Several months later, they had switched roles. It was Will who wanted to make it work while Stacy had come to doubt that it was possible. In the end, which person occupied which role didn't really matter. It led to the same conclusion. This dynamic ensured that the distance between them remained constant and, with it, their inability to make a commitment to marry.

We did individual and couples therapy for several months. They gained knowledge and awareness, but their destructive behavior patterns did not essentially change. They learned rules of communication that went out the window when their feelings were stirred up. They developed insight into their dysfunctional patterns, but continued to act them out. They delved into their childhood histories and saw the frustrated children inside of each of them. But the compassion they felt in the therapy room evaporated when they were in the grips of their power struggle. "I feel I can't make her happy," Will concluded sadly, "and what I offer isn't good enough." In almost the same words, Stacy concluded, "what I do is never good enough for him."

In desperation, they decided to try EMDR to see if it could forge a way out of their impasse. I asked each of them to reflect on what they believed was the primary issue standing in the way of their being open to the other person and thus capable of responding as adults, rather than reacting like children. They were keenly aware that it takes two to make a relationship work, but only one to break it up. They decided to let Will go first.

Will's Preparation Session

The issue that Will identified as the focus of his EMDR work was related directly to his jealousy and distrust. He stated his issue as follows:

> I want to stop assuming the worst and becoming suspicious and insecure with my partner.

He knew that the infidelities of two girlfriends in previous relationships had sensitized him to this issue in his current relationship. However, we decided to focus on a current example in his relationship with Stacy and allow the process-ing to direct us to the past in whatever way emerged as most relevant. The current example occurred at a party where Stacy was drinking tequila and Will noticed her talking with a couple of guys, then dancing with one of them. It bothered Will and, at his sister's suggestion, he went up to talk to Stacy about it. He even asked her to dance – something that was "not one of (his) favorite things." Stacy did not want to slow dance and was, as he put it, "bouncing around" on the dance floor. Shortly after, she went back to the guy she had been dancing with previously. This was the point when, in his words, "the bottom fell out" for Will. He tried to join in on their conversation and the guy asked who Will was. His sister piped up, saying he was Stacy's boyfriend. Then, Stacy proposed a drink shake. Will said "no," but she went ahead anyway. By this point, Will felt that Stacy was not considering his feelings and that the new guy was more important to her than he was. He walked away in a snit. When his sister informed Stacy that he was upset, she came to find him and he told her he was feeling jealous.

The <u>target</u> was the moment the bottom fell out for Will and he felt that Stacy disregarded his feelings.

The <u>feelings</u> connected with the target were:

> betrayal that he felt in his stomach (it felt sick),
> anger that he placed in his head (warm, sweaty),
> self-pity that he located in his lower chest and sternum,
> fear that he experienced in his throat (it had a lump),
> jealousy that was in his heart (it felt hollow),
> hurt that he placed in his shoulders and arms.

Will's <u>negative cognition</u> was:

I'm not good enough for her.

His <u>positive cognition</u> was:

I am capable of being in a loving relationship.

The <u>VOC</u> was three and a half.

His level of disturbance or <u>SUDS</u> was an eight.

Will established a set of Resources that included the following:

1. For nurturing and support, he chose:
   - his sister who was very supportive, patient and non-judg-mental;
   - and his cat who always loved when he showed up and crawled into his lap. She was always there for him.

2. For strength, he chose:
   - a friend, Malcolm, who had been diagnosed with cancer and remained positive and fought it off;
   - and another friend, Robert, who was big and very strong. He could fight someone off and be in Will's corner.

3. For wisdom he chose:
   - God who is all-knowing and, Will said, "since it's all in His plan, He would be a good resource for guidance;"
   - and his dad who was very neutral and open-minded in giving advice. "He guides without telling me what to do."

The quality he felt he needed most was self-confidence.

He recalled that when he was younger, he had been "the class clown" and one of the more popular kids. He had dressed funky because he was so confident and natural that he never worried about fitting in. He had a lot of friends and was highly thought of. He felt he had somehow lost this sense of confidence in his intimate relationships with women.

Will's Processing Session

When Will came into the processing session, he expressed deep feelings of doubt and skepticism about the method we were about to use. I reassured him that faith and certainty were not prerequisites for the work to proceed. All that was required of him was openness to his process and a willingness to share that process with me. I recall his palpable discomfort in the early stage of the processing work, but my hand-written notes do not capture his mood. Suffice it to say, he went forward with visible reluctance.

= I'm at the party, thinking about the dance area and me being on the outside.

= I'm picturing the area, looking over the crowd, wanting to be more involved than I am.

= I'm thinking about how I wish I could feel comfortable going up to Stacy and not worrying about how other people think of me.

= I'm thinking about just going for it, having the confidence to just grab her and dance with her, without worrying about failing or being judged or laughed at by other people.

[Initially, his concern is directed toward the judgments of *other* people at the party, not his girlfriend. I ask him what is holding him back.]

= I'm thinking of being a kid in elementary school, but no incident comes up. What I remember is a guy in junior high though. I was just getting into surfing and he was mean about it. He thought he was hot stuff and he wrote something on my board saying I was Z (which means zero).

[I ask what he might want to do or say to this boy.]

= I want to grab him and tell him and punch him in the mouth.
= I didn't punch him but I told him how he squashed my self-image. Not just him, but other kids too.

[I encourage him to tell them all how he feels. As he does so, his energy comes back and his voice expresses strength and confidence. He tells them he is proud of who he is and that they're just insecure. I invite him to notice how it feels in his body to be self-confident in this way. Then, he carries this feeling back into the target situation.]

= I walk up to her in front of the guy and say: "I'd like to dance with my girlfriend." We dance and I have no feeling of being watched or judged. There are no negative feelings associated with this experience.

[I ask him what made the difference for him.]

= The difference is in my confidence and lack of concern for others' reactions.

[We go back to the target and it is a five. He says he still has some anxiety about being rejected by her. I suggest he focus on that.]

= I'm thinking about Darlene (his first girlfriend). When she went away to Midland School, she started to write about another boy at school. I felt a hole in my chest and a little betrayed by her. I'd have preferred for her to say we'd just be friends, instead of receiving letters saying she missed me and loved me and then, she just went and found someone to replace me.

= I wished I had told her I cared about her and that I had been honest with her. I should have been more mature and not such a jerk.

[I ask him to visualize the boy he was at age sixteen and to talk to him directly.]

= You should have been more mature and not such a jerk! Then she would have understood better and you'd be less angry.

[I ask him to notice the reactions of the boy he was at sixteen to what he just said.]

= He's sorry, but a little defensive. His arms are crossed and I see that he's been hurt by Darlene. He appreciates what I'm telling him ... Now, I feel sorry for him and more compassion for him.

= I say: "Sorry you had to go through this. It must have been hard for you." I want to reassure him that he's a good person. The relationship didn't last, but it's not so serious.

= He says he's not so hurt by Darlene as by the fact that the relationship was special and not to be shared with other people.

[At this point, I invite him to see the reenactment with Stacy by placing the two relationships on split screen.]

= With Darlene, the other people were friends, but with Stacy there are a lot of people I know who might judge me, and I didn't want to face them.

[I suggest he round them all up and see what he might want to say or do to them now.]

= I want to tell them: I'M IMPORTANT AND MY FEELINGS MATTER!

[I ask him to notice whom he wants to say this to.]

= My mom. I tell her and she agrees, but she doesn't fully understand what I'm saying to her.

[I knew that Will had a hard time with his mother, particularly in his adolescence. We had tracked some of his passive aggression with Stacy back to his way of dealing with his mother. I encourage him to explain himself to his uncomprehending mother, and he continues with more feeling in his response.]

= I felt like your vision for my life was more important to you than my feelings about it. You never watched me surf, but it was really important to me. You wanted me to be on the soccer team, but it was important for me *not* to be on that team. You put your agenda first and it was not what I felt or needed.

[I ask him what he feels and needs now with his mother. He comes up with a logical answer first.]

= It would help me to understand that she was doing her best and had good intentions. But, just the same, it went sour between us.

[What will address his feelings of resentment toward his mother?]

= I need to tell her and have her be sorry. It was really hurtful to me and she just denies the importance of what she did.

[I ask if he wants to bring in a resource to talk to his mother or release his anger in some physical way. He chooses to bring in God to talk to her. God makes a case to his mother, pointing out to her how her son changed from before to after she had all those expectations of him. Presumably, he is referring to his reduced confidence and increased resentment and distrust.]

= She says she is truly sorry for the pain she caused.

[Since he has achieved the goal he had with his mother, we go back to the target to see where it is at. It is a two. I ask what prevents it from being a zero.]

= I feel calm and I'm smiling, but I still have some concern about the future. How will Stacy react and will I be able to make her happy?

[In any relationship, there will inevitably be a degree of uncertainty about the future and how one's partner will react. The truth is, we cannot control either the future or the other person. Therefore, I ask him to focus on what he *can* control.]

= My confidence. That's what I can control.

[I invite him to replay the scenario at the party, imagining how it would be if he had confidence in himself.]

= I smile and wave. I get out and dance. I get myself over to her and I'm saying inside: "I'm a good guy and I'm worthy and confident."

[This is a new positive cognition that has come up spontaneously. I ask him to repeat this statement while we do a Body Scan to install this new self-concept. Every part is able to accept it without any objection.]

He goes off with this new statement: "I'm a good guy and I'm worthy and confident."

Will's Follow-up Session

Will came in pleased and, one might even say, enthusiastic. He reported that he had left the processing session still doubtful about what had been accomplished. But, the next day, it all fell into place. He found himself having positive thoughts and feeling "good, real good" about himself. He had experienced a noticeable increase in confidence in social situations. Even Stacy had noticed the difference in him.

When we went back to the target, it was a zero. Will commented that he was no longer clingy and anxious in his relationship with Stacy. He felt ready now to get married to her. Stacy, however, was at the end of her rope with their relationship and this saddened him. Nonetheless, he was not reacting by getting upset and exploding at her. This work had, in his words, "connected the dots" for him. Whatever happened, Will said, he felt more confident about his future – with or without Stacy.

Postscript

Six months later on his EMDR follow-up form, Will commented that his goal had been to be a more confident person and he had seen that goal realized in his daily activities. Even at those times when he felt a <u>little</u> anxious (underlining his), it was nothing close to the way he used to react, and he was able to control it and reduce its impact. He recalled how uncomfortable and awkward he had felt in the first ten to fifteen minutes of EMDR. He remarked: "That may have been a result of my own anxiety. I would probably feel different if I did it today."

Stacy's Preparation Session

Stacy wanted to work on her anger at her father and at other men in her life. She realized that this would be important regardless of what happened in the relationship with Will. She stated the <u>issue</u> she wanted to work on as:

> I don't want to react with excessive anger toward the men in my life.

There were two different situations she remembered as distressing involving her dad. The first one she mentioned had occurred in her freshman year of college. Her father had lost his job, and she decided she should come back from the expensive private junior college she was attending. She was angry about having to do this, but felt it was a sacrifice she had to make for her family. One day, she came home for lunch and her dad was there, depressed, and he blew up at her. He demanded that she clean the house and do things to help out the family. She was irate. "I felt he was such a selfish hypocrite! He was doing nothing, but was accusing me when I had already helped and sacrificed so much. It was so unfair on his part."

The second example came from much earlier in her life and had a higher level of distress. At age six or seven, she had asked to go along with her father and her brother to the store. Her dad refused, saying there was no room in the car. She knew there was plenty of room. She felt unseen and unwelcome because she wasn't a boy. She decided to go ahead with this example as the <u>target</u> for her work.

The <u>feelings</u> that came up for her were:

> disappointment that she felt in her chest,
> anger that she experienced in her throat, and
> hurt that she placed in her stomach.

Her <u>negative belief</u> was:

> I'm not wanted.

What she would like to believe if the work was successful was:

> I deserve to be shown love.

This <u>positive cognition</u> had a <u>VOC</u> of one

Her <u>SUDS</u> or level of distress was a nine.

We created a set of Resources for Stacy that included the following:

1. For nurturing and support, she chose:
   - her dog who was always loving, attentive and positive with her;
   - and her mother "who always says she'll love me no matter what and shows that in how she acts."

2. For strength, she chose:
   - a friend we'll name Mrs. Bailey who was the most positive person, despite having lost her husband and her son having suicided;

- and an uncle who was a really strong person in her family who could "kick the crap" out of someone if he had to.

3. For wisdom she chose:
   - her sister who was always there to give advice and play the devil's advocate in a fair and non-judgmental way;
   - and Mother Teresa who was so peaceful and wise and giving, with a motivation that was pure.

The quality she felt she needed was equanimity.

She felt she had recently demonstrated this quality with Will when he had discovered she was getting messages from an old male friend and attacked her unfairly. She was able to express her feelings calmly, without yelling and screaming.

Stacy's Processing Session

Stacy had seen dramatic changes in Will since his EMDR therapy, so she had a positive attitude toward the work. Nonetheless, it was difficult for her to face an experience that had caused her so much pain over the years.

Her SUDS was still a nine.

= I feel something in my stomach and it's intense.

[Her stomach is the site of her hurt.]

= I'm thinking about my mom and dad together and an incident she told me about how my dad stopped talking to her when she got pregnant with my sister. He went out and got a vasectomy without telling her.

= I'm feeling what it's like to be ignored. My arms are really tense.

= (She has tears.) I'm thinking about wanting a hug from my dad and not getting it.

= My stomach is tight.

= My throat is tight.

> [Her throat is the site of her anger. It seems that she is in touch with the feelings in her body, but needs to get them out. I ask her if there is anything she might do in relation to wanting a hug from her dad.]

= I could just talk to him.

> [She identifies the "I" in the statement above as her adult self. I encourage her to get his attention and tell him how she feels.]

= I told him I wish he had included me more. He just looked at me the way he does and said he understood. But I'm not sure ... Then, he says he did the best he could.

> [His response feels flat to me and, from her tone of voice, seems to be less than convincing to her too. I suspect that we may need to ensure she is engaging with the father he was back then. I prompt her to talk to him about the past situation as if it were happening now.]

= She says to her father: "You have a little girl who wants to spend time with you. Why aren't you including her? She won't be any trouble."

= Then she continues: "Just because you provide for us doesn't mean you are a father. She's just a child!"

= I'm thinking he would give an excuse, but I don't accept it. I'm feeling irritated.

[I notice that her voice is flat as she says this and encourage her to sound more the way she feels.]

= "You need to try! She's trying to do everything little boys do to please you. Don't you see?"

[At this point, the little girl speaks up.]

= "I love you. I just want to be with you. Let me come too."

= (Her father answers:) "Your brother and I are going and there is no room for you."

= "Yes, there is."

= "No, we want to go fast."

= "I can go fast too."

= "No, your brother and I are going alone."

[I can see that her father is not responsive to the feelings of his little girl. Her adult self does not trust his answers. I ask if there is someone else who might be able to get through to him. She brings in Mrs. Bailey, one of her resources for strength.]

= Mrs. Bailey says: "Don, pull yourself together! You need to try harder. She's a great kid. You need to spend time with her. You're lucky to have your kids around. You're blowing it!"

= Dad says: "You're right, but I don't know what to do."

= She replies: "Start by making time each day to spend with your kids. Talk to them at the dinner table. Spend time with each one of them. Ask them questions. Try! You just have to try!"

= Dad says he's going to try. He looks at the little girl and says: "How about we go to your soccer game together and then get an ice cream after?"

[I check in with her body to see how she is receiving this new experience of her father.]

She reports:

> stomach is relaxed,
>
> arms are relaxed,
>
> throat is relaxed,
>
> chest is relaxed.

The little girl is excited and happy.

[I ask her to play out the fantasy as she would like it to have been. Then, I check her level of disturbance. It is a four. I ask her: "What prevents it from being a zero?"]

= It was just a fantasy. He wasn't up to the task. Or maybe it was me. Maybe I haven't been able to relate to him.

[At this point I think she has switched to her adult self from the little girl she was. I invite her to ask Mrs. Bailey if there is something that she might need to take responsibility for.]

= Mrs. Bailey says: "You can be guarded sometimes. You have to be true to yourself and express how you feel to others in a way they can hear you."

[I remind her of the time she had expressed her feelings to Will in a calm and level way when he was attacking her. I ask her what allowed her to have that quality of equanimity she felt she needed in order to communicate with the men in her life.]

= I was free and able to separate from the feelings I was having enough to express them calmly and receive his response without exploding.

[I ask what will help her to cultivate this quality so that she can be this way in the future.]

= I need practice. I need patience. And I need trust in myself.

[I direct her to talk to the little girl inside of her.]

= She says to the little girl: "I will take care of you and express what are our best interests. I will speak for you and I will take responsibility."

At this point the SUDS she reported was a zero. We ended the processing session with her feeling connected to her inner child.

Stacy's Follow-up Session

Stacy said she was feeling good about the processing session. The target had remained a zero. She noticed that she had no distress when she remembered other instances with her father.[35]

There had been a couple of arguments with Will since that session and she felt she had handled them well. As an example, the night of her processing session he had said something mean and she didn't blow up as she would have done before. She said: "I visualized the little girl on my lap and I was calmer."

Stacy had been thinking about how she had been "guarded" and "hostile" with men in the past. Maybe she had some responsibility for the way her ex-fiancé had pulled back during the wedding planning. She acknowledged that she had been too explosive with Will in the past. But she was clear that she did not want a future with Will if it was going to be like the relationship they had in the present.

She told me that she had been experimenting with being more open about how she was feeling in the moment and it had been working well. One time, she felt ignored by both Will and her sister and she let them know that she felt they were not listening to her. They both apologized.

Will was telling her he wanted to move forward and move in together, but she was not ready to do so. "I'm still on the fence," she said, "and I need time to reflect. I don't want to be

---

[35] This sounds like an example of Generalization – i.e. the processing of a particular issue transfers or "generalizes" to other examples of the same issue that were not processed directly.

with someone who doesn't trust me." She proposed that they take a break in their relationship.

This was not the fairy tale ending we all might have wished where the couple rides off into the sunset into perfect marital bliss. There were too many warning signs and problems in their relationship to assume that it would all work out happily for them. What was important was that each of them came to a place that was congruent with who they really were. And each of them could now contemplate the decision to be together or separate without desperation or neediness. Will and Stacy both knew they would be okay as people whether they were together or apart.

CHAPTER EIGHT

Social Anxiety:

They're Laughing Inside

Case of Melissa

Anxiety is one of the most common presenting problems in our therapy offices. Human beings, it appears, have the distinctive ability to visualize the future in either excited anticipation or in fear and dread. Other animals can prepare for the future as, for example, squirrels that bury nuts for the winter. But it does not appear that squirrels worry about their supply of nuts drying up, or their fellow squirrels judging them for gathering too many, or ostracizing them for their particular nut-gathering behavior. This type of worry seems to be the distinctive domain of human beings.

We humans not only worry about the future. To make matters worse, we also worry about our worry about the future. Will we be so anxious that we can't speak? Will we act like a fool? Ruin our chances of impressing the other - whether that other be a potential employer, lover or friend? The most prevalent type of anxiety that brings people into therapy is social anxiety – the obsessive concern about how other people will receive and judge us. At bottom, it is a fear of rejection and the loss of approval and love.

The case of Melissa is a dramatic example of how social anxiety can cripple a person's confidence and block their ability to connect with other people. The messages inside Melissa's head paralyzed her from behaving in a natural and spontaneous manner in social situations. She went through her life with very little contact with anyone. In her therapy sessions, she sat up very erectly on the edge of her seat, poised as if ready to jump up and run at the first opportunity. In all the months I worked with her – and I worked with her for almost a year - I never saw her settle into the cushions of the couch and look as if she was comfortable and at ease. She came across as withdrawn and reserved, rarely initiating conversation and responding minimally when addressed. Her answers were most often clipped and to the point, reminiscent of the one-word answers of resistant teenagers. While her attitude was not inherently oppositional, she was perpetually guarded, as if expecting she might need to defend herself at any moment. Perhaps she rationalized that the less she put out, the less there was to attack. So, she put out very little. There were long pauses when she said nothing at all.

To keep the conversation going, she needed to be coaxed and coached, prompted and prodded. It required an unusually high degree of intervention on my part. I found myself explaining, paraphrasing, and repeating myself on a frequent basis. I had to draw out her thoughts with accompanying messages of continuous support and reassurance. It seemed clear that something had gone wrong in her early mirroring to create such blockage in her ability to communicate. I felt like I was trying to make up for the attunement and validation she had somehow missed.

Background Information

Melissa was nineteen years old and in her first year of community college when she first came for therapy. She had been living with her father, her father's girlfriend (who barely spoke English), and her grandmother during the previous semester. She succinctly summed up her current living situation with the words: "I don't enjoy it."

She had very little contact with the adults in the household. She ate her breakfast in the car on her way to school and her lunch in the car at school or on her own in the cafeteria. The only meal that was shared with her family was Sunday dinner. She described the conversation with her family as "nothing deep or too personal." They rarely went out together or had any shared activities beyond watching TV. She spent most of her time at home in her room with no one to talk to.

Nonetheless, this living arrangement was, in her view, a vast improvement on her previous living situation with her mother. Since Melissa's parents had divorced when she was seven years old, she had wanted to live with her father, but her mother would not allow it. In Melissa's mind, this was because her mother was afraid she would be lonely without her daughter's company. However, Melissa and her mother had what she described as "a very bad relationship." She depicted her mother as "rude, opinionated, high strung, and a racist who talks trash and blows up at the smallest thing." Her brother had moved out of the house when she was fourteen, leaving Melissa as the target of her mother's rage. She wondered if the negative thoughts in her head had any relationship to her mother's extreme negativity.

Melissa reported that she had been anxious "ever since (she) was little." She had some friends in public school, but they had gone in different directions, and she found herself isolated in high school. She didn't like the high school or the other students at the school. Her saving grace was gymnastics that she loved and excelled at. She focused all her attention on gymnastics and socialized, to the degree that she did, with the kids who were involved with that activity. Unfortunately, when she had not won the scholarship she wanted for college, she had to quit gymnastics. She rarely, if ever, saw any of the friends she had had in the gymnastics world. "It was my whole life," she said, "but there is no club here and it's time to move on."

Moving on was proving difficult for Melissa because of her social anxiety. She found it hard to talk to people at school. Sometimes she would stutter or slur her words or forget words, she reported. Sometimes she would say things backwards and not make any sense. She was so worried that something like this would happen that she avoided talking to anyone. She lived a very lonely life.

In the months before our EMDR work, we had trained Melissa in self-hypnosis so she could put herself in a relaxed state at will. We set up a hierarchy of school situations that were increasingly difficult for her, and did hypnotherapy to allow her to experience managing them without anxiety. We identified the negative messages she was giving herself and taught her how to fight them. She dutifully did all the work I proposed, but she remained socially isolated. We looked at resources for her to explore in order to expand her contacts, but she did not follow up on the suggestions or found some reason not to pursue them.

Then, one day, she asked: "Is there anything else we haven't tried?" I reminded her that we had not yet tried EMDR, although I had suggested it. It was as a last ditch effort that Melissa reluctantly agreed to do EMDR regarding her social anxiety.

Preparation Session

The <u>issue</u> identified by Melissa for her EMDR work was:

I want to lower my anxiety level in social situations.

The situation she chose as an example had occurred during her high school years. She had been talking online frequently with a boy she liked whom we will call Todd. Online, she was able to communicate comfortably and with ease. In person, however, it was a different story. She would stutter and find herself at a loss for words. She felt like she was a different person and could not be herself.

On one occasion, she had gone out to a restaurant with a group of friends including Todd. Afterward, they had walked around together, hanging out with another girl named Courtney. By contrast to Melissa who was anxious and choked up, Courtney appeared confident and chatty and talked easily. Melissa found herself feeling jealous of Courtney's social ease. Todd seemed to be more interested in Courtney and this made matters worse. Even when Melissa would speak, Todd did not respond much to her. He was focused mostly on Courtney. Melissa avoided standing next to him because she felt so uncomfortable. At one point, no one was speaking. She remembered thinking: "What's the matter with me? Why can't I be the person I was online? Why am I so anxious? Why can't I speak right? No wonder he isn't interested in me!"

The most distressing moment in the situation was when she felt jealous of Courtney's ability to talk so easily and concluded that Todd was more interested in Courtney than he was in her. This formed the target for our work.

The feelings that came up as she recalled this memory were:

> anxiety that she located in her jaw (tight),
>
> jealousy that she placed in her heart,
>
> anger at herself that was in her head (self-attacking thoughts),
>
> anger at Todd that was in her stomach,
>
> hopelessness that she felt in her shoulders,
>
> sadness that she experienced in her eyes,
>
> self-consciousness that she felt in her chest.

Her negative cognition was:

> I'm just not good enough.

Her <u>positive cognition</u> was:

I am confident in most social situations.

The <u>VOC</u> was a two (not very true).

The <u>SUDS</u> was a nine (highly distressing).

Melissa's set of Resources were as follows:

1. For nurturing and support, she chose:
   - her grandmother who was very loving and always cared what she had to say;
   - and her dog, Susie, who was always happy to see her and loved her unconditionally.

2. For strength, she chose:
   - a scary monster who was big and ugly with flames in the background. This monster would scare away all the bad things;
   - and her dad who had helped her get out of living with her mom. He knew what she was feeling and had supported her through it. "He takes my side and sees my point of view when bad things happen."

3. For wisdom, she chose:
   - the inner self-helper from our hypnosis work because "he always gives me the right answer;"
   - and Rachel (myself) because she seems to have a lot of wisdom about anxiety and therapy.

The quality she felt she needed was confidence.

Her example of when she possessed this quality was when she was coaching gymnastics. She saw herself as talkative and as someone who could give good advice because she knew what she was talking about. She felt "valuable" and that she had a lot to offer, and "powerful" because people were listening to her.

Her safe place was up in the mountains in the snow just before she was about to snowboard down the hill. She was sitting on the ground by herself, hearing the wind and looking at the mountains covered in snow. She was at peace, comfortable and relaxed with no pressure – just a feeling of excitement about going down the mountain, flying like a bird, free.

In contrast to the tense and constricted impression she conveyed when you met her face to face, this was a powerful and compelling image of Melissa – one I would have liked to see her realize in her life.

Processing Session

Rachel: I'm going to review what we set up in the preparation session and you can tell me if there's anything you want to change.

The issue you wanted to work on is: I want to lower my anxiety level in social situations. The example you gave had to do with a guy you liked in high school named Todd. You and Todd communicated often online and it went well. However, when you were talking with him in person, your voice would be shaky, you would stutter, and you wouldn't know what to say. You felt like you couldn't be yourself, like you were a different person.

On one occasion, a Sunday night, you went to a restaurant with a group of friends and then walked around afterward with Todd and a girl named Courtney. She was confident, chatty and talked easily. And you were jealous. Todd seemed to be more interested in Courtney and focused most of his attention on her. When you'd speak, he didn't respond much. You were thinking: "What's the matter with me? Why can't I be the person I was online? Why am I so anxious? Why can't I speak right? No wonder he's isn't interested in me!"

The target is the memory of that girl talking so easily and you're feeling jealous because Todd seemed to be more interested in her.

The feelings that came up were: *anxiety* that you placed in your jaw; *jealousy* that you placed in your heart; *anger at yourself* that was in your head and *anger at Todd* that was in your stomach. There was *hopelessness* that you located in your shoulders; *self-consciousness* in your chest, and *sadness* that you located in your eyes.

The negative belief you had about yourself was: I'm just not good enough.

What you would like to believe about yourself, your positive cognition, is:

I am confident in most social situations.

Now what I would like you to do is to hold the target, the feelings it brings up, and the negative belief. Hold these three things in your mind and ramp up the level of disturbance to the highest degree you can experience at this moment in time. Then, tell me the number on a scale from zero to ten where zero would be no charge and ten would represent the highest possible disturbance. Once I hear that number, I will turn the scanner on. At that point, your job will be simply to observe whatever comes up in your mind.

(Long pause)

Melissa: Seven.

Rachel: Seven. And that's the highest, right? Okay.

(Very long pause) And what's coming up for you Melissa?

Melissa: Um ... kind of sadness.

Rachel: Mhmm.

Melissa: Because I don't know why I would tell myself that I'm not good enough.

Rachel: Mhmm.

Melissa: That's it.

Rachel: Okay. Go with that.

(Another long period of silence.) And what's happening now, Melissa?

Melissa: I feel still just kind of sad that I would tell myself I'm not good enough. Same thing.

Rachel: Okay. No images? No memories? Nothing else came up? No pictures?

Melissa: Um. Just other similar situations.

Rachel: I want to hear about those, then. Tell me about the other situations that you also noticed. Anything that comes up I would want to know.

Melissa: Nothing in particular. Just other instances where I felt the same feelings.

Rachel: And did you have a memory of some of those flash through your mind?

Melissa: No.

Rachel: Well, how did you think about those other situations then?

Melissa: Um ... I don't know I just felt, um, other situations ...

[During the early part of the session, Melissa is having great difficulty focusing. She says repeatedly that no specific images or memories are coming up for her. She gets distracted by the equipment, complaining that the sensors (kinesthetic reinforcement for the audio stimulation) are too strong for her, even though they are at the lowest possible setting. Therefore, we disconnect them. Later, she decides that breaking up the audio stimulation with periods of conversation does not seem to work for her. So, we leave it on the whole time. It is not altogether surprising that a person with high anxiety might have difficulty getting comfortable with the bilateral processing.]

Rachel: You thought: "Oh, this has happened before?"

Melissa: Yeah. But nothing popped in my head.

Rachel: Stay with that thought and see what comes up.

(Very long pause) And what are you getting now?

Melissa: Um .... I came up with images at school when I felt that I wasn't good enough.

Rachel: Okay. Any specific examples?

Melissa: Um. No.

Rachel: What kind of images? Did you see pictures of school?

Melissa: Um ... I kind of saw people. Um ... People just laughing.

Rachel: Were these people kids your age?

Melissa: Yeah.

Rachel: Anything else that you saw?

Melissa: No.

Rachel: Were they laughing at you or laughing among themselves? Or what did you believe?

Melissa: Um ... Laughing at me.

Rachel: Okay. So, think about that – situations where people were laughing at you and how that felt.

(Long pause) And what's coming up Melissa?

Melissa: (Pause) I don't know. Not much.

Rachel: Usually, there is something there. You might not want to speak about it, but it would be better if you could notice what's happening. Is something happening in your body? Are you remembering something? Are there feelings? Any memories? Any recollections?

> [This client is inclined to be very passive and requires continual suggestions, questions, and prodding to come up with anything specific. A very proactive therapist style seems to be required here.]

Melissa: Not really. I'm just kind of drawing a blank.

Rachel: Okay. So, have these kids that are your age that were laughing – have they disappeared or are they still there?

Melissa: Maybe, if the beeping went on while we were talking, that might help.

Rachel: You want to try that?

Melissa: Yes.

Rachel: Okay. So, go back to the kids that were laughing at you.

> [She does not volunteer any information. She seems to need to be invited to respond each time.]

(Very long pause) And you can just speak when you're ready.

Melissa: I thought of a memory at my school when I was talking to … when I was in a group with two people.

Rachel: Good for you.

Melissa: And I was feeling anxious and I just thought that they were laughing inside.

> [This is the first hint of the inner dialogue that plagues this girl.]

(Long pause)

Rachel: Uh-huh.

Melissa: I just felt like they could see that I was anxious.

Rachel: Uh-huh.

Melissa: And, at first, I was talking fine, but then, after awhile, I just felt anxious.

Rachel: And when you felt anxious, what happened to your ability to talk fine?

Melissa: Um … I stopped talking as much as I was in the beginning and I let them do the talking.

Rachel: Okay. And in the meantime, how were you feeling when you began to become aware that you thought they were laughing inside?

Melissa: Um … I just felt like … just like every other situation that I had to deal with before where I felt anxious.

Rachel: It sounds pretty awful. Is it?

Melissa: Mhmm.

Rachel: So, there are many situations in which you feel that people are laughing inside, even though they may not be laughing on the outside?

Melissa: Uh-huh.

Rachel: Have you asked yourself the question: "What makes you believe that they are laughing at you on the inside, when nothing is showing on the outside?"

Melissa: I'm sorry; can you repeat that?

Rachel: Have you asked yourself the question: "What makes you believe they're laughing on the inside when nothing is showing on the outside?"

Melissa: Um ... kind of, yes.

Rachel: What makes you believe that?

Melissa: Um ... just because of the way I talk.

Rachel: And how do you talk?

Melissa: I feel like when I get anxious I, um, just don't act like myself, and I don't make as much sense. I don't speak clearly.

Rachel: Have people told you this? That you don't speak clearly? That you don't make sense? Have you heard that feedback from others repeatedly?

Melissa: Um ... I have a couple of times.

Rachel: A couple of times.

Melissa: Yeah. I've gotten a few weird looks.

Rachel: That you interpreted it as people thinking that you weren't speaking sensibly?

Melissa: Yeah.

Rachel: But this is your interpretation.

[I'm beginning to direct her attention to the source of her anxiety that is *internal* rather than *external*.]

Melissa: Uh-huh.

Rachel: Is there any time, or times, when people actually said to you: "You're not making sense. You're sounding strange"?

Melissa: No.

Rachel: None. And yet you believe this?

Melissa: Yes.

Rachel: What comes up when you think about that? That you have no evidence, but you have this belief?

Melissa: Well, when I listen to myself, I know that I'm not making sense. So then, when that happens, I just stop talking much.

[Typically, the person who is anxious is self-consciously watching and judging themselves, rather than focusing on the people they are interacting with.]

Rachel: So, the reason that you believe this is because you listen to yourself and *you* make that judgment.

[Putting the locus of control back where it belongs – in her.]

Melissa: Yes.

Rachel: So, the person that is listening and the person that is speaking are two different parts of you or two different people, right? There is somebody who is expressing herself and someone else who is judging. Correct?

Melissa: Definitely. I think that's the superego, I guess.

[This client has done work on the superego (or inner critic) and how to silence its attacks, but she has not been putting it into practice in her life.]

Rachel: Uh-huh. Okay. So the superego tells you: "Oh, my gosh, you're weird and you're not making sense. Nobody can understand you." No one else tells you that, but the superego does. And how do you feel about this superego? Do you think that he/she/it is trustworthy and believable?

[I'm trying to remind her that the judgments of the superego are not reliable sources of truth.]

Melissa: Um ... No. I don't like the superego.

Rachel: Oh. Do you think that it has your best interest at heart?

Melissa: No.

Rachel: Do you think that it has a strong, reality-based picture of you? Do you think the superego is right about you?

Melissa: Um ... Sometimes.

[However, she's not ready to disavow it entirely.]

Rachel: It could be. It could be right. Sometimes you think it is. But who thinks it is right? It does or you do?

Melissa: I do.

Rachel: You do. So, you buy in.

Melissa: Sometimes.

Rachel: Sometimes it is right, you think. And sometimes it isn't.

Melissa: Uh-huh.

Rachel: Hold that thought for a minute. What makes the difference for you? When would you believe it and when would you say: "That's a crock? You don't know what you're talking about. I'm fine. I can speak like anybody else."

Melissa: Um ... I guess when it says I'm not good enough. Then, I wouldn't. I would not believe it.

[It's unclear at this point if she truly grasps what she is saying, but I go with it.]

Rachel: Oh. You would *not* believe it.

Melissa: No.

Rachel: I see.

Melissa: Um ... When it says: "Oh, you can't talk, you can't speak clearly, um ... you're not like everybody else." Then, I do believe it.

Rachel: Oh. And exactly why is it that you believe that you can't talk and you're not like anyone else?

Melissa: I just feel like I've been through less experience than everybody else. They've been through more social situations than me, so I feel like I am different.

Rachel: Uh-huh. You have less experience of social situations.

[She has, in fact, been socially deprived in her past history and continues to be so in her present circumstances. While this lack of social experience presents challenges for her, it does not necessarily preclude positive change in the future in the way that her negative beliefs about herself do.]

Melissa: Yes.

Rachel: And that makes you unlike everyone else.

Melissa: Well, different from everybody else. They've been through more than me.

Rachel: Okay, so there could be a few people who are also on the fringe, maybe a little bit shy, maybe they haven't had as much exposure. And you feel like you would be one of those people? Not one of the people in the majority?

Melissa: Yes.

Rachel: And what is the reason for that?

Melissa: Um ... Because I just feel like they have more of a social life than I have. They have been to more school dances and um, things like that, than I have.

Rachel: Mhmm.

Melissa: And get togethers and had boyfriends or girlfriends, which I haven't had. Which, I feel, just makes me different.

Rachel: Okay. And do you believe in your ability to learn?

Melissa: Yes.

Rachel: Uh-huh. Are there situations where you didn't know about something that maybe other people knew about? Like I don't know how to work an iPhone? I haven't a clue, but other people do. So I'm different if you compare me to iPhone holders, iPhone people. But do you think I might be capable of learning? Do you think I could pick it up somehow?

Melissa: Yes.

Rachel: Do you think that your social life is like the iPhone experience? That it's something that maybe you haven't had as much experience or exposure as others do, but you could learn?

Melissa: I feel like I can learn, but, um, I can never learn ... it's hard to explain ... I can never ... like I missed out still on so much, I can never go back in time and learn what they learned when they were, say, in high school when I missed out on a lot. I don't know if that makes sense.

[It is the belief that she is permanently disabled by her past experience that blocks her from moving forward and even trying to socialize.]

Rachel: What I'm hearing is that somehow you feel you missed out in high school and you can't catch up.

Melissa: Yes.

Rachel: Is that true?

Melissa: It feels that way. Yes.

Rachel: So, when you were in high school, what was the reason that you missed out?

Melissa: Um ... I was really anxious - it seemed like all the time - and I just thought, because I was so into gymnastics and everything, I just revolved gymnastics around everything. I thought: "Oh, I have gymnastics. I don't need these people." And I remember I was never really close to my friends, so I pretty much didn't bother to make new ones, even though I wished I had new ones. But I didn't make a big deal out of it.

[Here she describes her passivity and how she minimizes her own social needs and gives up easily.]

Rachel: So, you did have friends in gymnastics?

Melissa: I did have friends in gymnastics. Yes.

Rachel: And with these friends that you did have in gymnastics, did you ever have get togethers?

Melissa: Yes, we did, but a lot of them seemed like they were into their friends at school, so I still kind of felt left out, because they were into their friends at school and stuff. And they all had a bunch of friends at school, which I didn't, so I still felt left out when I was around them.

Rachel: When you were around them, you were still telling yourself that you were different and not as good.

[Even with her friends, the discouraging tape keeps playing in her head, preventing her from feeling accepted and at ease with other people.]

Melissa: Yes. Uh-huh.

Rachel: Just look at being around them. Were there any times that you were around them when you were not right in the middle of doing gymnastics, but were maybe on the sidelines talking?

Melissa: Yes.

Rachel: Were there times when you might have been joking around, kind of telling stories, talking about what happened on the weekend or the day before, before you got right into practicing?

Melissa: Yes.

Rachel: Were there ever any times when you went out together to a party, or to a restaurant, or to have a drink like a soda or something? Ever had times that you went out?

Melissa: Yes.

Rachel: Would you call those social times?

Melissa: Yes.

Rachel: I would call them social times too. So, you may not have had as many, but you did have social times with your friends in gymnastics. And when you were with your friends in gymnastics and you went out socially, were you more comfortable and more at ease than you were with kids at school?

Melissa: Yes.

Rachel: And did you talk?

Melissa: Yes.

Rachel: And interact socially?

Melissa: Yes.

Rachel: I'd like you to visualize the person that you were in that type of situation. You can pick any example that comes up in your mind where you're out with your friends in gymnastics and you're chatting, you're talking, you're feeling confident, you're animated, and you're socially at ease. Can you think of a time like that?

[Not only is it important to bring up positive aspects of her history that she may have selectively forgotten, it is also crucial for her to reconnect with her ability to be that social person she wants to be.]

Melissa: Uh-huh.

Rachel: Okay. And that person that you're visualizing, how old is she?

Melissa: Um, sixteen or seventeen.

Rachel: Okay, so this is the person you were in high school?

Melissa: Yes.

Rachel: And she has adequate, acceptable social skills?

Melissa: Yes.

Rachel: She does. Okay. She's kind of like the person you were describing who communicated online with Todd and communicated fine online and had social skills. Something changed when you got into social situations with kids in high school. What do you notice that's different about when you were with Todd in person versus online – or when you were with kids from high school versus kids from your gymnastics? What's the difference between those two? The social person is there, but somehow blocked.

> [We need to identify the difference between these two types of situations so that she can become aware of the obstacle in the way of her socializing comfortably.]

Melissa: Um, I almost felt like people at my gymnastics – or some people at my gymnastics, the ones I was closer with – they were different than people at my school. They had the same personalities, but they were just different

Rachel: Better or worse, in your personal opinion?

Melissa: Better.

Rachel: Ah.

Melissa: That's why I got along with them.

Rachel: So, what was different about them that was better?

Melissa: Um. They were just, um, more fun to talk to. More goofy. Not like the people at my school. It seems like the people at my school were so gossipy and into drama.

Rachel: Uh-huh.

Melissa: At least, the people I was around. I really didn't like the friends I hung out with.

Rachel: They sound like maybe they were kind of snooty, a little bit – the ones in high school.

Melissa: Um. I guess so. Yeah. But not the friends I hung out with. I just didn't like them as people.

> [So we see that she is judging not only herself, but also her peers. The superego criticizes the self and, at the same time, projects its judgments on others.]

Rachel: Okay. So, when you're around people that you don't really like, that have qualities about them that put you off, you aren't as at ease, you aren't as comfortable, you aren't as talkative.

Melissa: Yes.

Rachel: Is that true?

Melissa: Yeah. Uh-huh.

Rachel: So, you change when you're with them, as I would when I was with somebody that I didn't know really like or didn't feel comfortable with.

> [I'm thinking that I am making a rather self-evident observation that, if we don't like the people we are with, we may well be uncomfortable in their company. But Melissa does not see it that way.]

Melissa: Well, it varies, I guess.

Rachel: Well, yeah. But from what we're saying, you had social skills in high school. You were quite comfortable socially with some people, but there were other people who were different from you and from your gymnastic friends and you didn't like them.

Melissa: Yeah.

Rachel: And when you were with them, it was a lot harder for you to socialize.

Melissa: Yes. It was a personality thing. I get along with … it seems like … some personalities, and then, other personalities or the way people act or the way they say things, I just don't get along with. Almost like I'm a whole different person.

Rachel: Well, I think you're probably not a whole different person, but you're saying that these are people you don't like. So, what comes out is that dislike, that discomfort, that distance in terms of values. You're goofy. They're snooty. They're gossipy. They're more dramatic. There are features of them that you're judging and not feeling comfortable with. Is that true?

Melissa: Uh-huh.

Rachel: Okay. So, is it a problem for you that you have difficulty being really comfortable with people you don't like?

Melissa: Yes.

Rachel: You want to be able to be really comfortable with people you *don't* like and socialize easily with people you don't like?

[This seems to me to be unrealistic, but I choose to go forward with the client's values to see where they might lead.]

Melissa: Yes.

Rachel: So, could the girl that was able to socialize with the people at gymnastics bring out those same skills, if she wanted, when she was with people she didn't like? If she wanted to, could she do that?

Melissa: Well, I don't know if it would be people I don't like. Like sometimes, I feel like I'm not myself when people just have a different personality than me or they don't get me.

Rachel: Well, then, you're talking about people you don't like or can't connect with, that you don't seem to be like, or you don't have the same values as they do. Maybe I boiled it down too much by saying "don't like," although that sums up, in some sense, the lack of comfort, the lack of ease you have with these folks, right?

Melissa: Uh-huh.

Rachel: And I'm asking: "Is it okay with you that there are certain people that you just don't hit it off with?" Do you believe that you should be comfortable and happy with everyone?

Melissa: I believe that I should. Yes.

> [She articulates a pretty harsh standard in demanding of herself that she be able to socialize equally well with every person, regardless of who they are or how she feels about them.]

Rachel: Oh. And who told you that?

Melissa: Um. Myself.

Rachel: Hmm. Interesting. You believe that you should be comfortable with everyone. Now, is this the same person that was comfortable at age sixteen socializing with her friends in gymnastics? This doesn't sound like her.

Melissa: Mhmm.

Rachel: Is this the superego that's saying you should be comfortable with and like everyone?

Melissa: Um ... Well, I don't know. Maybe it's my superego saying I should be comfortable with everybody, because it seems like so many people are so comfortable with a lot of people. It seems like they're comfortable with everybody. Then, when it comes to me, it seems like there is a lot of people I'm not comfortable with. So I think that's why I'm telling myself I should be comfortable with everybody.

[As is often the case, a person may see their own anxiety all too clearly and imagine that no one else has the same experience of fear that they have.]

Rachel: I think that you have a picture in your mind that there are some people - I think you almost mean most people - who are comfortable with everybody and have no discrimination. They are comfortable, they like everyone, they get along with everyone, they feel the same as everyone.

Melissa: Yeah.

Rachel: I have difficulty with that point of view. I'm not sure it's true. I'm not sure that most people can relate to everybody equally, Melissa.

Melissa: Well, it feels like they can relate to people more than I can relate to people.

Rachel: Okay. And what do you think it is that makes it easier for them than it is for you? Do you think they're telling themselves that they're not good enough if they don't feel comfortable with everyone?

Melissa: Um. No.

Rachel: No.

Melissa: I don't think they have those thoughts in their mind.

Rachel: Right.

Melissa: They don't have the superego telling them stuff. They just go with the flow.

[Again, the superego is a universal phenomenon, but Melissa thinks she is unique in her struggle with its dictates.]

Rachel: So, if they were saying to themselves the whole time: "There is something wrong with me. I can't speak clearly. I'm not like everyone else. I'm not as good as anyone else. No one's going to like me. This is going to be a disaster. Socially this is not going to work ..." Do you think that they would be able to be relaxed and comfortable relating to people when they were thinking those thoughts?

[I'm directing her back to her negative belief system as the primary source of the problem.]

Melissa: Um, maybe, if they had the ability to block them out.

Rachel: Then, they wouldn't have those thoughts.

Melissa: Well, then, no.

Rachel: That's right. I have to agree. They would not be able to do it. The difference between you and them is that they're not engaging in self- attack believing that they *should* be able to be similar to everyone else. And they don't believe that there is something wrong with them if they are not at the same level of ease with everyone they meet.

Melissa: Hmm.

Rachel: So, where does that leave you when you realize that?

Melissa: Um. I don't know. Still kind of makes me feel different that I have these thoughts and they don't, or they have the ability to tell their superego to be quiet and sometimes it's harder for me to tell my superego to be quiet.

Rachel: So, the problem is that you are letting in these thoughts.

Melissa: Yes.

Rachel: And that's the difficulty.

Melissa: Yes.

Rachel: It's not that you can't catch up socially, that you missed out and you'll never get there. It's that the belief that you're not going to be able to make it is proving itself to be true because of your having that thought.

Melissa: Yes.

Rachel: Okay. Does that make sense to you? So just look at that thought.

Melissa: Well, partly, yeah, I think it's the thought, but other things too, why I can't catch up socially.

Rachel: Let's just look at this piece first, because this is what you've noticed is the difference between your ability to relate socially with the people in gymnastics, for example, or with other people that you like and feel comfortable with, and the fact that, with other people when you have those thoughts, you choke up, you get anxious, you can't speak and be yourself.

Melissa: Mhmm.

Rachel: Right? So, look at that thought that you're not good enough and you never will be because you missed the train or you missed the boat. Where does that thought come from? When you just hold it for a minute, where is it from? Who ever said that to you? Who comes up in your mind when you ask yourself: "Why do I think I'm not as good as everyone else socially?"

Melissa: Um. Where does it come from?

[I'm going after the original source of this negative belief system.]

Rachel: Yeah.

Melissa: Um. I'm just myself telling myself that.

Rachel: Check it out for a minute. Hear the thought. I'm going to repeat some of the things you said. "I'm so different. I'm not as good as everyone else. I missed out in high school. I don't have the same social skills. I'm never going to make up or be able to make up. I'm just not good enough."

Melissa: I guess, because I've told people I've never been to a school dance. Well, I've been to just one school dance. And I guess they're really shocked when they hear that. Maybe it's people's reactions.

Rachel: They're surprised. And do they say to you: "Oh, you're just not good enough and you're never going to be able to catch up"?

Melissa: No.

Rachel: Who says that?

Melissa: Myself.

Rachel: Okay. Go back farther. You were not born with this thought. This thought developed. It came from somewhere outside of you. And when I say that, let an image come up in your mind as to who it might have been who told you that.

Melissa: That I'm not good enough or different?

Rachel: Uh-huh. That's right.

Melissa: (Long pause) Um …

Rachel: Let an image come up. Do you see anybody? Whether you want to or not, whether you like the fact that you do or not, does anybody come up?

> [The client has shared with me, at length, how unsupportive and critical her mother is and was. I'm preparing her to let in the crucial implications of this fact.]

Melissa: Well, I guess, I just see the image of people not getting along with me as well as they do with other people.

Rachel: That's the image that follows the thought. But I'm asking you to go back to the source of the thought. "You're not good enough, Melissa. You're different." Who said that to you? Who gave you that idea?

Melissa: Um ...

Rachel: Who made you feel that there was something wrong with you?

Melissa: If I look back as far as I can, you mean?

Rachel: Just let yourself focus on that thought, and let an image come up from the past way, way back it may be, of someone who might have helped you to feel that way.

Melissa: Um ... Well, I don't know if this is relevant, but I remember back in kindergarten. Um, I had this girlfriend and she was like my best friend, but she had another best friend named Charlene. We were next-door neighbors, me and my best friend, but this girl Charlene lived a little bit out of the way. And I remember one day, we were playing tennis and she was like more friends or she was getting along better with Charlene than she was with me. And I remember just feeling that I am not good enough. That I'm different.

Rachel: Very good.

Melissa: That was in kindergarten.

Rachel: Can you go back even farther?

Melissa: (Pause) Um, I don't think so. I don't think I can think past kindergarten.

Rachel: As a child, as a very little child, did you feel different and not good enough, when you were little, little?

Melissa: Um, not really. I can't really ...

Rachel: Do you remember your mother telling you that you were wonderful, that you were great, that you were the most wonderful little girl in the world, and that people would love you? Do you remember that?

Melissa: No.

Rachel: What did your mother tell you about your lovability and your likability?

Melissa: I don't remember what. I don't remember anything.

Rachel: Bring up the image of your mother, just as a chance, and ask.

Melissa: When I was younger or older?

Rachel: When you were younger. And ask your mother. First, can you see your mother?

Melissa: Nope.

Rachel: Bring up her image.

Melissa: I can see her, but I don't see her when I was younger. I don't remember what she used to act like when I was younger.

Rachel: Okay. Bring up the earliest image you can of your mother.

Melissa: Okay.

Rachel: And ask her: "What did you feel about me when I was a little girl and what did you tell me about me and my value as a person?" And then, observe what she says. Is she listening? Does she hear you?

Melissa: Mhmm.

Rachel: She does. She's heard your question?

Melissa: Mhmm.

Rachel: What does she say?

Melissa: That I'm not good enough.

Rachel: Oh.

> [So here it is. Despite all the blocking and obfuscation, the knowledge is there and it comes to the surface at this point.]

Melissa: There's always going to be something wrong. No matter what I do.

Rachel: Now, isn't that a strange thing to say to a little girl? Why would she say that?

Melissa: Well, I don't know if she would say those exact words, but …

Rachel: But she felt it. They came up.

Melissa: Yeah.

Rachel: Okay. So that's what she felt – that there was always going to be something wrong with you, no matter what you did.

Melissa: Yes.

Rachel: Now, why on earth would a mother feel that way?

Melissa: I don't know. Because that's the way she is.

Rachel: That's the way she is. Which is what? Super critical?

Melissa: Yeah.

Rachel: And how do you feel about that?

Melissa: Um. Well, not happy.

Rachel: Makes me angry.

> [This was a spontaneous reaction on my part, but it also gave her permission to feel something similar.]

Melissa: Yeah.

Rachel: Does it make you angry?

Melissa: Yeah.

Rachel: And knowing that your mother isn't here – and I'm certainly not going to tell her what you did or said in this room – how would you like to express your anger at your mother for such a horrible thing she thought and felt about her little girl? Do you want to tell her how angry you are, scream at her, kick her, punch her, stab her in the heart?

Melissa: Well, if I did, she wouldn't acknowledge it. She wouldn't acknowledge what I say or do.

Rachel: If you expressed it, she would ignore you?

Melissa: It would just go in one ear and out the other and then, she would start talking about something else that's wrong.

Rachel: She'd ignore you and change the subject or she'd just go on with more criticisms?

Melissa: More criticisms.

Rachel: Wow. What a battle-axe. That's hard.

Melissa: Mhmm.

Rachel: Okay. So, it felt to you, and still feels to you, like the person who set you on this track was impenetrable. You could not get through to her when you were a little girl. She wasn't going to listen to you. She was just going to go on criticizing.

Melissa: Yes.

[In fact, her mother was so relentless in her attacks on Melissa that she had moved in with her father and grandmother just to get away from her.]

Rachel: Okay. So, is this still true today? If you were to say to her: "You know, the way that you felt about me and treated me as a little kid was horrible," would she ignore you and go on criticizing now?

Melissa: Uh-huh.

Rachel: She would.

Melissa: Uh-huh.

Rachel: Okay. So, you have taken in these views, and it sounds like you feel powerless to change them with your mother. Because she is not listening to you. Is that right?

Melissa: Yeah.

Rachel: Who might be able to talk to your mother and make an impact on her?

Melissa: No one. What do you mean? About what?

Rachel: About how she treated you.

Melissa: Nobody.

Rachel: That's hard to believe. There's nobody who could tell your mother and make her hear that the way she treated you as a little girl was terrible?

Melissa: Uh-uh.

Rachel: Well, let's review your resources. Do you think that your grandma would be a person who could do that?

Melissa: I don't think anybody would, because she doesn't really listen to anybody.

Rachel: Well, let's just go through the list. She may not agree, but we may be able to make an impact on her, if we try. And we need to find the person who could make that impact. Who would be the best person to stand up for you now with your mother, Melissa? You can pick anybody, but in your resources we have your grandmother, we have your dog, we have a scary monster, we have your dad, we have the inner self-helper which is the very best part of your adult self, and we have me.

Melissa: I guess herself would be the only person to tell her.

Rachel: Herself? I don't think she's listening right now. Could I possibly talk to her? (She shakes her head.) Nobody?

Melissa: No.

Rachel: If she can't be talked to, could she be destroyed? In fantasy, of course, we're not going to hurt her in reality. But it sounds like she's someone that you have a lot of anger at and that you need to be able, in some way, to stop giving her power. You need to have a way to express that anger and reduce her to the mean person she was. Do you agree?

Melissa: Well, it's kind of in the past right now.

Rachel: No it isn't, babe; it's in the present. It's right here in this room.

Melissa: Uh-huh.

Rachel: You are still listening and responding to the messages you got from your mother from the earliest days. You don't even remember when it started. Maybe you were just born not good enough for your mother. Maybe she didn't want to have a child. Maybe she didn't want a girl. Maybe she didn't want to be a mother. Maybe she didn't have the ability to understand that babies are very needy and they cry, they spit up, they poop, and they have problems like colic and, you know, diarrhea, whatever. Maybe she simply wasn't able to be a mother.

[She has so internalized these messages from her mother that she is having a hard time letting in the idea that the problem may lie in her mother, not in herself.]

Melissa: Mhmm.

Rachel: And then she made it about you. Do you think that's a possibility?

Melissa: Mhmm. I don't know. Um … Possibly. I mean, she did the motherly things that she was supposed to do – she did half the things that she was supposed to do – but her thought that I was not good enough was there.

Rachel: I hear that, loud and clear. And it seems to me that until you stop believing the horrible things your mother conveyed to you about yourself, you're going to remain stuck. It's your mother or you.

Melissa: Uh-huh.

Rachel: Whose side are you on?

Melissa: Mine.

Rachel: Good. Then, we need to make an impact on your mother. We need to let her know in some way that what she did to convey to a little girl, an innocent little girl with the same capacities as everyone else, that she wasn't good enough, was not okay. Was totally unacceptable.

Melissa: Uh-huh.

Rachel: Do you want a message from God? Is there anybody that could let her know that, or shall we just burn her?

Melissa: (Pause) I don't know. Maybe a message from God, since she's a religious person.

Rachel: She is?

Melissa: Yeah.

Rachel: That would be a good choice then. She might listen to God?

Melissa: Yes.

Rachel: Okay. So I would like you to imagine God, in whatever form that makes sense to you, telling her, standing by your side

- and when I say *your* side, I mean the side of the little girl you were as well as all the time in between, including the person you are today. So, there's going to be you as a little child and there's going to be you today, standing behind God. And God is going to face your mother. What do you imagine He says?

[I see the helpless look on her face and add:]

Do you need me to help you with that?

Melissa: Um … I need you to help me.

Rachel: Okay. Well, I'm not God, but I certainly have a strong view in this case, and I'd be inclined to say to her: "Anne Marie, I am God speaking and you are a religious person. You need to listen to me. Without meaning to, perhaps, you have done some terrible damage as a mother. Because you have allowed your daughter, Melissa, to believe that she's not good enough. That there's something wrong with her and that's she's different and is never going to be as good as anyone else. And that was a horrible thing you did. And you need to apologize to her, and you need to tell her that you were wrong. That it was not her fault. That it was an unloving, undeserved thing that you said. And I want you to recant. And I'm God speaking to you so you better listen."

Notice what happens. Is your mother listening, now, finally?

Melissa: Yes.

Rachel: I would think so. Has God gotten through to her? I mean, it's God. It's hard to argue with the omnipotent, omniscient force in the universe.

Melissa: Uh-huh.

Rachel: And God has told her that she was wrong to say that about you and that she needs to apologize now. What happens,

Melissa? What does your mother do?

Melissa: I feel still like … part of me feels that she'll never change, no matter what.

Rachel: Give her a chance Melissa. I know that you've been so deeply hurt by this person that it's hard for you to believe. But God just spoke to her. And let yourself imagine that, you know, if she had God actually talking to her straight up like that, maybe it would have an impact.

[I suspect that Melissa needs some corrective experience with her mother, so I give it another try.]

Melissa: Uh-huh.

Rachel: And see if you can imagine the remote possibility that she would actually turn to you and have an apology on her lips or even a sad, remorseful look on her face. Anything that would let you know that God had affected her. What do you see? What do you hear?

Melissa: I do see her feeling sorry.

Rachel: Ah. Good.

Melissa: She's, um, sorry for what she did.

Rachel: She is?

Melissa: I don't see her being a completely different person.

Rachel: Well, maybe not, but let's just go with her feeling sorry God has demanded an apology from her. So, I'd like you to imagine listening to your mother apologize to you and repeating what you hear her say.

(Long pause) And what is her apology?

Melissa: Her just saying: "I'm sorry. I don't know how it came to this."

Rachel: Anything else?

Melissa: I see an image of her hugging me and crying.

> [This is what the child in her needed, but never received.]

Rachel: And how do you feel? She's hugging you and crying. Is that good enough for you or do you need more from her? I don't hear that she's taken full responsibility. She said, "I don't know how it came to this." Do you need her to be more accountable? Or are you satisfied with this hug and quasi apology?

Melissa: I'm satisfied.

Rachel: Do you feel that she's truly sorry?

Melissa: Yes.

Rachel: Do you believe that? Do you let that register?

Melissa: Yes.

Rachel: Okay, let it register that your mother said horrible things to you that made you believe you were not good enough. And you've had that belief your entire life. And now, she's sorry, and she's hugging you, and she's crying, and you believe her. You believe her?

Melissa: Uh-huh.

Rachel: And if you were to believe her, what would you now believe about yourself?

(Silence.) If it isn't true that you're just not good enough, what *is* true now, when you realize that this was a messed up thing that your mother led you to believe? What would be true? And if you're not sure, ask your mother.

Melissa: I just feel more accepted.

Rachel: More accepted by her? Or do you mean more accept-able?

Melissa: More acceptable.

Rachel: You feel more acceptable. So, is it true, then, that you could be good enough, just as good as anyone else?

Melissa: Um, I don't know.

Rachel: Well, if it's *not* true that you're just *not* good enough, does that mean that maybe you *are* good enough?

[I may be spelling out what seems patently obvious, but it is a radically new perspective for her.]

Melissa: Yes.

Rachel: Hard. It's a new thought. It's a new sense of self. It's going to be a big shift in your way of thinking about yourself. But I'd like you to try it on. I'd like you to try on: "I am good enough. Good enough. I am good enough." Or if it seems more real: "I'm as good as anyone else" or "I'm just as good as anyone else." Which would feel true right now?

Melissa: I'm just as good as anybody else.

Rachel: Okay. I want you to say that sentence over and over. As you say it, I'm going to ask you to focus on each part of the body in turn that was affected by the target. So, if you would say that sentence: "I'm just as good as anybody else" out loud please.

Melissa: "I'm just as good as anybody else."

Rachel: And focus on your jaw. Is it relaxed or tight?

Melissa: Um. In the middle.

Rachel: So, it's not really tight?

Melissa: No. But not really relaxed either. It's in the middle.

Rachel: Okay. We'll come back to the jaw. Focus on your heart. Is it all contracted and tight or is it okay?

Melissa: Like in the middle.

Rachel: What about your head?

Melissa: My head is good.

Rachel: What about your stomach when you say the statement?

Melissa: "I'm just as good as anybody else." My stomach is good.

Rachel: Focus on your shoulders and say it again.

Melissa: "I'm just as good as anybody else."

Rachel: Shoulders okay?

Melissa: Yes.

Rachel: Focus on your eyes. Say it again.

Melissa: "I'm just as good as anybody else."

Rachel: Eyes are okay?

Melissa: No.

Rachel: Eyes are not okay?

Melissa: No.

Rachel: Okay. Focus on your chest.

Melissa: "I'm just as good as anybody else." It's fine.

Rachel: Okay, now go back to your jaw. Repeat the statement: "I'm just as good as anybody else" and notice what happens in your jaw.

Melissa: "I'm just as good as anybody else." It's the same.

Rachel: And what is the objection to that statement from your jaw?

Melissa: For some reason, I still feel kind of sad.

Rachel: You feel sad?

Melissa: Uh-huh.

Rachel: Now, sadness was in your eyes. So, first look again at your jaw. That was the seat of your anxiety. What is the objection from your jaw about believing: "I'm just as good as anyone else"?

Melissa: Um … I don't know. I guess part of me still believes that I don't talk as good as everybody else.

Rachel: It's an old idea that you've been with for … how old are you?

Melissa: Twenty.

Rachel: Close to twenty years. So, it might take a little while to change. I don't hear that your jaw has a major objection, but it is just not used to this idea, it's new. And maybe a bit scary.

Melissa: Uh-huh.

Rachel: Now let's look at your eyes. Your eyes seem to have the biggest problem. There is sadness and what's that about? Is it for all the years that you believed something that wasn't true?

Melissa: Yes.

Rachel: And that *is* sad, isn't it?

Melissa: Yes.

Rachel: Is there anything your sadness needs in order to feel a little relieved?

Melissa: Um … No.

Rachel: What would allow your eyes to relax?

Melissa: Um. If I went back in time and fixed this problem.

Rachel: What I'm hearing, Melissa, is that, in a way, we *are* going back in time and fixing it, but there is grief and sadness for the years that you believed this and suffered as a result.

Melissa: Yeah.

Rachel: So, maybe you need to grieve for those lost years and for the suffering that your mother's mistaken ideas caused you. Would that be okay with you? Do you understand that that might be necessary for you?

Melissa: Yes.

Rachel: With a little time to get used to a new idea, and with grief for the years of misery that were caused by this mistaken thought, it's possible that you could begin to integrate a new picture of yourself: that you're just as good as anyone else. And if that were true, would it also be true that you could be confident in most social situations, if you were just as good as everyone else?

Melissa: Um, I think so.

Rachel: So, I think we might want to say: "I *could be* as confident as anyone else in social situations" rather than "I am," because it's not quite true for you yet.

[We are modifying the positive cognition to fit better with the place the processing has taken her.]

Melissa: Uh-huh.

Rachel: We could make that statement "I could be" and then, would that seem true right now?

Melissa: Part of me is still kind of set back a little bit.

Rachel: You might have to live with it a bit. You might have to live with that idea that you could be confident in social situations because you are just as good as anybody else.

Melissa: Yeah.

Rachel: And then, when we get together for the follow-up, we'll come back and see where you are with it at that point in time.

[I sense that even when she gives verbal acquiescence, it may take some time to evaluate to what degree the processing has actually integrated this new picture into her experience of herself.]

Now, if you were at this moment to go back to the target – that time when you are walking along with Todd and Courtney and she's all chatty and you're unable to speak clearly and you feel like Todd is not paying attention to you – what level of disturbance does that experience have for you now on a scale from zero to ten?

Melissa: Um …

Rachel: Let a number pop into your mind. Is it still disturbing to you?

Melissa: Not as much.

Rachel: Where would it be?

Melissa: Maybe a four.

Rachel: And what prevents it from being a zero?

Melissa: It just still bugs me that I acted that way. That I couldn't be different.

Rachel: Do you understand why, with the belief system you were holding from your mom, that it was impossible for you to be different then? Do you understand that?

Melissa: Yes.

Rachel: And could you be different now?

Melissa: I'll try.

Rachel: So, you could be.

Melissa: Yes.

Rachel: Part of what you're struggling with is: you can't go back and change the past. But you can change your response to it.

Melissa: Yeah.

Rachel: And recognize that when you were all frozen up like that, it was because your mother had communicated to you – probably in a thousand different ways – that you were just not good enough.

Melissa: Yeah.

Rachel: And when you drop that idea - when you really let it go – then you can see that you don't have to be that way going forward. Can you get that?

Melissa: Yes.

Rachel: And when you get that, does the level of disturbance change? Or does it stay the same?

Melissa: Um. It changes.

Rachel: And where does it go?

Melissa: Uh … I don't know.

Rachel: Well, just ask a number to pop into your mind.

Melissa: It still bugs me a little bit.

Rachel: A little bit, so what would that "little bit" number be? What number would be a little bit?

Melissa: Like a two?

Rachel: A two. Okay. Let's live with a two for now. And since the processing may continue, by the time you come back, that may have adjusted lower, or there may be something else that's needing to come up that we may have to look at.

Melissa: Uh-huh.

Rachel: Okay? Is this a good time to stop then?

Melissa: Yes.

Rachel: Okay. It's very hard to shift a deep belief coming from someone you were totally dependent on and someone you loved, because all children love their parents. Even if their parents are abusive.

Melissa: Mhmm.

Rachel: It's very difficult. But I think you've made a huge step in that direction, Melissa.

Melissa: Okay.

Rachel: So, good for you! And now, because you are as good as anyone else, because you matter, you need to take really good care of yourself. Okay?

Melissa: Okay.

Follow-up Session

In the processing session, we had introduced and developed the new positive belief for Melissa that she was as good as anyone else. She had learned that her negative beliefs about herself were fed by her mother's criticalness, and it was time to let them go. It is as if we had constructed a bridge into territory that was largely unfamiliar to her, based on her prior set of beliefs and experience. Now, we needed to shore up the bridge to ensure that it would be solid enough to stand up in situations that had previously been anxiety provoking for her.

It happened that a new school year was about to begin. This presented a perfect opportunity for Melissa to put her new learning into effect. I decided to use a combination of hypnotherapy and processing with bilateral stimulation to prepare her for the new school term, and to move forward from there into her life in the future.

Melissa had experienced hypnosis in our prior therapy and already had a safe place up in the mountains in the snow. I had her visualize herself as "the new Melissa," the real Melissa who was relaxed and calm, with the new positive thoughts that had been installed in the processing session. We then added the resources she had chosen for her EMDR work into her safe place so that she would know that they were always there, inside of her, and could be called upon any time they might be helpful to her.

We proceeded to visualize the first day of school, going through each element of her day, step by step, the way she would *like* it to be. For example, she imagined making contact with another student and feeling comfortable with the conversation. When other students arrived, she mentioned that she was feeling "calm, confident and comfortable." "I don't feel out of place," she commented. "I feel like I belong here."

Throughout her day, Melissa imagined keeping a running dialogue in her head of positive thoughts such as: "I'm as good as anyone else," "I'm calm and confident," and "I belong here" as she went to each class; then, to work after class; and then, to her cross country practice after work. In each situation, she smiled and reached out to other people, initiating conversation, and reminding herself that she was just like everybody else.

We looked forward in time - a day, a month, six months – to a time when she had friends and was going out with them to a barbecue. Melissa said: "I'm feeling fine and ready to have a good time at the barbecue, knowing I've changed. And reminding myself to keep calm and relaxed, just like I was the last six months." This approach had, by then, become second nature to her. She didn't need to think about it. It was her true self coming through.

Then, I asked her how she would respond if a circumstance arose where she began to doubt herself and feel anxious. Melissa replied: "Not put myself down about it. Just go on and deal with it and not hide in the corner like I would usually do in the past." The part that used to hide in the corner she identified as a child of thirteen whom she could now support and mentor. That child part had always felt alone and afraid. Now she felt "uplifted" with the adult part of Melissa to turn to for support and guidance. "We are living a happier life now that we know we have each other."

They ended the session hand in hand, feeling, she said, "comforted and comfortable." "I think she's just like everybody else," Melissa concluded. "She just needs a hand."

If that hand was not there in the way we needed when we were children, the work may bring us to the place where we can learn to be there for ourselves. Melissa's mother, like Ryan's mother, was unable to deliver the support and empathy that would have fostered autonomy and self-confidence. But whereas Ryan preferred to give up on himself rather than give up on his mother, Melissa was able to look inward and to learn how to parent her inner child in the way she needed now.

There is always the possibility that human beings can transcend the trauma of the past to become the fully func-tioning adults we were meant to be. Therein lies the hope for all of us. [36]

---

[36] The transcript of the follow-up session with Melissa is located in Appendix C.

Concluding Remarks:

Why EMDR?

Why EMDR?

This is the moment to look back over what has been written and put on the finishing touches. What I want to offer are some reflections on what has been presented in the last eight chapters of this book.

I have detailed the process of working with nine different clients on nine different issues. You have been given an inside view of EMDR therapy with each of these cases. You have seen how they all started out in a stuck place characterized by negative beliefs, feelings and behavior patterns that were adversely affecting their lives. And you have watched as they transformed these beliefs, feelings and behaviors to move forward in the direction of the goals they had set for their therapy. How could one doubt that change is possible? You have been an eyewitness to the intimacy of the drama as the change process unfolds.

But, you might wonder, how long will the change last? I, too, felt a need to track this for myself, just to be sure. Therefore, I sent out an EMDR follow-up form to eighteen of the EMDR clients I had worked with at least six months after their work. Ten of the eighteen responded. Here are some sample questions I asked and the results I received:

Do you feel that you accomplished the goal you had for this work?

    not at all ____ somewhat __1__ most definitely __9__

Would you recommend this therapy to others?

    never ____ maybe ____ most definitely __10___

Overall, what is your level of satisfaction with the EMDR therapy you received?

dissatisfied _____ satisfied __1__ very satisfied __9__

I also inquired about whether any of their symptoms had come back. The results were split between "none at all" and "some" (with nobody saying they were back where they started).

Some comments from the group that said "none at all" were:

1. *I can look back on the situation/problem as if I am an objective observer. I don't feel angry or upset about it anymore. Not only that, but it has generalized to many other situations. It has helped me to not take others' actions so personally.*

2. *I felt free from the negative thoughts I was having consciously and most likely subconsciously.*

3. *I'm no longer stuck in the life I had made for myself that I was afraid to change. I know I will never go back to the place I was before the EMDR, and that I'm a much happier person now.*

For these clients, as you can hear in their own words, the EMDR work they did was a life-changing experience. These are clients like the clients you have met in this book. They were all struggling with major problems – acute recent trauma, depression, social anxiety and so on – problems that deeply affected the quality of their lives. To think that they felt freed from the grips of their issue in the course of – not years or even months – but in five hours is simply astonishing.

What about clients that answered that "some" of their symptoms had come back? What I learned is that while symptoms may recur, the key question is not whether they recur, but how the clients are handling them.

Consider the following four examples:

1. *I felt like I had a physical block, something that was stopping or sabotaging me from taking positive action. I don't experience that block anymore. I still sometimes have challenges doing the things that are positive for me in my life, but now I feel like I have more choice, rather than being blocked internally.*

2. *Mostly I'm pretty good with keeping the focus in the proper place. There are a few lapses - but very infrequent.*

3. *EMDR has definitely instilled a new sense of self-confidence in me: I know I can handle crises well. The reason I wrote "somewhat" (to the first question) and "some"(to this question) is that I still have thoughts about my traumatic experience and my attacker every day - this is the part that I think will go away with time. However, I can usually remember the incident without experiencing the trauma all over again, which is where the EMDR helped.*

4. *At times I feel a <u>little</u> anxiety in social situations, but I am able to control it and reduce its impact. Nothing close to the way I used to react to anxious feelings.*

What is to be concluded from these comments is, first, that EMDR does not erase memory. The client will remember what has occurred, whether they do so frequently or infrequently. However, the level of disturbance will have changed dramatically. As the client in #3 recognizes, she can remember the incident without experiencing the trauma all over again. In the case of acute recent trauma, as in her particular example, one would expect that the frequency of memories would decrease over time. However, the *moral* nature of the trauma will not change as a result of the EMDR work. If it was a horrible event such as an assault, an attempted rape or a suicide, it will always be a horrible event. What is new and significant is that, following the work, the survivor will be in a mental state that allows them to cope with it.

Second, EMDR opens up the possibility of new ways of thinking, feeling and behaving. One is no longer condemned to repeat the same mode of reacting every time one is triggered. But while EMDR opens new options, it does not compel one to follow them. We have stressed this point in Chapter Six. It will always be a matter of choice. As the clients in #1 and #4 above acknowledge, the symptoms may arise, but they can react to them differently. Most often, people will decide to adopt these new, more positive alternatives, since constructive change of this sort is the reason they undertook the therapy. They may have "lapses" due to life stressors and human frailties, but generally they, like the client in #2, can "keep the focus in the proper place."

Finally, we need to keep in mind the remarkable time frame in which these changes have been realized to truly appreciate the dramatic impact of this work. Normally, therapy for these issues would take months and often years to resolve. And for some clients, even after spending months and years in therapy, they still may not have accomplished their goals. For example, earlier I spoke about a woman with a major depressive disorder who had spent fourteen years in therapy and was hospitalized twice for extended periods of time with no improvement. After EMDR, her depression lifted and she was able to move on with her life. For all the cases in this book, as well as in my practice since adopting this format, only **five** hours of EMDR work have been utilized to accomplish these monumental changes. I consider this fact alone sufficient reason to write a book.

Admittedly, this is still an extraordinarily small sample and the follow-up evaluation in no way constitutes a significant experimental result. I am not claiming to provide research data. All the same, the follow-up reports offer anecdotal evidence of the life-changing experience that clients have had in their EMDR therapy and how that experience has endured.

Why, we might ask, does this therapy work so remarkably well? I believe there are two elements to be taken into account in response to this question.

The first lies in the EMDR theory itself and, specifically, in the elements of the protocol. Even when I was not making explicit reference to the protocol during the processing with a client, it was always there in the background, informing the work and, so to speak, lighting the path. It is the substructure on which the work is grounded.

In the writing of this book, I not only exposed my therapeutic process to the reader, I also exposed it to myself. I got to stand back and take a frank look at what I had actually said and done in each therapy session. There was nowhere to hide. I couldn't help but notice when I had left things out, forgotten specific elements of the procedure, gone off on a tangent, or made a questionable remark. But, despite any shortcomings on my part, the protocol kept me on track. It was the compass I needed in order to be a companion and, at times, a guide for my client's journey.

In the protocol, the *issue* provides the focus. It defines the contract we have with the client and what they are there to address. The issue tells us where the client is lost or stuck and where they hope to end up. If the issue is defined too broadly, we can open up a myriad of channels – much like different paths in the woods – each heading off in a different direction. Following a jumble of paths may keep us wandering around for a much longer time than is helpful or necessary. Since time is deliberately condensed in this model, maintaining focus on the issue is critical.

The *target* gives us an X-ray of the difficulty. What is causing the block? What is holding this person back? What needs to be released so that the client can move forward in the direction they want to go?

The *feelings* flesh out the form in which this difficulty is experienced by the client on both the affective and somatic levels. They are touchstones we can turn to in order to assess our progress. Have we taken steps in the right direction, or are we going around in circles? Are we still lost in the woods, or is there an end in sight?

The level of disturbance, as represented by the *SUDS*, indicates the depth of the difficulty experienced by the client at the starting point. It operates as an indispensable gauge – a way of calibrating our progress. I tell my clients: you will know it is working when the level of disturbance goes down. At bottom, that is the litmus test for success of the process.

The *positive cognition* represents the goal of the work as understood at the outset and, possibly, as modified at the end point. The level of truth as expressed in the *VOC* is like the inverted correlate of the level of disturbance. As the former goes up, the latter goes down.

Thus, we are not left to wander aimlessly in the woods looking for proverbial breadcrumbs. The territory can be charted, measured and appraised by the key ingredients of the protocol. They form our guidebook for the change process.

I think of myself as a companion and guide for the process. I would call my approach "interactive." It can be non-directive when the client's process is moving forward readily, as in the case of Sam. When the client is stuck and looping, or has difficulty seeing options as, for example, in the case of Trevor or Melissa, I will make suggestions which they can accept or refuse. I prefer not to call my style "directive" in as much as I offer suggestions rather than commands. In the end, it is the client's process that determines the direction of change.

The other factor that accounts for the effectiveness of EMDR is, undoubtedly, the bilateral stimulation. It allows our brains to make new connections that move us forward. It supplies an energy that fuels the process of change. Once I had a client who doubted that the bilateral stimulation was making any difference. I readily agreed to turn the scanner off. Within a few moments, she noticed an appreciable difference. Her doubts allayed, she asked me to "please, turn it back on again."

Whatever explanation finally comes to dominate our thinking about what makes bilateral stimulation effective, the fact that it *is* effective is self-evident to anyone who has experienced this work, either in the client or therapist role. What may look like "ordinary therapy" in a transcript is actually powered by the bilateral stimulation that accompanies it. Bilateral stimulation galvanizes the work and takes it to a new level.

In the more than thirty-five years I have been a therapist, I have never experienced a methodology as fast and effective as EMDR. Consider this book as three hundred pages of testimony in response to the question: "Why EMDR?" The inescapable conclusion is that Eye Movement Desensitization and Reprocessing allows us to find a way out of deep personal suffering at lightning speed. It is an elixir of change.

Submissiveness: Case of Danielle

Follow-up Session

Case of Danielle: Follow-up Session

Rachel: Okay. So, I'd like you now to just let go of what's going on at work, what's going on in your outside life, what's going on in your relationships with everybody except Nils, and just focus your attention on your relationship with Nils. That's what you're thinking about right now. The things that you love about Nils. The things that frustrate you. The times that work really well between you. And the times that seem to be problematic. It's all a package. Just think about the relationship with him. And when I turn on the scanner, I'm going to ask you, based on the work that we've done, how do you see the relationship moving forward in terms of what you would like to accomplish with Nils? In terms of what you need in order to be more honoring of yourself with him? Got it?

Danielle: Yes.

Rachel: Okay. And just let me know what comes up for you.

Danielle: Well, the first thing that comes up is that I need to spend a good amount of time every day reflecting on my needs. I don't do that right now. I don't look at what I want with him or how I want our days and nights to be. I think that's one of the biggest things that I need to do for myself.

Rachel: So, like you were saying, you can't really put in effect what you want or need if you're not aware of it.

Danielle: Correct. I think that looking at and making sure I'm addressing and, you know, putting it down is really important. Like journaling in the morning. I think would be an amazing thing to look at - what happened the day before, how I felt about it, how I'm feeling this morning, then the next day – I think that would be just an amazing, amazing thing. And then, being able to talk with him about certain issues that come up that I feel need to be addressed.

Rachel: Okay. So the first obstacle that you will overcome is the need for you to take the time to figure out what you want and feel. And to be in touch with yourself.

Danielle: Exactly.

Rachel: And the suggestion that you made was that you could journal in the morning. That would be one possibility.

Danielle: That's one possibility.

Rachel: Okay. What would get in the way of that?

Danielle: Being tired. Not getting up early enough. Like: "Oh, I don't feel like doing it." You know. Things like that. There is no reason why I couldn't, because I read the paper every morning, which I thoroughly enjoy doing.

Rachel: So, reading the paper is like a reward for you. You really like it.

Danielle: It really is a big reward for me. I really enjoy it very, very much.

Rachel: Could you imagine yourself setting it up that you don't get to read the paper until you've done at least some journaling?

Danielle: Yeah. That's what I'm thinking is to get up, grab a coffee, have my journal pad somewhere safely put away where he can't get it and look at it, because I don't want him reading it.

Rachel: That's right. You need to have your privacy.

Danielle: And I really, really need to be doing that. And then grab it and go. And that's another reason why I need my computer to be separate from his. I want to either be able to type in a password or not have him in there at all. He just follows me around all the time when I get up and it bothers me.

Rachel: And do you think that you might be able to find an affordable computer? Does it seem reasonable to expect that you could find one in the next so many months?

Danielle: I think it is reasonable, because I'm getting a commission check and I'm getting this refund from Mary Kay. I'll be able to get a laptop and bring the laptop with me wherever I go in the house, because we have wireless. So, if he's in the room, I'll just leave him and say I need to be alone.

Rachel: Okay. So, it seems like you're trying on this idea and it fits for you. Is that your feeling about it?

Danielle: Oh yeah. It fits really well. I'm too tired at night. I just know I won't do it at night. I'm more emotionally aware in the morning. I think that, by the nighttime, my ego's taken over and walls have gone up.

Rachel: Okay. It sounds like this is a plan that feels right for you.

Danielle: It does.

Rachel: And what it does is it tunes you in to what's going on inside of you - what you're wanting and needing. You just make the space available. The very fact that by opening your pad to journal, you're committed to knowing is what provokes that material to come up. It's like you've expressed interest in it and, then, it arises. "Well, actually, this is bothering me." "Well, actually, that's okay, but that's not." You know - it comes. So, it's putting yourself in that position that will probably be sufficient, if you can do it on a regular basis.

Danielle: Yeah.

Rachel: Okay. Now you begin to become aware, on a regular basis, of what you need and want. And what are some of the things that you think you might want to deal with differently with Nils? What do you anticipate? You do know some of those now.

Danielle: Yeah. I think that I'd like to have … well, gosh, it's his teasing. He always teases me, and sometimes I just lose patience with him, because he teases me all the time. I need to be able to either deflect it or not care and just joke back. That's one thing.

Rachel: Okay. So, handling his teasing is the first thing that comes up.

Danielle: Yup.

Rachel: And what you said was that you need to find a way to deal with it. Maybe the way you find varies depending on how you feel about it in the moment. So, let's look at several different possibilities.

Danielle: Well, I could just say that I'm not in the mood for the teasing right now and walk away.

Rachel: You could walk away. Because at that moment in time, you just don't want to hear it.

Danielle: Right.

Rachel: Okay. So, that's one possibility.

Danielle: I could sit down and talk with him and say: "You know what? I know teasing is a part of who you are. It's how you show affection. But for me, sometimes it doesn't feel that way. Sometimes it feels bad, and I feel like I have to defend myself. Sometimes I don't even understand that you're teasing. It's very dry humor and I just don't understand. So, if you start doing something that I feel is teasing and I'm just not able to deal with it, I'm just going to say: "Now is not a good time to be teasing me, okay? And I ask that you respect that and not keep teasing me."

Rachel: So, that puts it in his court - whether he's going to do that or not.

Danielle: Yup. But I can walk away if he doesn't.

Rachel: And, then, you would walk away if he doesn't cooperate. Are there also times when you might even tolerate his teasing?

Danielle: Sometimes. Yeah. Sometimes I'll tease him back.

Rachel: Is there any time when it's fun? Where you actually could say it's kind of a game, and you don't mind? Is it sometimes okay with you to tease each other, or is that a stretch?

Danielle: Yeah. Sometimes it is. Sometimes. It depends on what he's teasing me about.

Rachel: Right. Okay. You could imagine situations where it could be okay.

Danielle: Yeah, sometimes.

Rachel: Okay. So, how will you know which situation it is? Is it one where it bugs the hell out of you and you have to walk away? Is it one where you can tolerate it? Is it one where you can give it back or even enjoy it?

Danielle: Well, I think I have to just be aware of how I'm feeling right then.

Rachel: And then, when you're aware of that …

Danielle: Then, I have to react accordingly. Either I tease back or I tell him it's not a good time. That it's not a good time to be teasing me. I'm just not in a good space right now, so I'm not receptive to your teasing right now.

Rachel: Exactly. So we come back to being in touch with your own feelings and responses.

Danielle: When it's happening.

Rachel: Which means you might have to take a moment to check it out. Not just react.

Danielle: Right.

Rachel: And that there isn't a single way to handle his teasing. It depends. Sometimes it's fun. Sometimes it sucks. Sometimes it's okay.

Danielle: Well, I don't think it's ever fun.

Rachel: Okay. That's a stretch.

Danielle: Yeah. Sometimes it's kind of like: "Oh, okay," you know. I don't think I'd ever wake up in the morning and want to have a teasing match with Nils.

Rachel: Okay. It's not your favorite. Do you feel like you could walk through in your mind how you would react when Nils is teasing? Imagine a situation and how you would react. Look at a couple of possibilities.

Danielle: Well, what I could do is … kind of … 'cause a lot of times what he does is – it's just offhanded remarks. He's not turned towards me totally or whatever, but I could turn him towards me and hold his face and say: "Nils, this is just not a good time. I love you. I need you to not tease me right now." And, then, he'll probably make a joke. Whenever I'm talking seriously, he always makes a joke. He doesn't like getting that close, so he'll make a joke. And that's hard. But if he makes a joke, I'll just say: "You know, I know maybe you're uncomfortable with this, but this is serious for me, so I'd appreciate it if you would respect that."

Rachel: Let's imagine that Nils makes a joke about something that you feel is no joking matter. And look at how you're going to handle a situation like that which could happen with him.

Danielle: Oh, yes.

Rachel: And, you know, sometimes he's joking because he's defensive. You know, sometimes he's joking because he doesn't want to acknowledge his accountability.

Danielle: Right. He just wants to deflect.

Rachel: Exactly. And sometimes it may be because he's stubborn.

Danielle: Yeah.

Rachel: So, what does that say about you?

Danielle: I don't understand the question.

Rachel: Exactly. What does it say about you that sometimes he deflects, sometimes he won't be accountable, and sometimes he is stubborn. What does that say about you when he's joking?

Danielle: Just that he's Nils. I don't think he does that to be mean. I don't feel badly. I don't feel guilty about it or anything. Is that what you mean? I don't have any emotional attachment to his joking, except for just being frustrated that he's always joking.

Rachel: So, you could have a variety of different responses to it. But all of them would start with: "It's not about me."

Danielle: Absolutely.

Rachel: Can you imagine actually saying that in your mind?

Danielle: "It's not about me." Yeah, I could.

Rachel: "That's Nils. That's what he does. It's not about me." Try that on and see how that feels for you.

Danielle: "It's not about me." It feels good.

Rachel: Now, visualize a couple of different scenarios where he's joking, and you start with that statement, and then follow it with different responses depending on what feels right.

Danielle: Saying "it's not about me" would center me more. So, when he is joking, I can just look at him with this twinkle in my eye and just say: "Nils, it's not really a joking matter, but you can go ahead and joke. I know you're uncomfortable with this." Just be very straightforward like I want to be. Like I am. And not get upset about it and frustrated because…it's not about me.

Rachel: And it sounds like that sentence – that statement – is actually very helpful for you.

Danielle: Yeah. I don't assume that I know why he's doing what … why he's joking.

Rachel: Or that it has anything to do with you as a person – your value as a person, or that you've just blown it. You've just done something stupid. You've just let him down. You're a bad wife. You're a bad woman. I almost said "mother." Well, you are kind of a mother in some ways. That it really isn't about you, and if you get that he's just doing his thing.

Danielle: Right.

Rachel: Then you don't have to be – you might be annoyed that he acts like that, but it isn't something that reflects on you.

Danielle: Well, I'm trying to get water from a stone, you know. It's stupid. It's like always doing the same thing and expecting a different result. It's just not going to happen with him.

Rachel: So, sometimes it sounds like the statement: "That's how he is" or "You can't get water from a stone" or "I can't change him" might also be helpful. Like: "It's not about me."

Danielle: Yup.

Rachel: Which statement would you pick that feels the most powerful for you – the most helpful?

Danielle: "Oh, that's just Nils."

Rachel: "That's just Nils." Okay.

Danielle: "There he goes again." I could make him like a cartoon. I've always thought he'd make a great cartoon character.

Rachel: I think of Popeye.

Danielle: Yeah. I know.

Rachel: Okay. Imagine yourself moving forward armed with three new tools. One is you're aware of what you want and need, and that's because you're spending time journaling and processing so you know what you feel. The second is that much of what goes on is not about you and you can remind yourself of that. And the third is: "That's just Nils. There he goes again." And let's look at a couple of circumstances that have bothered you in the past and how you might handle them in the future with these three different options. What comes up? Maybe you could pick that he wants you to dress sexy. Or maybe you could pick that he's mad that you're late.

Danielle: Okay. Well, the first one that came up is that he wants to have anal sex. He always talks about it and, instead of being upset because I'm not giving him everything he wants or I'm not as open minded or kinky as he would like or as other women might be or whatever - that his desire for that is just Nils being Nils, and I don't have to do anything that I don't want to do. I don't have to feel less because of that. If he says it to me like last time when he said it, like begging me during sex - gosh, I don't know what I would do.

Rachel: So, with many of the circumstances, just saying no and refusing and recognizing that you don't have to feel less because you don't want it would work. But what happens when he pulls out all stops and starts begging for it?

Danielle: I would just tell him it's not going to happen. It's not going to happen, so stop begging. And try to divert him, I guess. Do something else, instead of him being so fixated on it. There are two things. There's the moment when you're having sex when you could stop everything and start talking – which is a drag. Or I could divert him into being interested in something else. We could do a different position or just do something else, so that he stops thinking about that. And, then, I would talk to him later about it and say: "This is not a good time for you to be asking for that. It just puts a damper on the whole experience."

Rachel: So, what he'd be learning is that it actually affects you in a negative way that makes you less sexual and less willing. He probably didn't understand that or he wouldn't be pushing for it.

Danielle: Exactly. Right. It's a downer. It's a total downer for me. And I would explain to him that he doesn't like when I watch country music videos – it's a real downer for him. He just really doesn't like it. So, it's like that. It's like, in the middle of sex, me putting on a country music video – how would he feel?

Rachel: There you go. Perfect. Great. And in none of those responses, did I hear you feeling guilty or bad.

Danielle: No. It's never with that situation. It's not very hard for me to say how I feel and what I want. I wish that I could be okay with it, but I don't feel bad for not wanting it. I guess that's the difference.

Rachel: Are there any times when you think you would be okay with it? The face says "no."

Danielle: No.

Rachel: No. It's not something that sometimes is okay with you and sometimes isn't. It's really just *not okay*. It's not like dressing up sexy is sometimes okay. It's not your thing. Period.

Danielle: No. It's not my thing. It's dirty. It hurts. I just don't like it. And did you want me to imagine another situation?

Rachel: Yeah.

Danielle: Let's see. Well, I guess about doing the house – painting and doing décor in the house. He could be resistant about doing a particular thing. So, instead of thinking he's just doing that to be resistant on purpose – I don't think he objects because he doesn't trust what I'm doing. I think it's because he doesn't want *me* to spend any money on it because *he* doesn't want to spend any money on it. And he's kind of lazy, so he doesn't want to do the work himself. For example, I need him to help me get rid of this rug. I can't do it myself because it's too big, and he just constantly refuses. I probably could get somebody else to help me, so that's maybe what I'll do.

Rachel: Well, perhaps if he's lazy and he's cheap, you'll find out which is the more important if you say: "Well, I'm going to pay somebody to do it." Then either his cheapness will make him say: "No, I'll do it" or his laziness will say: "Okay. Pay somebody." Right?

Danielle: Exactly.

Rachel: But, then, it's his choice and you still get it done. And it doesn't reflect on you.

Danielle: I get it out. Take it to the dump. You know, after my session last time, he actually said: "Well, let's talk about redecorating the back room."

Rachel: (smiling) Was he listening in?

Danielle: No. But I told him it's so frustrating, because I just want our home to be pretty and he's just a stick in the mud, stick in the mud, stick in the mud, and I don't understand. It's so frustrating. So he started changing his tune a little bit. I do think a lot of it is laziness or cheapness or both. Yeah.

Rachel: Okay. Remember our statement: "That's Nils."

Danielle: "That's just Nils."

Rachel: "That's just Nils. That's how he is."

Danielle: Doesn't mean it's not going to happen because that's just Nils. Let's just figure out some way to go around it. Yup. That was exciting. I can't wait to redo that room! Oh God, it's terrible.

Rachel: We're down to the last few moments. Is there anything else that you feel you want to run through that may have been blocked for you in the past, but maybe could be different for the future? Any other example that you feel we need to cover where it's been frustrating with him?

Danielle: Well, I mean, there are so many different things that are frustrating with him.

Rachel: Pick your biggest.

Danielle: Well, let me think. Always telling me how to put the coffee filter in the coffee pot. Every day he'd ask: "Did you fold the coffee filter?" That really bothered me, so I got a new one that has a permanent filter and now, I don't have to put a coffee filter in it or fold it anymore. That kind of solved the problem.

Rachel: Well, that was a great way to deal with that problem! So, if he harps on something repeatedly …

Danielle: Yes. He harps. He corrects me all the time. He always tells me how to do things.

Rachel: Okay. That's a good one, because it can happen a lot. Sometimes you can find an alternative. Like in this case, he can't talk to you about folding the filter anymore because there isn't one. But sometimes he's still going to be correcting you.

Danielle: Even on stuff that he's told me about a million times. Just last night he did it. He has this way of wringing out a wet towel. And he does it like this. And I do it like that. (She shows two different movements.)

Rachel: How dare you!

Danielle: I know. He goes: "This is just better because you do this." I go: "Oh, that's cool. You've shown that to me before. I just can't really do that very well." "Well," he says, "it's just so much better, you know." It's like I say: "Okay. I'm not going to do it, but you can show me."

Rachel: Okay. So, it sounds to me that what you're doing is you're basically tolerating that it's just Nils and not changing your behavior.

Danielle: Yeah. Exactly. And not like: "Oh my God, here he goes again!" because I would be dead of frustration if I kept doing that. Expecting something else from him is unrealistic. I'm not going to change who he is.

Rachel: So it's back to: "That's Nils. That's who he is." That's where that came in. Are there any circumstances where you feel like that wouldn't be enough? Where his correcting really bugs the hell out of you?

Danielle: Yeah. I can see some times where it would be construed as insulting - like I don't know what I'm doing - and I could just look at him and say: "You know, I know what I'm doing. I know you're trying to help, but I'd really just appreciate if you'd leave me alone with this right now. Let me fail if I'm going to fail. And let me succeed if I'm going to succeed. It's okay."

Rachel: So, you could actually stop him if you let him know that you found it insulting.

Danielle: Yeah.

Rachel: Okay. That could work. Will he stop?

Danielle: He might. He might complain about it a little. "Well, I'm just trying to help. I don't know why you're upset."

Rachel: If he complains, what would you do with that?

Danielle: I'd say: "I really appreciate you wanting to help." I think it's really important for him to feel valued and important. I think that is probably one of the biggest problems in our relationship. If we could figure out a way for him to feel more important, I think it would help, so he doesn't feel like he has to do that correcting all the time. I think he feels like - what is he contributing? I guess, because the money isn't really happening for him - but that's okay.

Rachel: And those are choices he's made.

Danielle: Exactly. So I can't fix it for him. He has to fix it for himself.

Rachel: Can you say that again?

Danielle: I can't fix it for him. He has to fix it for himself.

Rachel: So, if he's not contributing, that's not your responsibility.

Danielle: Exactly.

Rachel: Actually, you would like him to contribute.

Danielle: I would. I would like him to contribute more. It would be better. Instead of complaining about it or not doing a very good job, you know? I ask him sometimes to – you know, 'cause he's home a lot – I say: "Could you vacuum and dust the living room?" And he just doesn't do a good job. He does a shitty job. I don't tell him he does a shitty job; I just see. I tell him "thank you and I really appreciate you doing that" and, then, I go over and see this huge amount of stuff that he missed, and I just leave it. He tried.

Rachel: Is that okay with you? Does that feel okay that sometimes you just accept his best efforts?

Danielle: Sometimes. Sometimes I want him to pay a little bit more attention. I think part of it is just short-changing, just being lazy.

Rachel: So, you might at some point say: "Yeah. That's great that you did that, but, you know, if you did it over here too, that would be even better."

Danielle: Right.

Rachel: You might point it out. You might not. It depends.

Danielle: Yeah. It depends. He just doesn't do a very good job, so I might just get a house cleaner.

Rachel: And then, you can't take responsibility for the fact that he doesn't feel he's contributing because, if you get a house cleaner, he won't be doing the housework. Right?

Danielle: Right. But he doesn't do it anyway. I mean, he doesn't like doing it. He doesn't do a very good job.

Rachel: Okay. So, what you need to say again: "It's not my responsibility if he chooses not to contribute."

Danielle: "It's not my responsibility if he chooses not to contribute."

Rachel: How does that feel? Is that true?

Danielle: It helps. Yeah. Yeah. It's kind of sad. I feel sad. Sometimes I feel sorry for him, you know, 'cause … that's *his* fault.

Rachel: Yeah. I know you wish something better for him.

Danielle: I do. I wish he would just get off his duff. He's a smart guy, you know.

Rachel: And, you know, a lot of times people that we love do things to disappoint us, and it's sad.

Danielle: He's better than that. And he's better than what he's exhibiting.

Rachel: I understand. So there's a sadness about that. But you can't make it different.

Danielle: No, I can't.

Rachel: And any attempts you made backfired. They didn't work. We tried to make it different. So, it's about accepting that's his choice.

Danielle: Exactly.

Rachel: My son smokes. It makes me crazy. But it's his choice. I can't stop him. You might want to think about it like that.

Danielle: Yeah. I don't really … you know, Nils smokes too. It bothers me, but … (she blows out) it's like that.

Rachel: What you went was: "Pooh!" (the sound of her blowing out). I think that was great. That may be the thing that you can do. You know? Blow it off. Literally. That – what you just did – "Pooh!" – blow it off, because there's nothing you can do.

Danielle: Exactly.

Rachel: So, that might be our last one: "Blow it off." Do you know what I mean by that now? "Nothing I can do."

Danielle: Yeah. "Nothing I can do." It's kind of a relief.

Rachel: Yeah. It is.

Danielle: People like me, we carry around a lot of a big load of responsibility for everything.

Rachel: For things that you can't be responsible for.

Danielle: Yeah. It's so silly.

Rachel: Right. You got it.

Danielle: It's so silly! It's like: "What made me so important? I can control the world." Woo-hoo!

Rachel: You're right, you can't. Exactly. Okay, I think this is a good stopping point.

Danielle: Thank you. Thank you.

Despair: Case of Ryan

Follow-up Session

Case of Ryan: Follow-Up Session

Rachel: So, I want to remind you about the issue that you were working on. And what you're hoping to accomplish in your life. That issue had to do with feeling comfortable with the connections you make with people and feeling that they were genuine. And, before you did your processing, your belief system was: "I'll never be able to connect with anyone."

Ryan: Uh-huh.

Rachel: When you finished the last EMDR processing session, you stated in your own words: *"I know I can connect with people and I need to have more experience connecting with them."*

Ryan: Okay.

Rachel: That's where we left the work the last time. So, when I turn on the scanner, I want you to reflect on how you feel about your ability to connect with other people. What comes up about that? And what are the problems that you had in the past connecting with people that made you feel that you weren't able to do that?

Ryan: Okay.

Rachel: So, think about the issue of connection with people and just let me know what comes up for you. (Pause) And what are you getting?

Ryan: I can't focus at all.

Rachel: Okay, where is your mind going?

Ryan: I'm just thinking about thinking about stuff, and why I can't think about what I'm supposed to be thinking about.

Rachel: So, maybe, start with some examples of where you feel in the past that your connections didn't work.

Ryan: Like – always. They never work.

Rachel: So, who's an example?

Ryan: Everybody I've ever met and talked with.

Rachel: Everybody you've ever met?

Ryan: Uh-huh. I don't know. I just limit my connections with people.

Rachel: And how do you do that?

Ryan: I don't know. I just don't like to include them in a lot of things. I consider myself separate from other people, and I like to keep things that way.

Rachel: And yet there obviously is a part of you that wants something deeper, and better?

Ryan: Right.

Rachel: In terms of connecting.

Ryan: Well, I imagine that exists. I mean, that would be nice to experience.

Rachel: Uh-huh and, if that were to happen, what do you feel would need to change?

Ryan: I don't know, I would have to …um … I don't know.

Rachel: Stay with that for a minute.

Ryan: I would have to not be in my head so much. I feel like there's just too much that happens in my own head to possibly ever share with another person. There's this, you know, endless divide that I'm just always … no matter what, I'm always going to be completely different from other people.

Rachel: So, there is some sense that your difference is more marked, more extreme, than the differences between other people?

Ryan: Maybe, I don't know. I feel like other people have the ability to sort of bridge that gap or something ... or ... ignore that difference or something. Um, I don't know.

Rachel: So, somehow other people don't have this obstacle, or don't believe they have this obstacle that you believe you have. And was there ever a time in your life when you felt like the obstacle wasn't there? Where you actually did connect with someone, even briefly, the way you would like to be able to connect?

Ryan: I don't know, maybe.

Rachel: And when you say "maybe," were there any examples that flew into your mind?

Ryan: I guess.

Rachel: And what examples would they be?

Ryan: This one time, I had one time with my friend Sarah. And we kind of connected, but ...

Rachel: Okay. Can you bring up that one occasion when you connected with Sarah?

Ryan: Okay.

Rachel: Do you remember that?

Ryan: Uh-huh.

Rachel: And as you feel into that situation, what do you notice about yourself?

Ryan: Um ... I don't know what you mean.

Rachel: Well, what is it that you notice about how you're feeling, thinking, acting, and behaving that's different for you than the rest of the time? What's happening for you with Sarah? Are you in your head? Partly? Completely?

Ryan: Yeah, but it seems like, I don't know ... I don't know what's different about it.

Rachel: Well, what feels different when you go there, when you remember it, Ryan? How did you cross the "endless divide?"

Ryan: I don't know, maybe I didn't. I just think I did.

Rachel: Well, when you think you did, what was different?

Ryan: I don't know; it just felt different.

Rachel: Uh-huh, so get in touch with that feeling – how it felt different – and what do you notice?

Ryan: I don't know. I don't think it felt that different.

Rachel: You're talking yourself out of it now?

Ryan: I don't know, I just can't explain it. I don't think that I really know what …

Rachel: Did it feel different because of maybe how she was being with you? You spoke a lot about not being able to get through to people, not feeling that your feelings were important to them, not feeling that other people really liked you. Those are things you've mentioned in previous sessions. Was that different with Sarah?

Ryan: I don't know. I guess I really wasn't thinking about it, you know.

Rachel: You weren't thinking about the problems?

Ryan: Maybe not.

Rachel: Uh-huh. Well, that would make a difference.

Ryan: I really don't know though. I mean, it's just … for some reason, I'm really not wanting to think about it.

Rachel: I'm sorry?

Ryan: I really don't want to think about it, for some reason.

Rachel: Can you, at least, let yourself know why thinking about it is so difficult? Or why you are blocking that?

Ryan: Um … because it's not something that I can have.

Rachel: Ah.

Ryan: So I don't like thinking about it.

Rachel: Are you sure you can't have that?

Ryan: Well, pretty sure.

Rachel: What about the statement you made after your last session that you know you *can* connect with other people?

Ryan: I don't know. I feel like it hasn't really happened much since then, so I don't know.

Rachel: What we need to get into is: what would allow that to happen? You said that when you felt a little different, in that example with Sarah, one of the things was that you weren't thinking about the problems. In other words, you weren't putting up the objection that it wasn't possible. So, what would happen if you let go of that belief that you can't connect and really let yourself imagine that you could?

Ryan: I don't know how to let go of beliefs.

Rachel: Well, you don't focus on that, you don't commit to that, and you go …

Ryan: I feel like those were extenuating circumstances that allowed me to sort of overcome those problems. I don't feel like I've ever been in a situation where the circumstances allowed me to do that. So, okay, maybe I can connect with people, but only under the right circumstances. And those have never really come about … Other than, maybe, one time.

Rachel: So, what special circumstances do you require, Ryan?

Ryan: I don't know. I guess it just needs to be the right person or something.

Rachel: What would the "right" person possess in the way of qualities or characteristics that would make them "right"?

Ryan: I don't know. Just someone I feel I could trust.

Rachel: Definitely. Someone you could trust. What else would be necessary? Or: what would allow you to trust someone?

Ryan: I don't know. What does it take to be able to trust someone? That's what I've been asking for like a hundred years.

Rachel: Yeah, and I think you've given some very good answers to that question. But you've given them in the negative – in terms of the things that stop you from trusting. Do you know what kinds of things you've mentioned that made it, for example, very hard for you to feel like you could make a connection with your mother? There's a case, a pretty clear case, of your frustration.

Ryan: Right.

Rachel: So what would be different if you could connect?

Ryan: Uh …

Rachel: Well, what is it that stops you from feeling like you connect with your mom? What does she do that blocks you?

Ryan: I don't know, just stuff.

Rachel: What stuff, Ryan?

Ryan: Um …

Rachel: Remember the things you said in the session?

Ryan: Kind of. It feels like I'm backtracking … I don't know …

Rachel: Well, there is a block up right now.

Ryan: Yeah … um …

Rachel: It's almost like you're afraid to believe this could be different for you.

Ryan: Well …

Rachel: Do you think everybody is going to be the same experience as your mother?

Ryan: No, not the same … Yeah, kind of.

Rachel: "Yeah, kind of." So, everybody has the same problem that your mother has?

Ryan: It seems like it.

Rachel: Everybody has the same problem?

Ryan: Pretty much.

Rachel: Well, I suppose that kind of whitewashes your mom, then, doesn't it? Because that means that the problem she has is just the same as anybody else.

Ryan: Right ... but you expect that ...

Rachel: Do you feel better?

Ryan: Her being my mom would allow her to sort of overcome that, I guess. I hold her to a different, maybe slightly higher standard than the rest of the world.

Rachel: Well, it sounds to me like, on the contrary, you're bringing everybody and the rest of the world down to the level of frustration that you have with your mother. And expecting that everyone will be as defensive, self-protective, unwilling to accept responsibility, unwilling to listen to you, unwilling to empathize with you, unwilling to stop and see when you're hurt. That's what you're imagining everyone in the world will be like.

Ryan: That's what it seems like.

Rachel: Yeah. Does it? Well, even in the processing work you did, there were two people in the situation you envisaged who were very different. Remember that? Who were they?

Ryan: They were made-up figments of my imagination.

Rachel: No, they were people that you brought in whom you knew personally.

Ryan: Well, yeah, but I mean ... you know ... in that circumstance.

Rachel: So, how did they behave? How were they different in your imagination?

Ryan: I don't know. They behaved in the way that, I guess, I would like them to.

Rachel: And how would that be? That was the question I was asking.

Ryan: Um … I don't know … sort of … like they cared.

Rachel: Uh-huh. So Uncle Carl and even Julia acted like they cared.

Ryan: Right.

Rachel: Okay, so that one thing that would make a difference. What else did they do?

Ryan: That was it. They cared.

Rachel: How did they show that?

Ryan: I don't know … by caring, by doing something.

Rachel: What was their caring behavior?

Ryan: I don't know how else to describe it.

Rachel: Do you remember how they acted and …

Ryan: Well, yeah …

Rachel: What did they do? Each one did different things.

Ryan: I don't know.

Rachel: You don't remember?

Ryan: Not specifically.

Rachel: Okay. Well, you remember yourself crying and "bleeding to death"?

Ryan: Right.

Rachel: And your mother being adamant that you deserved what you got? And what did Uncle Carl do?

Ryan: He … came to me and, I guess, helped me out.

Rachel: Uh-huh.

Ryan: Yeah.

Rachel: And?

Ryan: And … sort of, I don't know, he was trying to help me.

Rachel: Uh-huh. How did he do that?

Ryan: By trying to help me, I don't know. By protecting me from my mom, by trying to get her to … I don't know … look at what she did and …

Rachel: Uh-huh, right. Right, he did. He was defending you.

Ryan: Like he cared about the stuff that I cared about, I guess, basically.

Rachel: So, he could see what was important to you.

Ryan: Yeah.

Rachel: Right? And he could see that you were hurt.

Ryan: Yeah.

Rachel: Well, that's important.

Ryan: Right.

Rachel: And, he tried to stand up for you with your mom.

Ryan: Right.

Rachel: Okay, so those are some behaviors that sound like they would lead to your feeling cared about and, eventually, maybe lead to your trusting a person like that.

Ryan: I guess.

Rachel: Okay. And is there any way that you could imagine the circumstances that would allow you to trust somebody in the world? You don't need to be bleeding to death, but those characteristics would be important, I would think.

Ryan: Right, well, it doesn't seem like I can get anyone to give a shit unless I am bleeding to death.

Rachel: So, if you were to connect with someone, you would look for someone who seemed to be caring regardless of whether you were bleeding to death?

Ryan: Yeah, I guess.

Rachel: A person who recognized what was important to you and was able to protect you and empathize with your feelings.

Ryan: Uh-huh.

Rachel: Okay, so those are some of the characteristics of someone you could trust.

Ryan: Right.

Rachel: If you try to connect with people who are acting more like your mom was in that circumstance, what would be your chances of feeling a solid connection?

Ryan: Probably not so good.

Rachel: Correct. If you wanted to connect, then, the first important learning would be selecting people who seem to have characteristics that would give you hope that they would be more like uncle Carl and less like your mother was in that situation.

Ryan: Yeah.

Rachel: Have you met anybody who ever seemed to be able to understand or care about what was important to you?

Ryan: No.

Rachel: Ryan, I, for one, protest. I know you're in one of your *"Life sucks and then you die"* moods, but truthfully …

Ryan: Truthfully, not really. I don't know, it feels weird now, but it just doesn't …

Rachel: Well, I don't feel seen and heard then. Do I count?

Ryan: No, 'cause I pay you so …

Rachel: So, therefore, what I experience is invalid.

Ryan: I guess, yeah.

Rachel: Oh. So, you've eliminated me.

Ryan: Well, yeah.

Rachel: I want to share that I disagree with that because, while I do need to be paid for my time and services, my caring is my own feeling and not something you can buy.

Ryan: Right.

Rachel: And it's not just for the purpose of getting paid.

Ryan: I understand that. But it convolutes that. It just, I don't know, it invalidates it or something?

Rachel: Well, you can invalidate it if you choose. So, one of the things that we talked about is selecting a person who seems to show empathy and care and concern for your feelings. And also that you not imagine it is impossible and therefore defeat the possibility before you even begin. And you also need not to invalidate the person that you're relating to in the way that you just invalidated me.

Ryan: Right. But, how do I not do that? And also, if it's just that easy, I don't know, it just seems *too* easy.

Rachel: Well, maybe it's a lot easier than you thought.

Ryan: But then, it doesn't seem worth it.

Rachel: You don't think it's worth it to find someone whom you could trust and connect with? I thought that was your goal.

Ryan: I don't know, it was. But, for some reason …

Rachel: You're minimizing it right now in exactly the way that you do *not* want your feelings and goals and priorities to be minimized by other people. In the way your mother did.

Ryan: Right. Well, I mean, I don't know … It's just that with trust, it's not like I can just … People get invalidated. I can't control that. It's not like I choose not to trust people. It's just that I don't trust people.

Rachel: I think it is a choice, Ryan.

Ryan: Well, maybe, but …

Rachel: It doesn't become possible if you believe that everyone is going to be like your mother.

Ryan: Right, but how do I change? It's not like I choose to believe that. This is just how I see things.

Rachel: I think you do choose to believe that. I think it's easier for you to believe that everybody is as blocked and defensive as your mother is rather than face the fact that it is her particular problem. And that it's a deep-seated problem. It probably goes back to the loss of her own mother in a most horrendous way.

Ryan: Probably.

Rachel: So, you face a crossroads at this juncture. You have to make a choice.

Ryan: But then it seems like I basically already have everything that I want, and it doesn't seem that fulfilling. I mean, I have friends and whatnot who I … I don't know … I have plenty of connections, and it just doesn't seem like they're that valuable.

Rachel: Well, what I would imagine is that, as long as you're proceeding on the assumption that people basically don't, as you said, "give a shit" about you, and that, if they seem to, then you will invalidate it – it can't be trusted either because they're just a therapist that's getting paid, or because they're pretending and they don't really mean it – then, you can't have an experience of true connection. And you will do as you said – you will hold back. You will limit your connections with people.

Ryan: Right.

Rachel: So, if you want to have those beliefs, if you want to maintain them to defend and protect your mother, then you will have very limited connections going forward.

Ryan: Yeah.

Rachel: Or, do you see an alternative? And what would that alternative be?

Ryan: I don't know, to change my beliefs about that stuff, but I just don't see how to do that.

Rachel: Well, at least suspend the belief that *all* people are going to be impossible to connect with in the same way that your mother has been for you. And when you suspend that belief ...

Ryan: I don't know how to suspend my beliefs.

Rachel: That is, not take it as a foregone conclusion.

Ryan: I know what it means. I just don't know how to do that.

Rachel: You move forward, first of all selecting people who look to be potentially people that you can trust.

Ryan: But that's the thing, I never find those people.

Rachel: Well, they are out there. What would you look for? Do you remember what we said? What would you look for if you were interested in looking for people that you could connect with?

Ryan: I don't know how to connect with those people, because they know how to connect with people and I don't.

Rachel: What kind of people would you look for first? Let's start there.

Ryan: I don't know, caring, nice people. Who would ... I don't know ... listen, give a shit? Would seem interested in things?

Rachel: And, specifically, who might seem interested in you.

Ryan: There you go.

Rachel: So, you see somebody that looks like they have potential, right? Meaning, they seem to be pretty nice and caring and empathic, and you test the waters a little – that is, you share something that's important to you.

Ryan: Right.

Rachel: You talk with them. You tell them about something you're feeling or something that matters to you …

Ryan: But this never happens. I never make it. I never even meet anybody.

Rachel: Going forward in the future. Could you imagine a situation where you meet someone who has the potential?

Ryan: Yeah.

Rachel: And you test the waters by sharing with them something that's meaningful to you, some feelings that are important to you.

Ryan: Uh-huh.

Rachel: Some goals or priorities that matter to you. Okay?

Ryan: I never talk about that stuff with people.

Rachel: That's right. That would be a change in your behavior. Instead of limiting your connection by not sharing anything, you begin to open up just a little. You don't necessarily open right to the very bottom of your heart, but you open a little, and you watch and notice what happens. One possibility is that they say: "Yeah, well …" and change the subject. Or, they turn away, or walk away. Or they come back with something akin to the kind of put down that you got from your mother like: "This is bullshit" and "You don't know what you're talking about" and "You just want to …"

Ryan: Uh-huh.

Rachel: You know what I'm talking about? So, let's say they don't do that. Let's say they act more like Uncle Carl. That would be confirming. And then, maybe you decide that it would be safe to open a little more. Can you visualize that?

Ryan: Uh, I don't know. Usually I open up a little bit and then, kind of retreat again.

Rachel: Okay, that's what you did in the past.

Ryan: Right.

Rachel: If you ever opened up at all – and it sounds like you were implying that you rarely do that – you then close up like a clam right away. So we are looking at an alternative way of proceeding. You open up a little; the person shuts you down, makes you feel bad, it's game over, end of story. But, if you open up a little and the person is empathic, confirming, affirming, makes you feel like they care about you …

Ryan: I don't know; I don't trust it.

Rachel: Let's say you don't trust it *absolutely* and *completely*. But perhaps you allow yourself to wait and see if it's going to be consistent.

Ryan: Okay.

Rachel: So, if the first time, you didn't get blown out of the water by their responses, then you have the opportunity to try a little bit more …

Ryan: Okay

Rachel: On a different occasion, or on a different subject matter, or at a different time, or maybe at the same time going a little more deeply. You raise something that is important to you, or you talk about how you feel. And you do the same test.

Ryan: Uh-huh.

Rachel: Did they shut you down, make you feel stupid, tell you that you didn't know what you were talking about, minimize you, become verbally abusive? End of story. Not someone you want to go forward with. Not someone you can trust.

Ryan: Right.

Rachel: But supposing that you got the same empathic, listening, caring response as the first time. Can you begin to see how, step by step by step, you could begin to develop a connection?

Ryan: Yeah, I see theoretically how that can happen. It's just … it's just practically that I don't see.

Rachel: Okay, but you're seeing practically the process that you would be following that is different from the way you've been up till now.

Ryan: I don't see that it's any different from the way that I have been. I feel like I open up to people, and eventually they do something and it's just like: "Okay, well, that's clearly as far as I'm going to open up to this person." And that's happened with everyone. So, I mean, you know, there's a point where eventually I draw the line and realize clearly, I'm not going to get closer to this person.

Rachel: Well, that's different from what you have said up till now. You've said that what you do is you pull back and don't share what's important to you with people most of the time.

Ryan: Right.

Rachel: And, when you do, you close up right away. So, I'm envisioning a different way that you might go forward. Bit by bit trusting as long as …

Ryan: Right. But it seems that never, never …

Rachel: Up till now. So you don't see how that would cumulatively create the elements of a connection, an ongoing connection.

Ryan: Right, I see how it could. It just never happened.

Rachel: Okay, I get that. And had it happened in the past, you wouldn't need to change your approach to allow it to happen in the future. You would already know how to do that. So, of course, this is going to be new territory for you.

Ryan: But I don't think it's that. I think it's the same thing I've done a thousand times. It's just that it never happens, it never ...

Rachel: There are only two possibilities that I can see. One is in the selection process. If you choose people like your mother – or enough like your mother that it's obviously going to abort in the way that it does when you try to connect with her – then you will have the validating experience that you need in order to hold on to the belief that everyone is like your mother. If on the other hand, you choose people fundamentally different from your mother ...

Ryan: I don't know how to spot those kind of people.

Rachel: Well, you mentioned it yourself, Ryan. You said: "Well, I could look for people who seem to be nice, seem to be empathic ..."

Ryan: Well, that's what I do, but my mom seems to be nice and seems to be empathic just as everybody does. I open up to people and connect with them at first, but then, after a while, suddenly I realize, you know, how limited that is.

Rachel: So, you either have chosen badly in terms of the people you've tried to connect with or, what is more likely, is that you've shut down yourself prematurely.

Ryan: Okay.

Rachel: If you were not to shut down, you would also let them know a little about what you need and want from a relationship. And if they were not delivering that, you might still give them a chance. You might say: "Ugh, that kind of hurt my feelings ..." or: "I don't feel like you're listening to me ..." or:

"I get the idea that you don't care about how I feel ..." or something of that sort. And if they say: "Oh ... up yours!" or whatever, then, that would certainly prove that's a person not to continue to pursue a relationship with. However, if they say: "Oh my goodness, I didn't realize that you would respond that way. I didn't mean that. That was not my intention. That was a misunderstanding ..." then, you might be willing to allow them another chance, remembering that *everyone may not be like your mother.* They may not be, Ryan.

Ryan: Right, then, what are they like?

Rachel: Well, I think that they might be more understanding, more caring, more empathic, like Uncle Carl. Even like Julia in the particular circumstance you imagined. And like myself. Since I don't know any other people in your life, I can't pull on other examples, but they might be like me in that they do care about how you feel and that they are trying to help you. And that they do genuinely empathize with the place you're stuck, or the feelings you're having, or the places where you're hurting. In my experience, there are people in this world who are like that.

Ryan: Uh-huh.

Rachel: And there are people who would be like that with you. Letting yourself open to the possibility that there are people – maybe even right around you – that you're not seeing or trusting or giving a chance would mean to you that your worldview would have to change.

Ryan: Uh-huh.

Rachel: You would have to begin to allow in the possibility of connection, and the possibility that your picture has been contaminated by your experience of an extremely self-protective and defended parent. When you think about that, what comes up for you?

Ryan: It just seems like, I don't know … it just seems that most of the people I meet end up being that way. So, at some point or another, they either get off the bus really quickly, or it's months later that I realize that they're an extremely defended and protective person. And, yeah … it's been like that.

Rachel: Sometimes.

Ryan: Everybody I've met. Eventually I realize where they get off the bus, and it's just like … I realize that any connection I have with someone is only going to last so long and, then, eventually it's going to be very obvious how far they'll go.

Rachel: I'd like you look at the possibility that *you* have been invalidating them, or that you've selected people who will fulfill - like a self-fulfilling prophecy - the belief system that you are operating under.

Ryan: I think that makes sense, but I don't know how to pick other people. I don't feel like I can pick people.

Rachel: You observe their behavior and you take a risk.

Ryan: Right.

Rachel: And maybe you try and look at how you've shut down. Or how you invalidate them because they don't give you exactly what you want when you want it. Perhaps you say: "Oh, well, there you go; they are just like everyone else."

Ryan: Right.

Rachel: And maybe you eliminate them? Or you don't share, as you said earlier. You don't share the things that are important to you. Or the feelings you have that make you vulnerable.

Ryan: Right.

Rachel: If those things were to change, then there is at least the possibility of a different experience of connection. And with it, the pain of recognizing that your experience with your mother is not necessarily going to be duplicated everywhere else. And that *is* painful. Because we do not want to see problems, limitations, or defects in our parents.

Ryan: Uh-huh.

Rachel: Particularly in the primary caregiver – your mother.

Ryan: Uh-huh.

Rachel: And so, in your way, you may be protecting her by believing everyone is going to be just like her. And forgetting about the Uncle Carl's of the world or the Rachel's who are interested in knowing how you feel. Who are interested in being there for you. And who would want to have a genuine connection with you. Look at how you've been today in our relationship, Ryan. Would you say you've been holding back?

Ryan: Yeah.

Rachel: Do you think you could imagine doing something different in this particular circumstance, just as an example? And if you were different, what would that look like – right from the time you walked in?

Ryan: I don't know. I can't really see it.

Rachel: Are you … are you sure? Maybe you don't want to see it?

Ryan: I don't know; it seems like a lot for …

Rachel: If you were to see that you could open up in our relationship in the way that you have other times, but not today, you could begin to get a handle on what you can do that would make a difference.

Ryan: Uh-huh.

Rachel: For example, making a decision, answering a question, being interested in doing the work, believing that this is going somewhere that could be helpful for you, trusting me and, more importantly, trusting yourself. When I suggest that, what comes up for you?

Ryan: Wow, that sounds like a good fairy tale existence.

Rachel: "Fairy tale existence." So, do you hear the minimizing and putting down that becomes part of how you describe the difference?

Ryan: Yeah, I just don't know how to do anything else, really.

Rachel: You've done it with me in other sessions without a problem, Ryan, so I know that you're capable of this. I know you can. And you knew at the end of the last processing session that you were able to connect with people. But somehow you've lost that realization.

Ryan: Well, I just ... it seems like the world is basically made up of people who are like my mom, so it's not even an issue of me being able to choose the right people versus the wrong people. It's an issue of ... not having a choice to make.

Rachel: Okay, Ryan, this is what you do and how you do it. It's happening right now. You're back to that negative belief system. As long as you hold on to that belief system, that's exactly what you will experience.

Ryan: But, I mean, you're telling me not to choose people that are like my mom, but I'm saying that there are *only* people like my mom.

Rachel: And I gave you different examples in our experience together this morning.

Ryan: Right, but I don't know how to spot those people just on the street.

Rachel: I wouldn't expect you to spot them on the street. What I was saying was that, if you were to behave differently in the session we had today, it would have opened up connection. You do really close down the possibility of connection.

Ryan: It's not what I was deliberately doing, but I don't really know what I was deliberately doing.

Rachel: It seems to me that you need to reflect on what you are doing when you relate to other people. In terms of our relationship, it is possible for us to talk about what is happening and make it transparent. So it's a useful laboratory. I'm going to leave you with that.

Ryan: Okay.

Social Anxiety: Case of Melissa

Follow-up Session

Case of Melissa: Follow-Up Session[37]

Rachel: Visualizing yourself up in the mountains, smelling the pine trees, feeling the wind on your face, the cold air of the mountains and the snow. And sensing the person that you are - the real Melissa, the new Melissa, who is relaxed and calm and at peace. And for her, it is easy to accept into her truth the belief that "I," - meaning you, Melissa - "am good enough and just as good as anybody else." Let that belief repeat in your mind. "I am just as good as anybody else." And sense how that feels in your body as you allow that thought to be in your mind. Feel what it's like to know that this is true of the person you are, and the person you are is the person you're connecting with now. Letting go of the old, negative beliefs that got in your way in the past - negative beliefs that were fed by your mother's criticalness. You can remember that your mother had her own issues and, perhaps, let go of her judgments and the judgments of others that are unfair, like she was.

And imagine that all around you, in your special place, are the special resources that you chose for your work. There's your grandmother who always cares about you and what you say and is loving. She knows your value. She knows that you have no reason to be afraid or concerned. And there, too, comes your little dog, Penny, who's always happy to see you and loves you unconditionally. See Penny in your snowy mountain place. And your dad is there as well. He helped you get out of the situation with your mom, because he knows something about what you were feeling and what she's like. He always takes your side and sees your point of view when bad things happen. Your father knows you're just as good as anybody else. He never doubted that. He's always known that to be true - which may be part of why he rescued you from your mother. And then, your inner self-helper is there, who will always give

---

[37] We are doing a combination of hypnotherapy and bilateral stimulation in this session.

you the right answer, and who will, at this moment in time, reassert and confirm that you are a good person, Melissa. Just as good as anybody else. And Rachel is there, your therapist, who knows something about how you can turn away from negative thoughts. And in that way, reduce and eliminate the anxiety that you have felt in the past to move forward as this new person with growing confidence.

Let's imagine you moving forward now into the future. And we can start with some important events that are coming up next Monday. You will be going to school. First day of school. New term. New chance. New folks, perhaps some old ones. And I'd like you to imagine yourself walking into the grounds of the school from wherever you parked your car, saying to yourself: "This is going to be different. I'm just as good as anybody else. I'm going to be calm and I'm going to be looking forward to meeting people. And I'm going to be able to speak as easily as I could with people who liked me in gymnastics, with my grandmother, with my father, with Rachel, with people who already know my value as a human being." And as you visualize this, you're getting closer and closer to the classroom that you're going to have your first class in. And you walk in, and there's a little smile on your face because you feel the difference, Melissa. If those old, negative thoughts come up, you blow them away. You say: "I'm not listening to you. I don't want to hear from you. Don't bother me right now. I'm fine and I'm just as good as anyone else." And as you walk into the classroom, you can scan and notice if there's anybody that you might like to say hello to – anybody that you might be willing to sit beside, to chat with, to start a conversation. Choose someone who looks like they have a kind of niceness about them – as if they may also appreciate some contact. They wouldn't be in a group with a whole bunch of other people. They might be just by themselves, waiting for the class to start – someone that you might feel comfortable to sit near or to smile at or to say hello to. What would you like to do? Would you like to sit, say hello or smile, or sit beside her or him?

Melissa: Say hello.

Rachel: Say hello. Is it a boy or is it a girl?

Melissa: A girl.

Rachel: It's a girl. Okay. And you say hello and then, what happens then?

Melissa: They say hello back.

Rachel: Uh-huh. Play out the scene as you would like it to go. And tell me what's happening.

Melissa: We start a conversation and I'm comfortable with the conversation.

Rachel: Uh-huh. Do you have any idea what you might be talking about?

Melissa: Yeah. Our classes.

Rachel: That would be a good subject. "What are you taking? I'm taking this. How do you like that?" That kind of thing?

Melissa: Mhmm.

Rachel: Very good. Say some more about what's happening.

Melissa: Um … More people are arriving. I'm feeling calm, confident and comfortable.

Rachel: Very good.

Melissa: Everyone in the class seems friendly.

Rachel: Good.

Melissa: I don't feel out of place.

Rachel: Wonderful.

Melissa: I feel like I belong there.

Rachel: So, tell yourself again: "I belong here." Then, say it out loud a couple times.

Melissa: I belong here. I belong here.

Rachel: Feels true?

Melissa: Yes.

Rachel: Excellent. Continue the story as to what's happening in the classroom.

Melissa: Um. There's a full class.

Rachel: Mhmm.

Melissa: And then, I'll talk to someone else nearby. And then, the teacher walks in. And then, starts talking.

Rachel: Mhmm.

Melissa: I feel comfortable sitting in the chair.

Rachel: How far back are you in the classroom?

Melissa: The middle.

Rachel: Are you on one side or the other, or are you in the middle of the class?

Melissa: I'm kind of towards the right side.

Rachel: Okay. You're about middle of the classroom towards the right side and you're looking at the teacher.

Melissa: Yes.

Rachel: And the teacher's speaking? Okay. And what's going on for you?

Melissa: I feel fine and comfortable. Um. Just waiting for my next class, looking forward to the day.

Rachel: Excellent. So, now, I'd like you to go through your body as you're having this experience right now. Scan through your body, looking to see if everything in your body is relaxed. And then, I'd like you to install the thought: "I belong here. I'm comfortable and relaxed."

(Long pause) I'm going to turn the scanner off for a minute and just check in with you. How is that going for you?

Melissa: It's going good.

Rachel: No problems? Everything is feeling very clear and straightforward. Is that correct?

Melissa: Mhmm.

Rachel: Do you want to continue the class or do you have another class after this class? Let's go through your school day, your first day of school. You tell me what you're saying and feeling and hearing.

Melissa: Okay. (Long pause) Should I tell you?

Rachel: Yes, if you would please.

Melissa: I'll be going to the next class. Maybe I'll have a lunch in between.

Rachel: Oh. Good. Let's have a lunch in between then. And where do you go for lunch?

Melissa: Usually I'll bring a lunch.

Rachel: And where do you go to eat it?

Melissa: My car. Down by the beach.

Rachel: Is that what you want to do?

Melissa: Uh-huh.

Rachel: Do you feel like you might want to invite someone to join you? Or do you feel like you prefer to go by yourself this time?

Melissa: Well, since it's my first day, I'd rather go by myself.

Rachel: Could you leave that question open? This is a suggestion - you don't have to agree. You could leave the question open because - what if you really like that girl you were talking to in the previous class and you felt really comfortable with her and you might want to say: "Hey, do you have lunch now? Do you have a break now?" Is that a possibility?

Melissa: Yes.

Rachel: And if she said: "Yeah, actually, I do." What might happen then? Play out that scene.

Melissa: I don't know if I could see myself asking her to have a break with me the first day.

Rachel: It feels too overwhelming?

Melissa: Mhmm.

Rachel: What's the worst that could happen?

Melissa: Um … I end up not liking her and then I have to deal with her for the rest of the semester.

Rachel: You end up not liking her. That's so interesting, Melissa. You see it is possible that *you* might not like *her*. It's not always directed at you, is it?

Melissa: No.

Rachel: Okay. Now, you remember that some people you like and some people you don't, and some people might like you and some people might not. But it's okay to be confident and know that you're just as good as anybody else. It's possible that you might want to wait and have lunch with somebody in the future, but just not on the very first day.

Melissa: Uh-huh.

Rachel: So, visualize yourself going to your car to have your lunch. And what are you saying to yourself? And what are you thinking? And what are you feeling as you go?

Melissa: I'm feeling fine, just waiting for my next class to start.

Rachel: Okay. Are you enjoying sitting in the car looking out at the beach?

Melissa: Yeah.

Rachel: Okay. Take us now from lunch to your next class or activity.

Melissa: Then, I go to my next class and hopefully I'm still feeling confident from the last class.

Rachel: Would you like to imagine you're feeling confident from the last class?

Melissa: Yeah.

Rachel: Should you doubt that you would feel confident from the last class, since you had such a good experience?

Melissa: No.

Rachel: Okay. Do you want to choose to be confident going to the next class?

Melissa: Yeah.

Rachel: What are you thinking and saying as you go to the next class?

Melissa: That "I'm just as good as everybody else."

Rachel: Uh-huh.

Melissa: "I go to this school and I belong here."

Rachel: Uh-huh.

Melissa: "Just like everybody else."

Rachel: Absolutely. Very good. So, you walk into the next classroom and what happens then?

Melissa: Um ... I talk to someone else. Maybe introduce myself.

Rachel: Very good, Melissa. And who do you visualize this time? Just as a possibility?

Melissa: Maybe a girl again.

Rachel: Aha. You think it's best to start with females?

Melissa: Yeah.

Rachel: Okay. And what do you do? What happens?

Melissa: Um … Maybe a situation kind of similar to the last.

Rachel: Explain the details.

Melissa: It's the first day of school, so we'd be discussing our classes and how our summers went.

Rachel: Yes. That's a good thing to bring up as well. Good idea.

Melissa: And it's going good, and the teacher walks in, and it goes just as good as the first class.

Rachel: Wonderful. Are you getting a feel for this sense that it can be the same experience that you want it to be from one situation to the next? From one experience to the next? You get what you expect and you expect for it to work out fine.

Melissa: Yes.

Rachel: Is that the end of your school day?

Melissa: Yes, and then I have work.

Rachel: Do you want to take it into your work situation?

Melissa: Sure.

Rachel: Very good. Tell me the details of your going to work.

Melissa: Well, I go into work, and two of the girls just quit, so I'm working with two of the new people there.

Rachel: Uh-huh.

Melissa: And I'm feeling confident and telling myself they're just here to work, just like me.

Rachel. You feel calm and confident?

Melissa: Uh-huh.

Rachel: And when you walk in and see these new, new girls, do they smile at you? Do you smile at them? Tell me what happens next.

Melissa: Mhmm. I walk in, maybe smile. Ready to start work. Maybe ask how their day went.

Rachel: Play out your workday – the details. Let the scene play out.

Melissa: Okay. It's just like the other workday, like it was with the old people. No changes, just different people that I'm working with. It's going good. We're working well together.

Rachel: And what are you saying to yourself about yourself?

Melissa: I'm doing fine and I'm just as good as a coaching person as the people I'm working with.

Rachel: Good.

Melissa: I'm very relaxed and doing fine.

Rachel: Very good. Do you want to take that right through to the end of your workday?

Melissa: No. It's okay.

Rachel: When is the practice?

Melissa: Um. Before work.

Rachel: Oh, we skipped that.

Melissa: Or, actually, I don't know. After work, I think.

Rachel: So, you finish your work and what happens next?

Melissa: I go to practice, and I think these people are just the same people that were at school – and not different.

Rachel: Mhmm.

Melissa: And I'm the same person I was at work. And I'm the same person I was at school.

Rachel: And that person is?

Melissa: Melissa.

Rachel: And what about her? What's true of her?

Melissa: She isn't different, um, I forgot. (Pause) Oh, she's the same as everybody else.

Rachel: Just as good.

Melissa: Just as good as everybody else.

Rachel: Right. Is that true?

Melissa: Yes.

Rachel: Yep.

Melissa: She'll be fine carrying on her practice with these new people.

Rachel: Uh-huh.

Melissa: Maybe start a conversation and enjoy her practice.

Rachel: Yes.

Melissa: Have a good time. Not get stressed out too much about anything.

Rachel: Is that what's happening as you visualize yourself going through the practice?

Melissa: Yes.

Rachel: Everything is going fine? People are nice? You are able to talk? Your practice is going well? You feel comfortable and relaxed and you feel like you're just as good as everyone else?

Melissa: Uh-huh.

Rachel: And when the practice is over, what do you tell yourself?

Melissa: I say: "Good job for being different - different than I usually am."

Rachel: Than you used to be.

Melissa: Yeah.

Rachel: That's really important. That you used to be one way, but you can be different now.

Melissa: Yeah. Okay.

Rachel: And that is the person you're going to be from now on.

Melissa: Yes. That's the person I'm going to be from now on.

Rachel: "My life has turned a corner. I'm able to socialize and get along with other people in a calm and confident way." Can you repeat what parts of that seem true for you?

Melissa: "My life has turned around and I'm capable of being calm and confident in all aspects of my life."

Rachel: Excellent. Now look forward. This was Monday. You had a wonderful day – Monday – at school. You had a wonderful time at work. You had a great time at your practice. I'd like you to go forward in time. Visualize other days of the week, at school, at work, at practice. Can you hold the same image?

Melissa: Yes.

Rachel: Visualize a time of month from now at school, at work and in your practice. Can you hold the same image?

Melissa: Uh-huh.

Rachel: Visualize six months from now at school, at work and in your practice. Same image of yourself?

Melissa: Yes.

Rachel: Some time in there, I'd like you to imagine that you've made some friends, and that you've actually been invited out with them or invited them out. Visualize that and tell me the story of your going out with one or more of these new friends that you've made.

Melissa: I'm visualizing that I made new friends at practice. And my teammates, maybe we go to a barbeque.

Rachel: Cool.

Melissa: There are different people there. Maybe people from practice and some of their friends. Guys and girls.

Rachel: Mhmm.

Melissa: And I'm feeling fine and ready to have a good time at the barbeque. Knowing that I have changed. And reminding myself to keep calm and relaxed, just like I was the past six months.

Rachel: Absolutely.

Melissa: Not forgetting anything I learned in EMDR and therapy.

Rachel: By now, this has become second nature to you. It has become part of the person that you believe and experience yourself to be. So, you don't even have to think about it. It's natural. It's your true nature coming through, influencing and affecting your way of handling all situations that you come across - any situation - with calm and confidence.

What would happen, Melissa, in your future vision, if for some reason, a circumstance arose where you began to doubt yourself or feel anxious? Tell me what you will do. What this new Melissa will do to deal with some of potential anxiety from old Melissa. What does she do?

Melissa: Not put myself down about it. Just go on and deal with it and not hide in the corner like I would usually do in the past or run away from my problems. I would just go on with my life and remind myself what I practiced.

Rachel: So, if that part of you, that old part of you, wants to hide in the corner, what will you say to her in your inner dialogue?

Melissa: Don't hide in the corner, because you don't want to be the person you used to be.

Rachel: And what if she says: "But I'm anxious. I'm scared. I don't know if I can handle this." What will you say to her, then?

Melissa: You can't run away from your problems. You have to deal with them.

Rachel: Can you reassure her that she has support from you?

Melissa: Yes.

Rachel: So, would you tell her: "I'm here with you now."

Melissa: Yes.

Rachel: And "I handle things differently. And I can help you do the same." And I'd like you to say what words come to mind that you might say to that part of you that used to be scared and anxious.

Melissa: "I'm here with you now and I can help you through it."

Rachel: Does she hear you?

Melissa: Yes.

Rachel: Does she believe you?

Melissa: Yes.

Rachel: And can you let her know that you will always be there for her? Is that something you'd be willing to commit to her?

Melissa: Yes.

Rachel: That when she feels scared or anxious, if that ever happens, you will be her support. Can you tell her that?

Melissa: "When you're feeling scared and anxious, I will always be here for you."

Rachel: Okay. When you see her now, Melissa, the old person, how old does she look to you?

Melissa: Um. I don't know.

Rachel: Well, look at her. How big is she?

Melissa: Um ... Small.

Rachel: Would you guess she would be three, six, nine? What age would you guess by her height and her face and her body?

Melissa: Um ... Thirteen.

Rachel: Thirteen. Ah – a difficult time for many of us. Early adolescence can be a really hard time. Can you have empathy for the fact that this little girl is nervous and needs some support from you? You're now twenty. Can you understand how she might feel a little nervous?

Melissa: (Pause) Yes.

Rachel: Can you give her some pointers on how to behave, based on your new experience of dealing with social situations at school, at work, at practice and in social settings? Can you give her some tips?

Melissa: Yes.

Rachel: So, do that. Talk to her about it. How it could be easier for her.

Melissa: Tell yourself that it's okay and don't beat yourself up too much, because that's not going to help.

Rachel: Mhmm.

Melissa: Stay calm and relaxed and visualize the positives. Block out the negatives.

Rachel: Mhmm.

Melissa: Just breathe, relax, and tell yourself it's going to be okay… that, um, you can always be there for yourself.

Rachel: That would be very good.

Melissa: Uh-huh.

Rachel: You also advise her that sometimes it's okay to say hello to people, to start a conversation.

Melissa: Mhmm.

Rachel: Think that you could help her do that?

Melissa: Yes.

Rachel: How is she feeling about what she's hearing right now?

Melissa: She's feeling more uplifted. That she's not all alone.

Rachel: Very important. Did you know that she's been feeling all alone for a very long time?

Melissa: No.

Rachel: So, now that you know that, can you let her know that she's not all alone? That you are going to be there with her and for her?

Melissa: (Pause) Yes.

Rachel: Do you want to hold her hand, put your arm around her, give her a hug? Is there anything you want to do to reassure her of your presence?

Melissa: Hold her hand. Let her know that she's with someone.

Rachel: And how is that for her?

Melissa: She feels more comfort, comforted. Comfortable.

Rachel: Absolutely. Comforted and comfortable – both are right, I'm sure.

Melissa: Mhmm.

Rachel: She needed your support, and now you're committing to be there for her, to help her in those situations. To talk to her, to advise her, to hold her hand, to be her always-present friend and mentor. This part of you can be like a parent, a good parent. How do you feel about her as a person?

Melissa: I think she's just like everybody else. She just needs a hand.

Rachel: That's right. Feel that hand – her hand – in yours. And you're giving her a hand. Can you feel that in your hand?

Melissa: Uh-huh.

Rachel: Can you imagine her as this part of you that is always there by your side? Or, if you wish, you could imagine placing her in your body somewhere, maybe in your heart space.

She's the one that was scared. She's the one that was anxious. She's the one that used to believe the things that were told to her by your mother, the things that were negative. So she needs your support to know that that was all wrong and that, actually, she's okay. She's just as good as anyone else. And it's sad that it took all these years, these seven years for you to figure that out, but now you've got it and you can be there for your thirteen-year-old self. Is she trusting that you'll be there?

Melissa: Yes.

Rachel: Are you confident that you are going to be there for her?

Melissa: Yes.

Rachel: See what happens as the two of you, hand in hand, move forward in time. Where do you go? What comes up?

Melissa: Life is different now that she is there. I know she is there.

Rachel: How is it different, Melissa?

Melissa: We are living a happier life now that we know we have each other.

Rachel: Exactly. So, neither one of you is alone anymore and both of you can make friends and maybe, if you'd like, a boyfriend? How do you feel about that idea?

Melissa: Confident.

Rachel: Very good. Are there any other circumstances going forward in the future that you want to look at? That you want to address?

Melissa: Not really.

Rachel: Are you sure?

Melissa: Yes.

Rachel: Everything feels like it's smooth sailing from here on? This is not to say that there might not be some problems that arise in your life that you'll resolve, days you'll feel better than others. But, basically, do you feel like you're bringing a sense of confidence and self-worth into your future?

Melissa: Uh-huh.

Rachel: And I want you to see how different it is for you not to be anxious, not to be expecting problems, and not to be worried that things will go back. Now, give yourself a message of appreciation just for being you – this new you, hand in hand with the old you, helping her go forward into a new positive life. A life of social relationships, friendships, good experiences with other people – at work, at school, in your sports, and in your private, social life. Give yourself a message of appreciation for the work you've invested in getting to this point and for the confidence that gets expressed in the words: "I love you, Melissa. I like you. You're great just the way you are, and you're just as good as anybody else." Can you repeat those words one last time?

Melissa: "I'm just as good as anybody else."

Rachel: Does that feel true?

Melissa: Yes.

Rachel: Very good. And in a moment, I'll be counting you back very slowly and guiding you up to an alert state by the count of ten. When you come back, you'll feel energized, yet relaxed. You'll feel a sense of confidence and companionship having this new allegiance, this new alliance, with the child part of you. And a commitment to her that the two of you will go forward together, and you will support her to maintain the confidence and calm you're feeling right now. That's it. Very good.

Counting now: **One**. Letting the scenes of you at school, at work, at practice fade for now, as well as the scenes of your snowy place with resources that are always there for you to call upon. And keep a sense of this new relationship between you, the adult, and you, the child. Bringing both of you back, hand in hand. **Two.** As they fade, bringing yourself back to present time and present space. **Three**. Sensing your body stretched out on the chair and stool here in my office, and feeling your presence in the chair as the scanner goes off. **Four.** Beginning to wiggle toes and fingers, bringing energy back into muscles and limbs. **Five.** Half way there now. **Six.** Beginning to stretch your arms out in front of you and your legs towards the front wall. **Seven.** Shifting your weight from side to side. Rotating your neck very slowly back and forth. **Eight.** Sensing the light on the other side of your eyelids and your eyelids are fluttering and getting ready to open. **Nine**. Almost there. **Ten.** Awake and alert.

Bibliography of Books Cited

Aarons, Rachel B. *Journey to Home: Quintessential Therapy and Beyond.* Santa Barbara: Journey Press, 2009.

Bowen, Murray. *Family Therapy in Clinical Practice*, New York: Aronson, 1978.

Firestone, Robert. *The Fantasy Bond*. New York: Human Sciences, 1985 [and numerous other, more recent books].

Friedan, Betty. *The Feminine Mystique*. New York: Penguin, 1963.

Levine, Stephen. *Who Dies?* New York: Anchor Doubleday, 1982.

Minuchin, Salvador, Michael P. Nichols, and Wai-Yun Lee. *Assessing Families and Couples.* Boston: Pearson Education, 2007.

Parnell, Laurel. *Transforming Trauma: EMDR.* New York: W.W. Norton, 1997.

Parnell, Laurel. *EMDR in the Treatment of Adults Abused as Children*. New York: W.W. Norton, 1999.

Parnell, Laurel. *Tapping In: A Step By Step Guide to Activating Your Healing Resources Through Bilateral Stimulation.* Boulder: Sounds True, 2008.

Shapiro, Francine. *Eye Movement Desensitization and Reprocessing: Basic Principles, Protocols and Procedures.* New York: Guilford Press, 1995.

About the Author

Rachel B. Aarons MSW, PhD, began her professional career as a philosopher. She was awarded numerous scholarships and fellowships, including the prestigious Woodrow Wilson National Fellowship, the Horace B. Rackham Graduate Prize Fellowship, and the Canada Council Dissertation Fellowship. She completed her Doctorate in Philosophy at the University of Michigan in 1971 and then taught at the University of Toronto as a Lecturer and Assistant Professor of Philosophy from 1968 to 1973.

At this point, her career took a new direction. She received a Masters of Social Work degree from the University of Toronto in 1976 and completed a three-year training program as a Gestalt therapist at the Gestalt Institute of Toronto. She opened a private practice in Toronto which she maintained until moving to Vancouver B.C. in 1978. She was also trained by Virginia Satir as a conjoint family therapist and later became a faculty member of the Northwest Satir Institute.

In Vancouver, Dr. Aarons founded and coordinated a women's resource center for Capilano University and also served as a career counselor before returning to private practice in counseling and hypnotherapy in 1984.

Dr. Aarons moved to Santa Barbara, California in 1996 and was licensed as a clinical social worker for the state of California (LCS 18298) in 1997. She was first trained in EMDR in 1998 and completed her certification as an EMDRIA approved therapist in 2004. She continued her practice as a therapist first under the auspice of the Family Therapy Institute of Santa Barbara and currently in her own private practice. She published her first book, *Journey to Home: Quintessential Therapy and Beyond* in 2009. For over thirty-five years, Dr. Rachel Aarons has been a companion and guide to individuals and couples on their journeys to growth and healing.

Contact Information:

Dr. Rachel B. Aarons LCSW

1018 Garden Street, Suite 106, Santa Barbara, CA 93101

Tel. (805) 450-6365 Fax: (805) 617-1700

Email: rbaarons@yahoo.com

www.RachelAarons.com